READING WITH THE SENSES IN VICTORIAN LITERATURE AND SCIENCE

Victorian Literature and Culture Series

Reading with the Senses in Victorian Literature and Science

David Sweeney Coombs

UNIVERSITY OF VIRGINIA PRESS
Charlottesville and London

University of Virginia Press

Printed in the United States of America on acid-free paper

First published 2019

1 3 5 7 9 8 6 4 2

Library of Congress Cataloging-in-Publication Data

Names: Coombs, David Sweeney, author.
Title: Reading with the senses in Victorian literature and science / David Coombs.
Description: Charlottesville : University of Virginia Press, 2019. |
Includes bibliographical references and index.
Identifiers: LCCN 2019015593 (print) | LCCN 2019981430 (ebook) |
ISBN 9780813943428 (cloth) | ISBN 9780813943435 (ebook)
Subjects: LCSH: English literature—19th century—History and criticism. | Literature and science—Great Britain—History—19th century. | Perception in literature. | Senses and sensation in literature. | Criticism—England—History—19th century.
Classification: LCC PR468. S 34 C66 2019 (print) | LCC PR 468.S34 (ebook) |
DDC 820.00/80936—dc23
LC record available at https://lccn.loc.gov/2019015593
LC ebook record available at https://lccn.loc.gov/2019981430

Cover art: Hummingbird on finger, benoitb/iStock;
additional illustrations, Artur Balytskyi/Shutterstock

For my parents
and in memoriam
Marian Gaber Battenhouse, 1912–2006

CONTENTS

ACKNOWLEDGMENTS

In writing a book about reading, I have felt acutely grateful to all the smart and generous readers who have shaped this project in ways too numerous to reckon fully.

At its germinal stage this book found its earliest readers in my teachers and fellow graduate students at Cornell. James Eli Adams introduced me to Victorian literature and showed me how compelling a world it could be. I owe him a huge debt of gratitude for his mentorship. Laura Brown and Paul Sawyer read drafts and patiently helped me begin to figure out what I was doing without ever letting on that they could see I didn't know. Peter Bailey, Ashly Bennett, Karen Bourrier, Colin Dewey, Meghan Freeman, and Ana Rojas were not only good friends but also my first colleagues in nineteenth-century literary studies, and I still try to live up to their standard of brilliance and camaraderie. I am grateful to have been part of the wider community of Cornell graduate students in English. My thanks in particular to Anthony Reed for his friendship and readiness to talk through ideas.

An Andrew Mellon Postdoctoral Fellowship at Wesleyan University provided support at a crucial moment in this project's development. Under Jill Morawski's wise and tireless leadership, the Center for the Humanities at Wesleyan was a model of what a vibrant intellectual community looks like. I learned so much from the other scholars there, especially Sonali Chakravarti, Joseph Fitzpatrick, Courtney Fullilove, Courtney Smith, Laura Stark, and Eirene Visvardi. A special shout-out goes to my fellow Mellon fellow, the amazing Neetu Khanna. Conversations with Jonathan

Kramnick and Steven Meyer during their visits to the center were formative for my thinking about perception. Wesleyan also gave me my first opportunity to teach my research materials, and I remain in awe of the students there whose intellectual curiosity and talent made that class a high point of my experience as a teacher.

This project became a book at Clemson University. I have had the good fortune to work in a department chaired by Sean Williams, Lee Morrissey, and Susanna Ashton, and I am thankful for their mentorship and advice. My research was supported by a Clemson SEED grant. In ways large and small, this book has been shaped by my colleagues and students in Clemson English. My special thanks to Cameron Bushnell, Gabriel Hankins, Walt Hunter, Brian McGrath, and Sean Morey, who commented on drafts of articles and chapters.

The excitement of Victorian literature is for me due in no small part to the brilliance of my colleagues in nineteenth-century literary studies. The conversations sustained by the V21 Collective have been important to my thinking, and I am grateful to conveners Anna Kornbluh and Benjamin Morgan for inviting me to participate. Daniel Hack's response to my work in a *Victorian Studies* forum on fictional character helped me understand parts of my approach in a new way. Dustin Friedman, Devin Griffiths, Nathan Hensley, Caroline Levine, and Michael Tondre read work in progress with their characteristically wonderful insight and taught me things about the project that I would not have grasped otherwise.

I feel very fortunate that this book found a home at the University of Virginia Press. My thanks to Eric Brandt, Helen Chandler, Ellen Satrom, and everyone at the Press who shepherded the manuscript through the final stages to publication. I am very grateful to Herbert Tucker and the anonymous peer reviewers whose thoughtful suggestions for revisions made this a better book. My thanks to George Roupe for copyediting the manuscript and Enid Zafran for providing its index. Portions of chapter 2 appeared as "Does Grandcourt Exist?" (© Indiana University Press) in *Victorian Studies* 59, no. 3 (Spring 2017): 390–98. An earlier version of chapter 3 appeared as "Reading in the Dark" (© Johns Hopkins University Press) in *ELH* 78, no. 4 (Winter 2011): 943–66. Portions of chapter 5 appeared as "The Sense and Reference of Sound" (© The Regents of the University of California) in *Nineteenth-Century Literature* 72, no. 4 (March 2018): 487–514. I am grateful to these journals for permission to republish here.

Lastly, I am profoundly grateful to my family for their love and care. My parents, David Walsh Coombs and Joan Sweeney Coombs, were my first and most important teachers. From them, I learned that sharp and eager observation that preserves a sense of wonder at the world. My sister Jeanette and brother Robert never cease to impress me with the different ways they learned that same lesson. My aunts Mary and Martha Coombs taught me how to talk about stories seriously while the innumerable Sweeneys taught me never to be too serious about myself. Without the encouragement of my great-aunt Marian Battenhouse I might never have chosen to go to graduate school. This book would be unimaginable for me without Angela, my best, most intimate friend and reader. Finally, my children Davey Naimou Coombs and Lulu Naima Coombs were born while I was working on this book. The happiness they have given me will, to my eyes, always be legible in every word of it.

READING WITH THE SENSES IN VICTORIAN LITERATURE AND SCIENCE

Introduction

Shapes intrinsically simple become interesting in writing.

—Thomas Hardy, *The Return of the Native*

READING IS A BREATHTAKINGLY elegant adaptation of our basic perceptual capacities in the service of communication at a distance. Consider, reader, how my words are reaching you now. Most likely, you are seeing them as your eyes scan lines of text on a page.[1] If you attend to yourself closely, though, you'll notice that this scanning proceeds not smoothly in a line but jerkily, through a series of minute, very rapid eye movements that you make four to five times per second. These saccadic movements allow you to fixate letters in line with your foveae—the small indentations in the center of your retina, packed with photoreceptor cone cells that transduce light into sharply defined visual sensations. To proceed in an orderly way from left to right and then down to the next line of text, you need to coordinate these eye movements and focalizations, and to do so you rely on the sensory receptors inside your muscles that enable you to feel your exertions and body position (the neurophysiologist C. S. Sherrington gave these feelings the name proprioception).[2] As you read, you are in effect gripping one word on the page after another, not so much scanning as swinging lightly along this line of text as if on the monkey bars.[3]

Now, to see these words *as* words, you are also, more subtly, drawing from your competencies in auditory perception. Letters signify sounds first of all, and we learn to read by learning how to match graphemes with phonemes. If you are reading an academic monograph like this book, you are probably not audibly sounding it out. Still, there is a broad consensus in psychology and neuroscience that even practiced readers often (though not always) mentally sound out their visual perceptions of written words.[4]

Reading hotwires our capacity for visual, positional, and auditory perception with remarkable economy. As a medium, print is strikingly austere, consisting only of repetitive strings of small black shapes on a white background. Elaine Scarry has observed that the act of reading is "almost wholly devoid of *actual* sensory content."[5] When we read a book, of course, we are always at some level aware of more than just the look of the type—the heft of the volume, the textures of the binding and the pages, the sound of the paper, the smell of the ink and the glue, all of these are an integral part of the experience. But such features are nonetheless more peripheral to literature than the sensory elements of the other arts. In the relative austerity of writing as a sensory array lies the elegance of reading as a perceptual technology. Partly for this reason, literary critics have for the most part remained uninterested in the ways that reading repurposes our perceptual competencies.[6] They have lately, however, become interested in the ways that reading acts as an aid to perception of the world beyond the page. Scarry, for instance, notes that reading has almost no *actual* sensory content merely as a prelude to her dazzling account of how reading literature provides us with *virtual* sensory content. Literature, she contends in *Dreaming by the Book,* tacitly gives its readers a set of instructions for mentally reproducing the perceptual experiences it describes. Reading figures here primarily as a technology of perception in a second sense, as a way of revealing the world to us.[7]

Reading, then, comprises two different kinds of experience: the actual experience of letters printed on a page before us and the virtual experience described therein. These actual and virtual experiences seem to compete for the reader's attention. The words on the page fade into the background as we become absorbed in what those words denote and vice versa.[8] For a reader, words often seem to point to the world by pointing away from themselves. Hence even the critics who have begun to advocate a more hard-nosed, observational model of literary studies for the most part ignore the actual experience of reading. In an introduction to a 2009 special issue of *Representations* that quickly became a flashpoint in recent debates over how we read, Stephen Best and Sharon Marcus argued against what they characterized as a dominant literary critical mode of "deep" reading that sought to see through texts in order to expose their underlying ideological preconditions.[9] Pointing to Scarry's *Dreaming by the Book* as one key instance, they advocated a loosely defined method they called surface reading, which would look not *through* but *at* the text so as to attend to "what is evident, perceptible, [and] apprehensible."[10] In practice, though, surface reading has not redirected the reader's attention to the page itself so much as to the precise descriptive specifications of literary texts. Partly for this reason, surface reading has in more recent years been absorbed by an affiliated group of methods that often go by the name of description.

Description, too, is a method of reading that strives to attend to the perceptible. The critics advocating a descriptive turn in literary studies envision a disciplinary future for English as something akin to an observational science.[11] The most influential theorist behind literary studies' descriptive turn is Bruno Latour, the sociologist who advocates comprehensive description as a method of showing "what the *real* world is *really* like."[12] Heather Love cites just this goal as something we might achieve by reimagining close reading on the pattern of thin description—the "exhaustive, fine-grained attention to phenomena" displayed in social scientific techniques of detached microanalysis (404). Less metaphorically than surface reading, descriptive criticism trades on the axiom that reading affords us an opportunity to perceive the world with a new clarity. In this respect, literary criticism's descriptive turn also marks something of a tacit return to the early twentieth-century formalist Viktor Shklovsky's notion of literature as a tool for "intensifying the impressions of the senses" by describing the world in a way that "makes [its] perception long and 'laborious.'"[13] In a similar vein, Marcus, Love, and Best argue that description "can allow us both to see more and to look more attentively, more fully, *and* more selectively."[14]

But description is above all referential—it refers our attention away from the page and toward the object being described. When they are applied to literary texts, descriptive methods therefore prompt the critic to look through the text to the world it enframes (this is perhaps why narratology rarely features in arguments about descriptive methods in literary studies, which most often play out instead between historicists and advocates of a postcritical turn). I do not point out this omission in the spirit of critical one-upmanship ("You call *that* a surface!"). Rather, I want to call attention here to the way that reading exemplifies a larger difficulty for empiricism and scientific observation, namely that what is actual and what is virtual commingle in our experience.

Since the end of the eighteenth century, scientific accounts of perception have taken for granted that a great deal of interpretive work goes into our everyday perceptual experiences of the world. Take the example of the perceptual processes involved in reading that I describe above: we do not just see the words on the page, we see them by (sometimes at least) reflexively sounding them out. In such cases, a visual stimulus is briefly transposed into an auditory sensation en route to becoming the visual perception of a word. Even when we strenuously focus on our experience of the page actually before us, that actual page turns out to have much that is virtual in it.

Perception, like description, is directed toward an object. It is what philosophers and psychologists call an intentional state. A description that we read usually points to an object quite a bit further away than the one we perceive right here before us, but even the present object of a perception has its hidden obverse and shadowy recesses. Making the most of this parallel, nineteenth-century scientists argued that the experience of reading in this respect exemplifies experience more broadly. In this view, just as we mentally sound out the letters in order to visually perceive a printed word, we mentally supplement the stimuli through which an object is acting on us at any moment with what we know that object is probably like. In both cases, what is virtually present fills out what is actually present.

The emergence of this understanding of perception—that is, as an intentional mental act performed on the basis of incomplete sense data—profoundly shaped the scientific and literary history of the nineteenth century in ways that continue to reverberate in our own moment. Even as literary critics have begun exploring more empirical reading methods modeled on scientific description and observation, comparatively little attention has been paid to how the experience of reading itself might contribute to this larger project. Attention to the perceptual processes involved in reading words on a page no doubt risks highlighting the fact that literary critics' observational knowledge of the world can only be got indirectly and at second hand, courtesy of textual descriptions. But what nineteenth-century scientists came to believe as they began making more detailed studies of the nervous system was that our direct observation of anything, even the words on the page before us, includes much that is indirect and secondhand. Victorian psychologists and philosophers came to call these kinds of indirect inferences and judgments knowledge by description.

This book charts the intellectual history of knowledge by description as a perceptual epistemology of reading. That history begins with the philosopher Thomas Reid, who established the fundamental nineteenth-century approach to perception when he drew a categorical distinction among what he saw as its three basic parts: stimulus (the force acting on the nerves); sensation (the feeling arising from the nerves' response to the stimulus); and perception (the mental apprehension of the object causing the sensations). While Reid worked out his tripartite model of perception in the eighteenth century, its deepest effects were felt in the nineteenth, when it became axiomatic for scientific work on optics, acoustics, and neurophysiology and ultimately served as *the* object of study around which experimental psychology first constituted itself as a field. As they struggled to account for how these three elements combine in our experience of the world, many Victorian scientists turned to the act of reading for a model: the contrast between the phenomenal richness of descriptive imagery in literature and the phenomenal parsimony of its print medium seemed to dramatize the new and startling scientific findings that our finely detailed perceptions of the world are often elicited by incomplete and attenuated sensory stimuli. Victorian science thus became deeply invested in an analogy between reading and perception, even as the weak causality it discovered between stimulus and perception raised difficult questions about the objectivity of scientific observations more broadly. At the same time, Victorian science transformed perception into a powerful model for Victorian thinking about reading and reference in both philosophy and literature. Its formative impact on modern literary studies is evident in Shklovsky's claim that literature is a tool for restoring sensational vivacity to our perceptions and thus closing the gap between how we perceive things and how they physically affect us—the very gap, in other words, whose existence the scientific analogy with reading helped establish!

Shklovsky famously argues that literature enhances and corrects our perception of the world by defamiliarizing it, and in this regard his formalism bears genealogical links to the long philosophical tradition characterizing aesthetic experience as detached and disinterested.[15] The disinterested judgment of taste justified many a Victorian claim for the higher objectivity of art, and those claims highlight the fact that detachment was a key virtue in both artistic and scientific observation during the nineteenth century. While eighteenth-century science "began and ended in pleasure, even under arduous mental and physical conditions," Victorian scientists often displayed an aversion to pleasure and attachment in favor of a "will to willessness" that Lorraine Daston and Peter Galison have termed "mechanical objectivity."[16] Nineteenth-century artists and literary writers rarely adopted the image-making protocols that define mechanical objectivity. Nonetheless, they too frequently embraced an ethos of self-abnegation that aimed to "repress the aspiring, desiring, emotion-ridden self and everything merely personal, contingent, historical, material that might get in the way of acquiring knowledge."[17] Similarly, for Shklovsky, things that are close to us, that we are attached to (like, he suggests, "our wives"), are too familiar to be rightly felt; it is only when things have been rendered strange that we can feel them vividly (5). But detachment is only the first step in the process of defamiliarization: art estranges the familiar in order to revivify and ultimately reattach us to it, giving us a more intimate understanding of what we had come to take for granted.

In this regard, Shklovsky's account of defamiliarization gives a name to what Fredric Jameson has described as nineteenth-century literature's turn to affect. Beginning around the 1840s, Jameson suggests, the realist novel adopted defamiliarization as one of its central animating impulses, with authors striving increasingly to renew perception by representationally rendering affective experiences that exceed the capacity of language to name them. The clear internal contradiction within this impulse—to reproduce in language what resists reification within language—charges realism with an explosive dialectical energy, driving the novel on to new forms of description in the service of making affective experience present to the reader even as affective experience outstrips those forms and makes new ones necessary.

Although Jameson's discussion of affect leaves scientific history largely to one side in its steady focus on the history of the novel, his antinomies of realism nonetheless track quite closely with the scientific distinction between sensation and perception central to this book.[18] Moreover, I contend here that the recent critical turn to description necessitates the kind of attention Jameson pays to the longer history of descriptive practices in literature (and I would argue in science as well). For Jameson, though, affective experience always remains the site of a productive contradiction: sensation and perception are held fast in a dialectical tension that propels the history of realism. On this understanding, experience is a problem admitting only temporary solutions. In contrast, this book traces the history of efforts to think past the problem of the antinomy between sensation and perception.

As Victorian literary writers responded to developments in nineteenth-century perception science, they began modeling the experience of reading in ways that pushed at the boundaries of how perception was understood. For most Victorian scientists, the analogy with reading worked to make perception seem less immediate and more detached from the world. Many of them thus understood perception as a mental representation of the world, a notion that became the central target for powerful critiques of perception science from William James to James Gibson. For some of the Victorian writers in this study, on the other hand, the analogy between reading and perception tended to work the other way around, so that the world encountered in reading came to seem more immediate, more empirical, more present. Through their encounter with perception science, I contend, Victorian writers moved toward a robust empiricism of reading that marks them as heirs to the "dissident line" of antirepresentationalism that Jonathan Kramnick has identified in eighteenth-century literature and theories of perception.[19]

Before reaching the Victorian period at the center of this study, both that dissident line and the more dominant strain of empiricism from which it departs run through Romanticism.[20] In the eighteenth century, the analogy with reading and language licensed an antirepresentationalist view of perception. Reid, for example, identified the deep structural similarity of human languages as evidence for the fundamental universality of perception and thus, ultimately, for a direct perceptual realism.[21] The end of the eighteenth century, however, marked the rise of comparative philology, which turned away from theories of universal grammar and instead conceived of language diachronically, in terms of ethno-national histories. Consequently, philologists invested texts (especially historical texts) with an unprecedented authority that, in the related domains of literature and law, spurred new processes of textualization in which embodied discursive practices came to be displaced by writings.[22] This emergent shift towards textualization is one way to understand Romanticism's fascination with how literary texts mediate older oral verse traditions such as the ballad.

Seen in this light, William Wordsworth's famous appeal to empiricist accounts of perception in the preface to *Lyrical Ballads* looks like an early attempt to theorize the conditions under which literature could restore the sensational vivacity that it had lost by its textualization. For Wordsworth, poetry aims to make experiences present to the reader in a way that directly parallels what he describes as "the language of the sense": "the mighty world / Of eye, and ear,—both what they half create / And what perceive."[23] Dramatizing the simultaneous presence and absence of memory more broadly, perception here embodies the paradoxically intimate distances of Wordsworth's poetry. But by the middle of the nineteenth century, following new findings in physics, psychology, and neurophysiology, the distance separating both language and sense from the world had grown more acute. For Victorian writers trying to bridge that distance, problems of reference and descriptive accuracy consequently took on new kinds of salience. While such developments had an effect on Victorian poetry, questions of reference and description have historically been of more central importance to discussions of the Victorian novel and the Victorian Aesthetic Movement. This book therefore largely brackets poetry. Its account of Victorian literature and perception science accordingly remains a partial portrait. Even so, I hope that this study's account of the radical empiricism of the Victorian novel and the Aesthetic Movement can help sharpen our sense of how reading makes both the page and the world beyond the page available in literary studies more broadly.

The indisputable difference between reading about the world and observing and experimenting on it firsthand, it would seem, is one way that literature and science really are two cultures. This fundamental difference is one reason that the groundbreaking work on literature and science by scholars such as Gillian Beer, Sally Shuttleworth, and George Levine focused on discourse and narrative, rather than experiment and observation, as the shared domain that unified Victorian literature and science into one culture. A common discourse facilitated the circulation from writers to scientists and back again of ideas, tropes, and narratives making up, as Gillian Beer puts it, "the patterns through which we apprehend experience and hence the patterns through which we condense experience in the telling of it."[24] This study, too, attempts to show how the shared verbal structures of literary and scientific thought enframe experience.

At the same time, this study attempts to move beyond the opposition between verbal structures and experience that tacitly undergirds much earlier work on Victorian literature and science. Experience, Beer suggests, arrives belatedly—the patterns of narrative and discourse must be already there for it to be apprehended or recounted. This textualist approach has often been the price of science's admission to literary studies, since it allows literary critical methods to be meaningfully brought to bear on scientific texts. Here, though, I explore reading literature as itself a perceptual experience, one that folds together the actual sensory presence of words on a page with the virtual presence of the objects to which those words refer.

This book, then, follows recent work by Elaine Auyoung and Mary Favret in arguing that the dynamics of reading as a basic perceptual competency have important implications for the practice of forming wholistic interpretations of texts that likewise goes by the name of reading. "Before it can unleash its virtual wonders or elicit our identifications and sympathy," Favret observes, "reading depends fundamentally on sensory perception . . . embedded in a historically given world."[25] Reading is one of the various modes of sensorimotor engagement that the philosopher Alva Noë evocatively calls "styles of exploring and achieving, or trying to achieve, access to the world" (45). The history of the world and of the bodies that populate it necessarily render those modes of access uneven and various. That unevenness is the core insight of the social model of disability (in contrast to the medical model), whose unfinished project is the egalitarian reorganization of the built social environment so as to arrange for its maximal accessibility to those different styles. We might see that particular project as a signal instance of politics as Jacques Rancière defines them: an ongoing contest over "the distribution of the perceptible."[26] Tracking that contest through the history of aesthetics, Rancière argues that literature participates in that politics insofar as it is a "mode of intervention in the carving up of objects that form a common world, the subjects that people that world and the powers they have to see it, name it, and act upon it."[27] Resituating literary studies' interpretive practices in relation to the perceptual processes involved in reading thus opens up space for thinking about the political terms of access to the world, the ways that access is managed, neglected, or policed as a crucial element of how particular bodies are gendered, racialized, and disabled.[28]

Those lines of inquiry are important and necessary, but they are not my primary concern here. Instead of the political history of such differential terms of perceptual access to the world, this book takes up the intellectual history of how we came to think of perception in terms of access to the world in the first place. While particularized bodies are significant parts of that intellectual history, and while gender and disability in particular figure prominently in parts of this book, in the main I follow the scientific, philosophical, and literary texts that constitute my primary archive here in focusing on the abstraction that is the normative case. That abstraction likewise precludes sustained attention to book history and bibliography, the fields devoted to the concrete and particularized stimuli encountered by the reading body. My hope is that this history of how perception has been understood can nonetheless contribute something toward the theoretical justification of ongoing work on its material and political histories.

This study, then, aims to disclose how Victorian literary texts imagine, elicit, and model the experience of reading them. This fundamental question has been gaining salience in scholarship on nineteenth-century literature, with recent studies taking it up as key to understanding novel-form, book history, and contemporary theories of affect, among other concerns.[29] I argue that nineteenth-century perception science is critical to grasping the experience of reading Victorian literature. Victorian literature envisioned its own reading by way of analogies to various kinds of perceptual experiences but also as itself an embodied practice instantiating those perceptual experiences. I take those perceptual experiences—harmony in Pater, association in Hardy, empathy in Lee, hallucinations in Eliot—as nodes linking together scientists with novelists and experimental instruments with aestheticist manifestoes.

Chapter 1 sketches the scientific origins of the category of knowledge by description. There I give a detailed overview of the emergence of a scientific distinction between sensation and perception focusing on the work of four figures from philosophy and the sciences: Reid, William Whewell, John Stuart Mill, and Hermann von Helmholtz. I then turn to William James, whose radical empiricism reconfigured the relationship between sensation and perception by framing it in terms of two different categories of knowledge: knowledge by acquaintance and knowledge by description. For James, knowledge by description became key to his view of experience as radically continuous movement through a connecting world. In this regard, I suggest, the radical empiricism that James developed in conversation with Victorian perception science can help clarify methods in contemporary literary studies, such as literal reading, that similarly see in descriptive language a means of restoring literary texts to a connecting world.

Chapter 2 focuses on the historical figures populating *Romola* (1862–63), George Eliot's historical novel set in Renaissance-era Florence. Reading *Romola* alongside the epistemological debates generated by mid-nineteenth-century optics, it argues that Eliot's novel is an extended exploration of how readers can come to know the past conjured up in the historical novel. Linked circuitously to their referents via portraits, histories, and historical documents, *Romola*'s historical figures themselves require the kind of rigorous literal reading that recent critics have reserved for material objects and forces. But *Romola*'s historical figures overpopulate the world of the novel, overwhelming the novel's would-be readers and leading Eliot to reflect within *Romola* itself on how reference operates in the historical novel, as a form that strives to make its readers acquainted with a past that can be described but not directly experienced. Eliot's "resurrection-swarm" of obscure Florentines likely contributed to *Romola*'s famous difficulty in attracting the kind of wide readership enjoyed by Eliot's previous novels. But it is through this same act of dense narrative conjuring that Eliot tests the capacity of the historical novel to provide readers with a way of knowing the past. Ultimately, I suggest that the quattrocento Florence to which *Romola* strives to give its readers access shares a kind of second-order existence with perceptual illusions—both are present to experience, even as we (usually) know that they are not really there.

Chapter 3 accounts for a similarly recessive presence in Thomas Hardy's *The Return of the Native* (1878). Against the common critical narrative that Hardy abandoned novel writing in the 1890s solely because of the hostile critical reactions to *Tess of the D'Urbervilles* and *Jude the Obscure*, this chapter demonstrates that this earlier novel already manifested a deep unease with reading. *The Return of the Native* is famed for its extended descriptions of the landscape of Egdon Heath, but what is most striking about Egdon is its resistance to clear visual description. The chapter accounts for Egdon's visual obscurity by reading the novel alongside James's *The Principles of Psychology* (1890), which displays a keen interest in how darkness affects perceptions. What James and Hardy both found in obscurity was the conditions for a certain kind of perception, one that could curtail its sensory responsiveness so as to single out one particular sensation from a rich potential field of sensory inputs. Focalizing one discrete sensation in this way allowed the mind to read it metaphorically and thus made possible an inventive, personal mode of vision. But Hardy also worried that this kind of reading in the dark empowered his readers to transform his texts without regard to his own intentions, a fear that seemed to him borne out in the scandalized critical reactions to his later novels.

Chapter 4 turns to Vernon Lee to examine the complex relationship with description held by the Victorian Aesthetic Movement. Lee's early essays and fiction analyze the tension between description and acquaintance that defined the modern museum, which struggled institutionally with how to frame its display objects with explanatory text (titles, reference guides, and so on) for spectators who might otherwise lack the expertise needed to identify what they were seeing. The Aesthetic Movement scorned such descriptive mediation in its insistence on the primacy of a directly sensuous encounter with art objects, even as description was the signature style of aestheticist writings. Aestheticist descriptions generally took their warrant from the art object's perceptual suggestiveness—its capacity to call different objects to mind—but Lee's work strives to minimize her response to art's suggestiveness in order to perceive artworks formally instead. This chapter traces Lee's preoccupation with the perception of form from her first essay collection to her late work on aesthetic empathy and literary criticism. Reading her essays alongside her novelistic experiment with formal masochism, *Miss Brown*, I show how, for Lee, formal perception involves us in a relationship of intimate withholding, in which the artwork at once incites and frustrates our desire for what it perceptually suggests.

Chapter 5 explores the kinky erotics of literal reading by strategically fetishizing the recurring figure of harmony in Walter Pater's essay "The School of Giorgione" (1877) and his later writings. I read the figure of harmony literally with help from the acoustics of the German physicist Hermann von Helmholtz, which achieved immense popularity in Britain at just the moment when Pater made his famous declaration that all art aspires to the condition of music. Both Pater and Helmholtz understood perception as an act of reading sensations in which reference—our attention to the objects we infer to be present in the world around us—constantly threatens to overwhelm our awareness of the sensations themselves. In his work on acoustics, however, Helmholtz singled out musical harmony as an experience uniquely susceptible to the mental effort to distinguish discrete sensations during the act of perception. Oscillating between sense and reference, harmony exemplifies the rhetorical logic of what Pater calls literal metaphors—figures whose figurative significance can only be fully accessed by taking them literally. The most emblematic of Pater's literal metaphors is the Paterian figure itself, at once human form and trope. To take Paterian figures literally, I suggest, is to reimagine literal reading as a form of kink—a fetishizing of the sensory forces through which a figure affects and dominates us.

Pater's kinky literalism issues in thick, ekphrastic descriptions of art objects very different from the rigorous attention to precise technical detail in literal reading as it is practiced today in literary studies. In the epilogue, I suggest that attention to the complex ways that reading makes the world present in Pater's literalism, along with the other Victorian practices of reading with the senses limned in this book, nonetheless has something important to contribute to our current methodological discussions. In Oscar Wilde's *The Portrait of Mr. W. H.*, Willie Hughes—the hypothetical historical figure the novella identifies as the fair youth of William Shakespeare's sonnets—assumes just such a complex form of presence, existing as a master referent for readers of the sonnets even as he is almost certainly a fictional character rather than a historical person. Combining fiction with literary criticism, Wilde's novella imagines an alternative version of formalism that would not cleave the referential function of language from its figurative, poetic function in the way of formalists such as Roman Jakobson. Wilde's novella, I suggest, is a model of intentional reading, a mode of reading that recognizes both literature's and its readers' fundamental entanglement with the world and might thereby clarify our sense of why literary studies matters.

1

Knowing Things by Description in Victorian Science

A feeling feels as a gun shoots. If there be nothing to be felt or hit, they discharge themselves *ins blaue hinein*. If, however, something starts up opposite them, they no longer simply shoot or feel, they hit and know.

—William James, "The Function of Cognition"

THREE-VOLUME NOVELS AND CHEAP yellowbacks, parliamentary blue books and double-entry ledgers, illuminated Kelmscott editions and *The Illustrated London News:* Victorians enjoyed the kind of constant intimacy with print that we have with the digital devices we keep on our persons at all times. It is no surprise, then, that for Victorian studies it has become a truth universally acknowledged that, as Benjamin Morgan puts it, "Victorians read books with their bodies."[1] Nicholas Dames, for instance, has leveraged this insight into the bodily nature of how Victorians read into an account of a lost theory of the novel, one that flourished during the nineteenth century before it was supplanted in the twentieth by the New Criticism and its successors. Victorian novelists and novel critics, Dames suggests, conceived of the novel form in the terms of nineteenth-century physiology. "In ways both obvious and hidden," he writes, "physiology was the metalanguage of nineteenth-century novel theory, as perhaps linguistics is of twentieth-century literary theory."[2] Dames shows just how critically important the sciences of the nervous system and sense perception were to the Victorian novel. Here I build on Dames's work by restoring a bit of reciprocity into the relationship between literature and physiology. If it seemed so natural to Victorian critics and writers to conceive of reading in the terms of physiology, this was partly because Victorian physiologists conceived of perception in terms of reading.

This chapter sketches the history of how Victorian scientists came to think of perception as analogous to reading. Since my account here relies on technical terms, a brief summary of the historical narrative here may help to orient readers (a glossary of the main technical terms can be found with the reference matter). Beginning in the late eighteenth century, philosophers and scientists began distinguishing between sensations and perceptions. Sensations became identified with bare intuitions of sensory stimuli, like the experience of a blue patch in our field of vision or of a single auditory tone. Perceptions, on the other hand, became identified with the conscious mental apprehension of the objects supposed to be the source of those sensory stimulations, like a blue ball or a note played on a guitar. New experiments in neurophysiology ratified and even aggravated this basic distinction by revealing that even highly fragmentary and unstable sensory stimulations are still consciously perceived as consistent and relatively detailed fields of objects (a phenomenon now referred to as perceptual constancy). Victorian scientists thus came to think of perception as the act of reflexively inferring the presence of objects from sensory intuitions, a process they called unconscious inference. For nineteenth-century empiricists, in consequence, experience cleaved into two fundamentally different components—sensation and perception, intuition and inference—each one requiring its own specific mode of explanation. Repurposing the trope of the Book of Nature, philosophers and scientists began to account for the relationship between these two components by comparing it to reading—sensations were natural signs, and perceptions were their interpretations.

As the nineteenth century drew to a close, however, these "theories of sensation-based perception" came in for systematic criticism by emerging scientific and philosophical schools.[3] Gestalt psychology and phenomenology, for instance, developed from the insight that sensation-based accounts of perception had things exactly backward—that our bodily engagement with perceptual forms shapes our sensory experience and not the other way around. Instead of rehearsing the familiar history of phenomenology, however, this chapter explicates the critique William James made of sensation-based theories as part of his late turn to a radical empiricism. The second section of this chapter surveys the evolution of that radical empiricism from James's own sensation-based account of perception in his 1890 *Principles of Psychology*. With his radicalization of empiricism, I suggest, James reconfigures the terms of Victorian perception science—sensation and perception, intuition and inference, knowledge by acquaintance, and knowledge by description—in ways that shaped the subsequent history of perception science as well as the philosophy of language. This chapter shows how, by refusing to give either sensation or perception priority over the other, James opens up possibilities for imagining the difference between verbal description and direct sensory experience as one of degree rather than kind. In this regard, apart from its place within a broader intellectual history, Jamesian radical empiricism also reveals an important dimension of Victorian literary history. Specifically, James provides us with a conceptual framework within which we can begin to see how Victorians' reading books with their bodies enabled them to explore the continuities between descriptive and empirical knowledge. Taken together, I argue in the ensuing chapters, these wider experiments in a radical literary empiricism deserve attention from contemporary literary study as it tests out new methods that explore possible affiliations between reading and scientific observation.

Sensation and Perception: Reading the Book of Nature in Nineteenth-Century Science

The origins of the importance of reading to nineteenth-century physiology lie in the eighteenth century, when Thomas Reid laid the foundations for Victorian physiological psychology with an account of perception that emphasized its similarity to language. Reid undertook a simple but devastating attack on eighteenth-century empiricism by prying open a gap between what John Locke defined as simple and complex ideas in his *Essay Concerning Human Understanding* (1689). For Locke, simple ideas are the sensory atoms out of which we compose our knowledge of the world. The softness and warmth of a piece of wax, the coldness and hardness of a piece of ice, the whiteness and smell of a lily, each distinct, irreducible sensation is a simple idea that we usually encounter bundled together into larger complex ideas—in these cases, the ideas of wax, ice, and lily.[4] Locke was not particularly concerned with specifying the precise mechanism involved in bundling simple ideas together or with how exactly a simple idea (the sensation of a particular shade of whiteness) spontaneously generates a complex one (our perception of the lily). But Locke had followers who did try to fill in these missing details.

One of the most famous was David Hartley, who argued that simple ideas generate complex ones through association. In the account Hartley offers in his *Observations on Man* (1749), simple ideas that are similar to each other or that we repeatedly encounter in quick succession (like the sensation of the lily's smell that quickly follows the sensation of the lily's color) become linked to each other in the mind, so that one simple idea easily calls to mind its associates. What's more, Hartley speculated that association had a material basis in the nervous system. A given visual or olfactory stimulus supposedly creates vibrations that travel along a particular route to and within the brain, and these vibrations shape the brain in ways that allow each stimulus to trigger vibrations in an associated neural pathway so as to make possible the economical generation of complex ideas.[5] Hartley's speculations about neural vibrations quickly fell victim to advances in physiological knowledge, as the current consensus that nervous impulse transmission is an electrochemical process began to take shape in the nineteenth century. His theory of the association of ideas, however, was able to dominate Anglo-American psychology for the next century and a half.

Nonetheless, Hartley's association of ideas and his neural vibrations both left Reid unmoved. Reid rejected Locke's argument that perception is mediated by ideas or images, advocating instead for a direct perceptual realism. Hence no amount of backfilling could fix the main problem he saw with Locke's account of simple and complex ideas—that Locke made a category error when he referred to simple and complex ideas *as ideas.* By categorizing both simple and complex ideas as ideas, Locke had suggested that the only possible difference between them was the relative one of their complexity. In contrast, Reid argued that Locke's simple and complex ideas were two entirely different things. In *An Inquiry into the Human Mind on the Principles of Common Sense* (1764), Reid proposed a different terminology, renaming simple ideas as sensations and complex ideas as perceptions, although he worried even that act of rechristening didn't make the distinction he was drawing obvious enough:

> The same mode of expression is used to denote sensation and perception; and therefore we are apt to look upon them as things of the same nature. Thus, *I feel a pain; I see a tree:* the first denoteth a sensation, the last a perception. The grammatical analysis of both expressions is the same: for both consist of an active verb and an object. But if we attend to the things signified by these expressions, we shall find, that in the first, the distinction between the act and the object is not real, but grammatical; in the second, the distinction is not only grammatical, but real.[6]

With the benefit of hindsight, we can see Reid groping here for the concept that a hundred years later Franz Brentano would term "intentionality"—a kind of aboutness that Brentano describes as "reference [or] direction to an object."[7] Simply put, Reid argues that perceptions refer to objects out there in the world, while sensations do not. The tree I perceive refers to something really existing in the world, but the pain I sense does not refer but simply is.

Reid's introduction of a distinction between sensation and perception was a momentous event in the history of psychology, one whose importance is hard to overstate. As the psychologist Edward Reed observed, it was Reid who sharpened psychology's foundational categories of stimulus, sensation, and perception into their modern form, making the later development of the discipline possible.[8] Reid himself doubted that there could be any convincing account of the causal mechanisms that somehow transform a physical stimulus into a sensation and a sensation into a perception. "Can any man tell me," he asks, "how, in vision, the rays of light act upon the *retina,* how the *retina* acts upon the optic nerve, and how the optic nerve acts upon the brain? No man can" (303). Undeterred, nineteenth-century scientists adopted just this challenge as a core research question for optics, physiology, and psychology. Even so, each of these fields not only adopted Reid's terminology but also discovered that advances in neurophysiological knowledge ironically confirmed Reid's arguments that there was only a weak causality leading from stimulus to perception. Victorian neurophysiology and psychology demonstrated experimentally that even very impoverished stimuli could still yield relatively richly detailed perceptions; the mind seemed to be filling in gaps in some way, and to explain how this might take place scientists appealed to what they saw as the similar power of language to conjure up vivid mental images from similarly minimal visual or auditory stimuli. Here too, nineteenth-century scientists followed Reid, albeit in a way he would have disagreed with.

When Reid identified something like intentionality as the hallmark of perception, he effectively redefined perception in terms of reference. As a result, nineteenth-century perception science and the philosophy of language met on intimate terms over their shared concern with how words and percepts signify things. It is thus no accident that perception is central to the two most influential philosophical accounts of reference to come out of this period, Gottlob Frege's "On Sense and Reference" and Bertrand Russell's "On Denoting." Well aware of his argument's implications, Reid made the connection explicitly himself, claiming that "there is much greater similitude than is commonly imagined, between the testimony of nature given by our senses, and the testimony of men given by language . . . [because] the signs by which objects are presented to us in perception, are the language of nature to man" (295–96). When we perceive things, Reid suggests, we are simply reading the Book of Nature in the way that Francis Bacon had advocated in *The New Organon.* According to Reid, the universality and divine origins of that book guarantee the truth of our readings despite our inability to specify the precise chain of causes and effects leading from a physical stimulus to a perception. The Book of Nature was legible to us, he maintained, because God had created us to perceive a world in common and to have an irresistible belief in the reality of what we perceive. Reid thus didn't see reference or signification as a problem that should lead us to doubt the potential accuracy or truth of what we perceive; instead, he argued that science and philosophy should take the reality of our perceptions for granted as a premise derived from common sense.

It is one of the ironies of nineteenth-century intellectual history that the main arguments Reid enlisted to support his direct perceptual realism—his distinction between sensation and perception and his notion that perception was the interpretation of signs—undermined that realism for the Victorian scientists and philosophers who followed him. Over the course of the nineteenth century, the uncertain causal relationships leading from stimulus to perception that Reid himself had emphasized began to suggest to investigators that there was too much interpretation in perception—that the mind saw less what was there than what it wanted or expected to be there. As perception came to be understood as a kind of reading, its interpretations of nature acquired the same liability to *mis*reading that had long haunted the novel in the figures of fantasy addicts like Emma Bovary and Don Quixote. The epistemologically troubling dimensions perception assumed for Victorian science become clear if we turn to William Whewell's *Philosophy of the Inductive Sciences* (1840). Whewell wanted to renovate Francis Bacon's inductive method—the systematic process of carefully extrapolating general truths "from sense and particulars"—and to reaffirm its status as *the* scientific method for the Victorian era.[9] To do that, though, Whewell had to reconcile Baconian induction with new theories of perception that emphasized its tendency to impose preexisting ideas onto concrete particulars.

Whewell in fact reconceptualized induction in terms of the distinction between sensations and perceptions.[10] Reid had defined sensations as essentially self-contained and nonreferential, in contrast to perception's intentionality (its constant direction toward real objects in the world). Whewell, on the other hand, underscored the origins of sensations as reflexive responses to material forces. Because they occur at the level of neurophysiological response below the threshold of mental activity, sensations functioned for Whewell as a crucial interface with the material world. At the same time, Whewell foregrounded the interpretive aspects of perception, defining it as the mental act of ordering sensations: "Sensations cannot become perceptions of objects, without some formative power of the mind. By the very act of being received as perceptions, they have a formative power exercised over them, the operation of which might be expressed, by speaking of them . . . simply as *formed.*"[11] Whewell thus reimagines Baconian induction as the productive antithesis of sensations and perceptions, or, as he also puts it, "things" and "thoughts."

Whewell's understanding of sense perception ultimately leads him to define science as a kind of reading. In an extraordinary passage, he returns to Bacon's trope of interpreting the Book of Nature and argues not just for its metaphorical but also for its literal truth:

> [In this metaphor,] Nature is the Book, and Man is the Interpreter. The facts of the external world are marks, in which man discovers a meaning, and so reads them. Man is the Interpreter of Nature, and Science is the right Interpretation. And this image . . . exhibits to us the necessity of both elements;—the marks which man has to look at, and the knowledge of the alphabet and language which he must possess and apply before he can find any meaning in what he sees. . . . Indeed the illustration is rather an example than a comparison of the composition of our knowledge. The letters and symbols which are presented to the Interpreter are really objects of sensation: the notion of letters as signs of words, the notion of connexions among words by which they have meaning, really are among our Ideas. . . . The Sciences are not figuratively, but really Interpretations of Nature. (37–38)[12]

Reading is not just a metaphorical illustration of sense perception but its essence, its most paradigmatic example, and scientists are not figuratively but really reading the world. Whewell literalizes the Book of Nature here in a way that demonstrates just how fundamental reading was to Victorian theories of perception.

At the same time, in literalizing the Book of Nature Whewell tacitly suggests that scientists are liable to confuse "thoughts" with "things" and perceptions with sensations. The source of that confusion lies in the nature of reading. As Ian Duncan observes, Whewell identifies two stages in the development of scientific language: an initial "act of figuration," in which a phenomenon is described metaphorically, and a "naturalization of the figure" through which "the aura of its artifice" is worn away so that it can be used literally.[13] For Whewell, these two stages of figuration and literalization in scientific language correspond to the two stages by which scientific theories become scientific facts. Scientific theories are a conscious and effortful attempt to see the world differently, to bring new inferences to bear on our perception of it. Facts are what we see once these inferences become familiar and taken for granted: "In a Fact, the Ideas are applied so readily and familiarly, and incorporated with the sensations so entirely, that we do not see *them,* we see *through them*" (40). Whewell underscores that the established inferences making up facts are necessary if we are to see anything at all. We cannot read the inscriptions of nature without reading them in the language we are accustomed to. Nonetheless, the very familiarity of that language opens us up to a readerly kind of error. As Whewell knew very well, nothing is more natural to a reader than to "make, out of these elements [of black marks on a page], thought and feeling, without being aware of the act by which [she does] so" (114). And so when we perceive likewise, we do not just interpret the Book of Nature, we *unconsciously* interpret the Book of Nature. When it is guided by facts, Whewell suggests, perception is an act of "unconscious inference" (42). And the unconsciousness of those inferences presents inherent difficulties for any attempt to separate out "things" from "thoughts" in our perception of the world.

Whewell's account of perception thus helped make the obstacles we face in distinguishing what is actually, and not just virtually, present in experience into a central problem for nineteenth-century empiricism. *Philosophy of the Inductive Sciences* is in fact the founding document of the concept that Edward Reed called the logical unconscious—an unconscious that performs the same kind of rational calculations that the conscious mind does. Whewell's notion of unconscious inferences would go on to serve as the cornerstone of physiological psychology after John Stuart Mill inadvertently helped popularize Whewell's arguments by making him the key antagonist of his *System of Logic* (1843). Mill objected to the way that Whewell's account of induction seemed to suggest that certain ideas are innate rather than the product of experience.[14] The notoriety of the Mill-Whewell dispute tends to sharpen our critical sense of the disagreements between these two figures. But to contemporaneous German readers at a remove from the dispute's immediate social context, like Wilhelm Wundt and Hermann von Helmholtz, Mill and Whewell were much more important for their broad agreement that experience is a compound of sensory intuitions and perceptual inferences.

While Mill insisted that perceptual inferences could always be traced back to sensations experienced earlier, he also assigned those inferences an even bigger chunk of experience than Whewell did. "For in almost every act of our perceiving faculties," he wrote, "observation and inference are intimately blended. What we are said to observe is usually a compound result, of which one-tenth may be observation, and the remaining nine-tenths inference."[15] That 90 percent of what we observe derives from our own mind is an astonishing claim to find coming from one of the nineteenth century's most steadfast advocates of empiricism. However, Mill's generous estimate of the unconscious inferences at work in perception marks the direction of Victorian empiricism's subsequent development as it began to absorb the groundbreaking work being done in neurophysiology.

No one figure better exemplifies the growing importance of unconscious inferences in empiricism and science than the German physicist Hermann von Helmholtz. One of the most important figures in nineteenth-century neurophysiology, Helmholtz helped make some of the field's most significant breakthroughs. In 1849 and 1850, he adapted Charles Pouillet's galvanometer in order to experimentally measure the speed at which nerves transmit impulses and found that it was surprisingly slow—only about thirty meters per second, a fraction of the speed of sound. In 1851, he devised the world's first working ophthalmoscope to peer inside the retina. The anatomy he found—a central indentation packed with photoreceptor cells (the fovea) tapering off into a surrounding peripheral area—convinced Helmholtz that what we see at any given moment is a central point of clarity surrounded by a vague, washed-out blur, and that it is only by constantly shifting the central point of our vision that we manage to construct a stable visual field. Later that same decade, he developed the widely influential resonance theory of hearing by using specially designed resonators (including an electric device for producing and combining tones that was the first ancestor of the modern synthesizer) to experimentally analyze musical tones. These experiments demonstrated that what we typically hear as simple tones are in fact the complex, harmonic result of multiple tones layered on top of one another. The resulting picture of our nervous system and sensory organs led Helmholtz to the conclusion that our sensations at any given moment are necessarily belated, fragmentary, and incommensurate with our conscious experience of the world.

In his lectures and major statements on his research from the early 1860s on, Helmholtz therefore argues that perception can only be understood as an act of unconscious inference with which the mind constructs an interpretation of the world out of the cues provided by sensations. He conceived of unconscious inference as a syllogism in which "the major premise is formed from a series of experiences which have individually disappeared from memory . . . [so that] in present perception, the newly appearing sense impression forms the minor premise to which is applied the rule imprinted [in the mind] through earlier observations."[16] For Helmholtz, sense perception is quite literally a logic, but to characterize its rapid inference of a whole world of meaning from even highly diminished sensory cues he draws an extended analogy with language itself. We unconsciously infer things from our sensations, he suggests, in the same way that we understand the meaning of words and sentences—effortlessly, without any specific recollection of the long course of experience that taught us to do so.

Language served Helmholtz as a model as well as a metaphor for perception. Like Mill, Helmholtz advocated the empiricist position that even the most fundamental of perceptual inferences—such as extension in space—are acquired from experience rather than innate.[17] As he pressed his claims that we must acquire the ability to understand sensations through experience, he found a perfect model for sensations in language, a "System of Signs, which is not given by nature but arbitrarily chosen, and which must undoubtedly be learned before it is understood."[18] Like Reid and Whewell, Helmholtz defined sense perception in terms of reading and reference. In his view, perception is the act of recognizing "a compound aggregate of sensations as the sign of a simple object."[19] Helmholtz's empiricism thus led him in a roundabout way back to something like Reid's notion of perception as reading the Book of Nature.

Helmholtz's return to Reid was repetition with a difference, however, since Helmholtz's account ran the risk of making perception all too much like reading. To begin with, Reid conceived of sensations as a system of signs on the model of a universal grammar. Reid held that the structure of the language of perception as of language per se was founded on a stable, universally held common sense.[20] Working after comparative philology had displaced universal grammar with its diachronic model of linguistic development, Helmholtz exacerbated a growing disjunction between sign system and meaning in ways that pointed toward what Ferdinand Saussure would later construe as the arbitrariness of the sign. Helmholtz emphasized tirelessly that our sensations were not images and had no necessary likeness or similarity to the material objects or forces that caused them.[21] If our sensations were thus at best an indirect guide to the material world, Helmholtz offered consolation in the idea that experience over time would average out sensory anomalies so as to reveal the world's fundamental regularity. Evoking structural objectivity, Helmholtz suggested that, guided by unconscious inferences, "the loving and attentive observer" might thus learn to perceive "the law-like order in the realm of the real . . . [even if] this can only be presented in the sign-system of our sense impressions" ("Facts," 355, 362).

That relentless averaging out of sensory anomalies itself raised a different problem, however, since the unconscious smoothing away of specific irregularities would necessarily efface the particular sensations eliciting an act of perception. Helmholtz suggests that when we perceive, we subsume the actually present sensations under the rule of previous experience, forgetting the signs before us in favor of the thing we know from experience that they denote. This tendency to neglect the signs for the significations is, as we've seen, a specifically readerly kind of blind spot. Since Helmholtz thought our best chance of apprehending the real lay in revealing its lawlike regularity, he was not especially alarmed by the idea that where our sensations are concerned, we reflexively see only the rule and not the exception. At the same time, though, the physical facts of raw sensations were themselves what Helmholtz's scientific work in optics, acoustics, and neurophysiology was trying to explain. Hence the jarring divide in Helmholtz's work that Jonathan Crary notes: "His ontology is a physics, but his epistemology is a semiotics."[22] Just to establish the facts of that physics, Helmholtz had to maintain that observers could train themselves to apprehend at least some kinds of discrete sensations before the mind interpreted them. For nineteenth-century physics, then, sensations were not a gauzy, introspective category of experience. For scientists like Helmholtz, they were on the contrary something like a mathematical language, a privileged expression of the pure physics constituting the natural world.

Split between a physics and a semiotics, Helmholtz's scientific work illustrates the emergence of two different orders of facts in empiricism and perception science. On the one hand, there were the facts of order and system reflected by unconscious inferences, what we might call the facts *of* perception. On the other, there were the facts of forces and neural anatomy embodied in sensations, the facts *in* perception. The facts of and in perception required two different modes of philosophical and scientific explanation.[23] Responding to this need, Victorian empiricists developed two new epistemological categories: knowledge by description and knowledge by acquaintance.

Knowing Things by Description: Jamesian Radical Empiricism

First proposed by John Grote, knowledge by description (which was also called "knowledge about") and knowledge by acquaintance distinguished between verbal or propositional knowledge and the kind of knowledge we obtain by the direct presentation of an object to our senses. While the distinction between propositional and empirical knowledge seems straightforward enough, these categories circulated widely in science and philosophy precisely because the boundary between verbal and empirical knowledge had become hard to draw. The chapters to follow chart the ways that the relationship between description and acquaintance was configured and reconfigured across a range of literary texts, observational and reading practices, and scientific and philosophical theories. The remainder of this chapter teases out one particular strand within that genealogy—William James's founding of his radical empiricism on his own reconfiguration of knowledge by description and knowledge by acquaintance.

One unforeseen effect of Reid's distinction between sensations and perceptions was that sensations came to seem ever more remote and inaccessible to conscious experience over the course of the nineteenth century. Normally, we do not experience sensations; we experience the objects those sensations cue us to recognize as being present. In the terminology of Victorian science, the vast majority of our experience is of perceptions and not of sensations. Instead of a yellow blotch in the lower left side of my visual field, I see a yellow notecard resting on the desk; instead of a group of auditory tones, I hear a familiar voice. There are, furthermore, distinct limits to how far we can train ourselves to attend to sensations instead of our perceptual judgments about the objects giving rise to them. Sensations, then, are elusive; even as they constitute our most intimate connection with the world, they tend to vanish down below the threshold of consciousness.

As sensations disappeared, perception itself came to seem more anaesthetized, its contact with things more abstract and mediated. Like reading in a private study, the act of perception likewise seemed staged in solitary isolation as a representation in the theater of consciousness.[24] The Victorian-era scientific approach to perception as the mental interpretation of sensations continues to inform important work in experimental psychology and cognitive science.[25] Nonetheless, the tacit model of perception as detached and immobilized that enabled much of that scientific work comports awkwardly with actual experience—the world does not seem to pass in show before us while we sit still in the dark. James, who had played a key role in drawing the formal disciplinary outlines of perception science (he is cocredited with Wilhelm Wundt for establishing the world's first laboratories for experimental psychology in 1879), also levied an important critique of that science on just these grounds. His radical empiricism insists on the principle that perception emerges from the dynamic interplay between the body and its environment, and his work is in this regard an important forerunner of what James Gibson would term the ecological approach to perception. Jamesian empiricism assigns knowledge by description a role within the ecology of perception. In this regard, his radical empiricism can help us understand how even reading in a private study unfolds within a larger world.

James used the categories of description and acquaintance as the foundation for his account of sensation and perception in *The Principles of Psychology* (1890). The function of sensation, he writes, "is that of mere *acquaintance* with a fact. Perception's function, on the other hand, is knowledge *about* a fact."[26] Sensing a fact is simply becoming aware of simple qualities, like heat, resistance, or pain. For James, sensation is strictly speaking intentional, because it cognizes an object or fact, but that object is stripped of all its relations, so utterly nude that it lacks even a name (James calls it a *that*). Perception, meanwhile, recognizes that fact's relations to other facts that past sensations have cognized and so ties them together into "the unity of a *thing* with a name" (2:78; italics in original). James thus follows Reid in defining perception in terms of its stronger intentionality. Perception is a mode of knowledge that operates through the aboutness of reference, through apprehending the relations that lead transitively from one fact of experience to another.

To illustrate the difference between sensations and perceptions, James invites his readers to pause in their reading to stare at and repeat one word over and over:

> Let the reader try this with any word on this page. He will soon begin to wonder if it can possibly be the word he has been using all his life with that meaning. It stares at him from the paper like a glass eye, with no speculation in it. Its body is indeed there, but its soul is fled. It is reduced, by this new way of attending to it, to its sensational nudity. We never before attended to it in this way, but habitually got it clad with its meaning the moment we caught sight of it, and rapidly passed from it to the other words of the phrase. (2:81)

James here asks us to defamiliarize the text itself in order to encounter reading in its sensational nudity, a state that is typically all but invisible to practiced readers but also one that lacks both meaning and movement. The defamiliarized word, like the defamiliarized sensation, by itself does not lead us anywhere.

The strange inertness of bare sensations indicates that sensations must always come clothed with relations as complete figures rather than nude elements; hence James concluded that sensations are not a primary fact of experience so much as a secondary abstraction that isolates one part of experience.[27] Extending this line of thinking, his later essays on empiricism push the confusion over how to parcel out experience into two different kinds of truth—thoughts and things, sensation and perception, etc.—to its limit by suggesting that perhaps the difficulty was owing to the fact that experience held primarily only one kind of truth after all. The "essential homogeneity of thought with thing" explains why it is "so hard to tell, in a presented and recognized material object, what part comes through the sense-organs and what part comes 'out of one's own head' [since] sensations and apperceptive ideas fuse here so intimately that you can no more tell where one begins and the other ends, than you can tell [in a panorama] where the real foreground and the painted canvas join together."[28] James, in other words, came to take the mixture of thoughts and things as primary in experience.

We only arrive in retrospect at the distinction between thought and thing, James suggests, by following the transitions connecting a given experience along two different axes. In one direction, those transitions are the experiential conjunctions that together add up to the mental history of a knower (the branching network of her sensations, emotions, movements, judgments, and so on); in the other, they are the experiential conjunctions comprising the physical history of the known. The resulting understanding of perceptual experience as a collocation of relational processes unfolding in time is what James calls radical empiricism.[29]

Among other things, Jamesian empiricism fundamentally transforms how we understand what it means for an object to be present to perception. Each experience has a solid nucleus of knowledge by acquaintance, a fully present *that.* But it also has what James calls a fringe, a set of dangling relations that are themselves experienced but only as pointing to elsewhere: "Much of our experience comes as an insufficient and is of process and transition. Our fields of experience have no more definite boundaries than have our fields of view. Both are fringed by a *more* that continuously develops, and that continuously supersedes them as life proceeds."[30] The fringe of experience here is, properly, knowledge by description, but while James insists that such knowledge is present in experience, it is present as receding, like a vanishing point. In some cases—in particular, James points to the case of another person's mind—such inaccessibility is final, and following the conjunctions pointing to a thing can at best make us acquainted with the fringe lying in its nearest vicinity. In others, we can follow those conjunctions through a connecting world that leads to direct acquaintance with a thing. When, for example, we see the oblong crystalline opacity of an ice cube, the feeling of its coldness and hardness to the touch is also virtually present, there for us if we were to reach out and grasp it. James thus refuses to approach acts of perception as discrete units that can be understood in isolation from each other. Instead, radical empiricism insists that perceptual experience always includes the experience of transitions and therefore of what is virtually present immanent within what is actually present.

In his turn to radical empiricism, James helps reveal for us what Alva Noë calls the varieties of presence. At any given moment, Noë suggests, the world shows up for us in perception as both present and present as absent. In seeing a three-dimensional object like a tomato, he notes, we do not just represent it in our own minds by logically inferring that it has an unseen back, as the theory of unconscious inferences would have it. Instead, we have a "visual sense" of its back even as we cannot actually see it (Noë, 16). The back of the tomato is absent, but it is perceived as virtually present because it is available—we know that the right series of movements will bring it into view.

The Ecological Approach to Textual Perception: James Gibson and Literal Reading

In its attention to the varieties of perceptual presence, Jamesian empiricism can help us better understand how reading, too, makes the world present. This section sketches the outlines of that better understanding by way of a more recent Jamesian account of perception: the psychologist James Gibson's landmark study, *The Ecological Approach to Visual Perception* (1979). Turning to recent methodological debates within literary studies, I then go on to show how Jamesian empiricism clarifies the conflicted status of the perceptible within the literal reading advocated by Elaine Freedgood and Cannon Schmitt.

Gibson, like James, conceived of perception as a mode of actively exploring the world that unfolds in time. The observer, he argued, perceives by picking up what he called invariants of structure—in effect, the features that persist despite changes in lighting, angle, and so on—out of a flowing array of sensory information. The invariants of structure that an observer picks up are the useful ones, the features that elicit us to act with and on them. To describe these useful invariants of structure, Gibson coined the term affordances, a term that has become something of a key word in literary criticism thanks to its adoption by Caroline Levine as a way of thinking about forms and their effects.[31] Gibson's work suggests, though, that formal structures are at best relatively stable and invariant, their edges constantly lapped by the flowing sensory array from which they emerge. Seen this way, forms are the fragile achievement of an embodied actor working in concert with her environment. Gibson therefore insists that "an affordance is not bestowed upon an object by a need of an observer and his act of perceiving it. The object offers what it does because it is what it is."[32] For Gibson, affordances are the locus of ecological interaction, and perception has its own (specifically ecological) ontology. Its objects are real objects, not mental representations.

For this reason, Gibson flatly rejected the idea that perception is the interpretation of sensations. He rightly identified the roots of the sensation-based theory of perception in the Book of Nature, and he had no patience for its theological implications: "The environment does not communicate with the observers who inhabit it. Why should the world speak to us? The concept of stimuli as signals to be interpreted implies some such nonsense as a world-soul trying to get through to us" (63). The ecological approach, Gibson insisted, demonstrated that perception could not be assimilated to conceptual or propositional knowledge; it instead revealed that propositional knowledge is a species of perception. If perception is the ongoing awareness of persisting structures in the world, as Gibson defines it, then we can see how propositions simply describe those persisting structures at one remove from their initial abstraction out of a sensory array. Therefore, Gibson concludes, "knowing is an *extension* of perceiving" (258; italics in original). This is a point that has been echoed by Noë, who likewise maintains that the difference between perceiving something and referring to it in language or thought is one of degree, not kind. "Thought is sometimes a kind of extended perception," he writes, since "to see something—that is, for something to show up for one in conscious visual experience—or to refer in thought to something—that is, for it to show up in one's conscious thoughts—is [in both cases] a matter of skillful access to the thing" (27).

The Jamesian understanding of descriptive knowledge in terms of extended perception offers literary studies an important means of explaining how reading can yield empirical knowledge. A key challenge for descriptive methods of reading is that their claims to empirical validity ultimately rest on the credibility of the literary author—if her descriptions of fictional behavior, setting, and so on are not themselves based on careful empirical observations, the whole thing falls to the ground.[33] Gibson makes a similar caveat, noting that there is a crucial difference between the knowledge communicated by descriptions and "the limitless information available in a flowing stimulus array" (260). He notes that "information about the environment that has been put into words has this disadvantage: The reality testing that accompanies the pickup of natural information [in perception] is missing. Descriptions, spoken or written, do not permit the flowing stimulus array to be scrutinized. The invariants have already been extracted. You have to trust the original perceiver; you must 'take his word for it,' as we say" (261). This disadvantage to descriptive knowledge is inescapable, but it can be substantially ameliorated if, rather than considering descriptions in isolation so that our only recourse is to accept them or not, we attend to how we encounter descriptions within a flowing stimulus array that continues beyond them.

Descriptions have a fringe of their own; they do not terminate in themselves but rather, Gibson suggests, act to aid and facilitate the reader's further perceiving. If the objects described in a text are further away than the back of the tomato on the counter, it is nonetheless true that, as James notes, a person in North America reading about tigers in Southeast Asia can, at least for the time being, follow the relations present in the thought of them through a connecting world "into some ideal or real context, or even into the immediate presence, of the tigers."[34] In other words, if knowing things by description is an extension of perceiving, we can always do our best to shorten the distance involved. To conceive of reading along these lines is to grasp that it is not "a modality of detachment [but] rather . . . a modality of openness to the world" (Noë, 8).

This Jamesian picture of how we know things by description captures something important about the way we read in literary studies. Thin and thick description alike require us to follow the relations leading outward from literary texts through a connecting world into different contexts, and we generally do so with the aim of making both the text and the world it describes more fully present to ourselves. New Historicism typically characterizes itself in terms of detachment; Catherine Gallagher and Stephen Greenblatt thus describe the attitude of the New Historicist critic as "skeptical, wary, demystifying, critical, and even adversarial."[35] Even so, they have also professed themselves animated by the desire to make something like a perceptual contact with the past—to touch the real, to speak with the dead, and so on.

The heightened interest in affect, materialism, book history, and ecology among literary critics in the wake of the New Historicism gives new urgency to the question of how reading might help us restore literary texts to what James calls "a connecting world."[36] While perceptual concepts and metaphors figure saliently in recent methodological debates for this reason, they have also tended to act as lightning rods because there has been relatively little critical attention to the longer history of thought about the relationship between reading and perception. Take, for example, the method that Cannon Schmitt and Elaine Freedgood call literal reading.

Ambivalent toward historicism and the descriptive turn, literal reading is a research program aimed at rigorously examining the descriptive language that abounds in the realist novel. Literal reading focuses primarily on the precise specification of features in the story world whose apparent insignificance for the larger narrative famously led Roland Barthes to call them reality effects—notations whose entire purpose is to seem to bypass meaning altogether so as to simply proclaim, "*We are the real.*"[37] Instead of skipping over a novel's opaquely technical or gratuitously pedestrian details as significant only for their apparent insignificance, literal readers painstakingly following the tracks of where such referential language points, looping out from the literary text along a circuitous pathway through dictionaries, technical manuals, maps, charts, and first-hand accounts before arriving back at a literary text whose global significance then seems remade. In this regard, literal reading is a model for critical attention to the text's fringe of relations.

Freedgood and Schmitt state categorically, however, that "the literal is not the surface or thereness or the perceptible."[38] By this, they mean that the literal is not what is actually present in perception—the letters on the page, which by themselves do not reveal anything. But that is just to say that what is actually present in perception is by itself meaningless. Without knowledge by description, the relations that connect one moment of experience to others, the perceptible cannot be meaningful. Insofar as they are both defined by intentionality, by reference to an object, the literal and perception are much closer than this statement suggests. To read literally is to insist on the sufficiency and rigor of our critical knowledge by description. A literal reading of mountains, for example, requires "the slow and painful disentangling of [the mere nebulous concept of mountains] from the perception of certain mountains from a certain vantage at a certain moment in time: the chalky Dolomite Alps in the early morning light; Emei Shan after a winter storm, every bamboo leaf encased in ice" (6). We can only attain to this kind of literal reading by carefully following the fringe of relations that lead from a text's description of an object through a connecting world so as to make (or approach as near as possible to) its acquaintance.

In its rigorous attention to referential language in literary texts, literal reading is an important critical paradigm for what it means to read with the senses in the chapters that follow. At the same time, though, the radical literary empiricism practiced by this book and the Victorian writers it considers brings literal reading's techniques to bear on figurative language. Literal reading operates by suspending figurative significance during its long detour into reference, and Freedgood and Schmitt suggest that this suspension is necessary because figurative language, especially metaphor, does two things. First, metaphor "defines and stabilizes" by firmly anchoring one thing to another; the metonymic path typically followed by literal reading, in contrast, names a relation of contiguous connections that branch out in a potentially endless succession of one thing after another.[39]

But secondly, we "flounder . . . around in [metaphor], comparing this to that, unable to think directly about things we do not already know (and not even about those things)" (Freedgood and Schmitt, 4). Metaphor is, then, somehow at once too stable and too slippery.

We can make sense of metaphor's apparently contradictory tendencies by thinking of metaphors as liable to act like what Devin Griffiths has recently described as formal analogies—comparisons that map the attributes of one thing top-down onto another thing. Formal analogies are stable, but they also tend to let their objects slip away as the tenor disappears beneath the vehicle. But crucially, these tendencies describe the ways that analogies can be used; they are not necessary functions of analogy itself. Griffiths stresses that analogies can also work harmonically, sounding objects off against one another and letting them resonate until unexpected similarities and contrasts emerge.[40] Harmonic analogies do not define and stabilize their objects and they do not propel us along a chain of substitutions so that the referent disappears. Instead, a harmonic analogy holds two referents together and generates new ways of understanding them from the unpredictable play of identity and difference.

This book itself centers on an analogy between reading and perception. If that analogy was sometimes formalized in Victorian literature and science, it could also be used more harmonically. As the Victorian writers in this study used that analogy harmonically to reimagine the continuities between reading and perceiving, that analogy also pushed them to reimagine the relationship between literal and figurative language. In the next chapter, I show how the overabundance of literal language in George Eliot's *Romola* (specifically, the names designating historical persons) reflects that historical novel's meditation on the conditions under which description can conjure up a historical past in a reader's perceptual present.

2

Getting Acquainted with Description in *Romola*

> Attempts at description are stupid: who can all at once describe a human being? Even when he is presented to us we only begin that knowledge of his appearance which must be completed by innumerable impressions under differing circumstances. We recognize the alphabet; we are not sure of the language.
>
> —George Eliot, *Daniel Deronda*

FOR A VICTORIAN NOVELIST, George Eliot sometimes didn't seem to think much of description. In the foregoing epigraph, Eliot's narrator suddenly breaks off in the middle of introducing Grandcourt as a character in *Daniel Deronda* in order to issue her memorable summary judgment on the stupidity of trying to describe people. The accent of Eliot's complaint here is on description's aspiration to timelessness—its aim to present a complete picture "all at once." This complaint has echoed down to us in the persistent charge that description is ahistorical. We can hear Eliot's criticism of description here reverberate faintly in Georg Lukács's 1936 essay "Narrate or Describe?" Narration, he argues, sweeps its objects up in the flow of human history by representing them as always intertwined with the long arc of the destinies of the novel's protagonists. In contrast, by aiming instead for detached observation in a misguided attempt to make literature scientific, "description contemporizes everything."[1]

Lukács's criticism of description in the novel has taken on a new resonance now, as historicist critics work to preserve the dominant position historicism has enjoyed in (especially Victorian) literary studies over the last three decades by fending off the challengers, including proponents of descriptive methods of criticism, among others. Hence the editors of a special issue of *Victorian Studies* on the current status of historicism suggest that descriptive criticism, especially when it models itself on scientific methods, suffers from "chronic presentism."[2] If, for instance, thin description aims to help us see with something like the scrupulous neutrality of the camera, that neutrality potentially commits thin description to stripping its objects of context in just the way that the camera's instantaneous images have long been criticized for doing.[3] Ahistoricism, then, seems to have long been a liability for description as a rhetorical and critical mode.

In the epigraph, though, Eliot contrasts the presentism of description with the kind of superior historical knowledge acquired not through long hours in libraries and archives but rather through direct acquaintance, through having Grandcourt not just descriptively but actually presented to us for observation. Direct acquaintance with Grandcourt paradoxically seems to involve some kind of verbal mediation since what we learn over the course of that acquaintance with him is how to read the language of his features. And then the passage breaks off from describing Grandcourt's features only by tacitly promising that the novel will go on to give us that fuller acquaintance with them and that it will do so using—what else?—descriptions of how they alter (or, in Grandcourt's peculiarly unresponsive case, do not alter) under the changing conditions of the plot.[4] Despite its summary judgment on the stupidity of description, then, this passage folds together description and direct presentation in ways that pose questions about how (and even whether) reading a novel's descriptions of the world differs from experiencing the world firsthand.

Eliot's career as a novelist coincided with epistemological debates around the distinction between knowledge by description and knowledge by acquaintance, a distinction she seems to call into question in *Daniel Deronda*. In *Exploratio Philosophica* (1865), John Grote observed that most European languages (English is a notable exception) have two different kinds of words for knowing: *wissen* and *kennen, savoir* and *connaître,* and so on. One signifies conceptual or propositional knowledge, the other acquaintance or "the kind of knowledge which we have of a thing by the presentation of it to the senses or the representation of it in a picture or type."[5] Grote formalizes this vernacular distinction into two separate epistemological categories: the sensory/pictorial "knowledge by acquaintance" and the logical/verbal "knowledge about" (later called knowledge by description). Highly portable, Grote's categories spread quickly, picked up by a range of figures in the late nineteenth and early twentieth centuries, including William James, Bertrand Russell, Hermann von Helmholtz, and, closer to Eliot, G. H. Lewes. The categories of acquaintance and description had ready appeal for philosophy and the sciences, where perception science had made established boundaries between verbal and empirical knowledge seem increasingly hard to draw and maintain.

Grote's categories of description and acquaintance are less directly linked to literary history—"Acquaint or Describe?" won't pass as the kind of fundamental stylistic choice Lukács names in "Narrate or Describe?"—but they nonetheless offer us an explanation of why some Victorian writers chose the latter of Lukács's two options as well as the difficulties entailed by that choice. Lukács himself suggests as much, in fact. In the advanced capitalist countries of western Europe, he contends, the novel underwent a strange evolution after 1848 when novelists began to prefer describing to narrating. The deep structural force at work in this development was the consolidation of bourgeois rule and the emergence of a new, alienated, and apolitical intellectual class, but Lukács proposed that the two more proximate causes of the novel's descriptive turn were science and, curiously, history itself. Lukács wrote "Narrate or Describe?" concurrently with his famous survey, *The Historical Novel* (1937), which diagnosed the genre with a slide to formal decadence in just this mid-century period.[6] The key symptom of this decline was the hypertrophy of the descriptive rhetorical mode. Lukács contends that the Victorian historical novel's overreliance on description stems from its turn away from narrating the historical transitions that brought the present into being in favor of settings chosen on the basis of their remoteness, such as the ancient Carthage of Gustave Flaubert's *Salammbô* (1862). Such purposefully exotic settings demand and serve as justification for the lavish, almost archaeological description of period details. Abandoning the form's earlier goal of telling the living history of the present, the Victorian historical novel is given over to what Lukács calls "a ghostly illusion of life."[7] The historical novel, then, turns to description in proportion to the distance that divides its setting from its initial readers.

Whether or not we accept Lukács's characterization of the fortunes of the historical novel in general (and there are good reasons to demur from some of his claims), it does account well for one historical novel in particular: Eliot's *Romola* (1862–63).[8] While Eliot's other novels could rely on her readers' acquaintance with England and its recent past to conjure up their respective story worlds, she set *Romola* in Florence during the 1490s, a place and historical moment that enjoyed no such easy familiarity for readers in Victorian Britain. Eliot consequently leans more heavily on description in *Romola* than in her other novels, and that makes *Romola* an especially good place to get acquainted with the function and effects of description in her fiction.

In this chapter, I read *Romola* alongside the intellectual history of the distinction between knowledge by acquaintance and knowledge by description. Tracing that history through mid-nineteenth-century optics and early twentieth-century philosophy, this chapter shows how the categories of description and acquaintance shaped both the science of perception and the philosophy of language. The formal logic of the historical novel, I contend here, leads Eliot to take up questions that are crucial to that intellectual history. In *Romola,* Eliot struggled to describe the past in a way that makes it feel present. She responded to those difficulties, I suggest, by writing them into the novel itself, exploring the formal conditions of the historical novel through an analogy with the experience of visual illusions and hallucinations, which are, like the characters of historical fiction, present to us even as we also know they are not fully there. Ultimately, I contend, *Romola*'s visions are Eliot's way of understanding how the world becomes present for us in fiction.

Romola's References: Historical Characters and the Philosophy of Language

Eliot famously remarked that she began *Romola* as a young woman and finished the novel as an old one, but in terms of her career as a novelist it is more accurate to say that *Romola* signaled the onset of a midlife crisis. Published serially in the *Cornhill Magazine* in 1862–63, *Romola* initiated a midcareer slump between Eliot's hugely successful early rural realist novels of 1859–61 (*Adam Bede, The Mill on the Floss,* and *Silas Marner*) and her hugely ambitious novels of the 1870s (*Middlemarch* and *Daniel Deronda*). *Cornhill*'s editor and owner, George Smith, offered Eliot unprecedentedly generous terms for *Romola* to lure her away from *Blackwood*'s at a time when publishing anything by Eliot promised to boost subscribers. It didn't work.[9] Commenting on the novel's chilly reception by the public, Eliot herself, in a letter to Sara Hennell, remarked defensively that "of necessity, the book is addressed to fewer readers than my previous works, and I myself have never expected—I might rather say *intended*—that the book should be as 'popular' in the same sense as the others."[10] *Romola* has scrupulously carried out Eliot's intention to avoid popularity ever since.

Romola, then, has suffered from the common fate of Victorian historical novels. Like Charles Dickens's *Barnaby Rudge* (1841) and Thomas Hardy's *The Trumpet Major* (1880), *Romola* has attracted far fewer readers than its author's other novels (with the possible exception of *Felix Holt, the Radical*). Since the novel's initial publication, the most enduring criticism of it has been that it is excessively descriptive. The novel is notorious for including too much of the prodigious research into Florentine history Eliot undertook (in her quarry for the novel there are extensive notes on the fine points of medieval Florentine attire under the running heading "Costume"). Anthony Trollope warned Eliot in a letter as soon as the novel's first installment appeared that the flood of historical details, if unabated in the novel's subsequent installments, would overwhelm all but a fraction of her audience.[11] Henry James, who was surprisingly one of *Romola*'s most steadfast admirers and frequently named it as his favorite Eliot novel, nonetheless issued the withering judgment that *Romola* "is overladen with learning, it smells of the lamp, it tastes just perceptibly of pedantry."[12] Eliot's noxious pedantry manifests itself, James had already suggested elsewhere, in a formal disproportion: in *Romola,* "there is too much description and too little drama."[13] In this regard, the novel seems to conform to Lukács's judgment that in the historical novel after 1848, "the description of objects . . . the dead environment of men, overwhelms the portrayal of the men themselves" (186).

But to judge from its first reviews, *Romola*'s excessive description becomes most acutely excessive not when the novel portrays the dead environments of history but rather when it portrays the dead historical figures who lived in it. One of the complaints about the novel that features saliently (and sometimes comically) in Victorian reviews concerns the difficulty for readers posed by the Italian names of its characters. The *Reader,* for example, interrupts its recounting of the novel's plot to propose "translating the sound of [Tito Melema's] name into homelier English," and decides to refer to him as "Titus Mealymouth."[14] The *British Quarterly Review* framed its negative review of *Romola* by contrasting Eliot's historical novel with those of Walter Scott, which "only exchanged Scotchmen for Englishmen" and thus prudently kept from veering too far away from the familiar worlds of their readership. "But how different is it in *Romola,*" the reviewer complains: "Bartolomeo Scala, Marullo, Piero di Cosimo, such names have little interest to the English reader of the nineteenth century; nor much greater do we feel in the better known names of Politian and Machiavel, while even Savonarola himself awakens an interest slight, indeed, compared with what we feel when the German or French reformers are referred to."[15] The parochialism on display here notwithstanding, *Romola* itself suggests that Eliot was alive to the challenge of generating readerly interest in the names of persons from a distant time and place.

As she grappled with the challenge of securing readers for *Romola,* Eliot wrote many of her difficulties into the novel itself. Despite (or perhaps because of) its enduring unpopularity, David Kurnick has observed that "one has only to read *Romola* to realize that *Romola* is all about reading."[16] Littered with books and parables of readerly extrapolation, the novel endlessly thematizes its own consumption. But *Romola* is equally replete with moments of readerly failure that thematize its difficulty in reaching an audience. Of the three main characters who are scholars and therefore serious readers—Bardo, Tito, and Baldassare—two, and the two most serious at that, spend most of the novel unable to read. Bardo's scholarly career is cut short by blindness, and Baldassare is stricken by a stroke-like neurological ailment that leaves him illiterate for long stretches of the novel.

Illiteracy likewise dogs many of the parables of readerly extrapolation, especially when those parables involve the kind of physiognomic reading of facial features that proved impossible on our first introduction to Grandcourt in *Daniel Deronda.* Consider the narrator's remark about Tessa, the peasant that Tito bigamously marries: "Tessa had not been slow at learning a few small stratagems by which she might avoid vexing Naldo and yet have a little of her own way. She could read nothing else, but she had learned to read a good deal in her husband's face."[17] The irony here, of course, is that even Tessa's limited form of literacy is dubious at best, since by this point in the novel it has been thoroughly established that the duplicitous Tito is virtually indecipherable. Tito's face is a "cipher with more than one key," and this illegibility is what makes all his machinations in the novel possible (98). His illegibility to Tessa is underscored here by the fact that, as the narration slips into her voice, it refers to Tito by his nom de guerre, Naldo. In other words, Tito's deeper illegibility crystallizes here in a false name.

In *Romola,* illiteracy bears insistently on the meaning that proper names might or might not have, which is to say that illiteracy in *Romola* is a problem of reference.[18] In this regard, *Romola* shares a key preoccupation with the philosophy of language. To grasp the way Eliot approaches questions of reference in *Romola,* it helps to have in mind John Stuart Mill's discussion of names at the opening of his *System of Logic.*

Mill's account of names inaugurates the modern philosophy of language, staking out initial arguments for both the descriptivist theories of Gottlob Frege and Russell and the causal theories of Saul Kripke and Hilary Putnam. Mill divides names into general and singular (we would call them common nouns and proper names). While single names denote an individual, general names denominate a class on the basis of the attributes shared across a variety of individuals. Mill calls the attributes signified by a general name "connotations." The difference between general and singular names, therefore, is that general names are connotative and singular names are nonconnotative. The word man, for instance, is applied to an object only if it possesses the connoted attributes of "corporeity, animal life, rationality, and a certain external form, which for distinction we call the human."[19] To Mill, this suggests that the meaning of a name lies not in what it denotes—one particular man—but rather in what it connotes—the attributes making up the human.

Mill's account of connotative names looks forward to the descriptivist theory of reference that predominated in analytic philosophy from the 1890s to the 1970s. Where descriptivism developed Mill's notion of connotative names, the powerful critiques of descriptivism made by Kripke and Putnam in the 1970s drew instead on Mill's account of what he called "non-connotative names."[20] For Mill, proper names have none of the connotations that determine reference in the case of common nouns. As Mill explains in a passage that Kripke cites approvingly, the town of Dartmouth in Devon was originally named for its location at the mouth of the Dart River; but if an earthquake or other geological event were to change the course of the river, Dartmouth would still be called Dartmouth even if its name came to connote ideas about the town's location that had become misleading. Proper names, Mill concludes, "are not dependent on the continuance of any attribute of the object" (20).

Building on Mill's reasoning here, Kripke famously conceives of names as rigid designators: markers that, after an initial baptism, stick persistently to their objects as long as they remain in currency within a linguistic community.[21] In this argument, an individual speaker does not determine the reference of a name by treating it as a description; rather, she simply uses the name to refer to the thing she has been told it refers to. For Mill, nonconnotative names therefore lack semantic content and so are actually quite meaningless.

> The only names of objects which connote nothing are *proper* names; and these have, strictly speaking, no signification. . . . If, like the robber in *Arabian Nights*, we make a mark with chalk on a house to enable us to know it again, the mark has a purpose but it has not properly any meaning. The chalk does not declare anything about the house . . . the object of making

> the mark is merely distinction. . . . Morgiana chalked all the other houses in a similar manner and defeated the scheme: how? Simply by obliterating the difference of appearance between that house and the others. . . . When we impose a proper name, we perform an operation in some degree analogous to what the robber intended in chalking the house. (22)

Semantically empty, proper names are merely a means of differentiating things.

One of the main ways that *Romola* alienates its potential readers lies in how the novel takes this power of names to differentiate past its limit. The greatest challenge for a reader of *Romola,* it seems to me, lies in the more than one hundred historical persons wandering through the novel, each denoted by an Italian name that therefore lacks the familiarity (and connotations) of common names in English.[22] Even for a contemporary reader armed with the scholarly apparatus provided by Penguin or Oxford University Press, to read *Romola* is to be sent flipping back to the explanatory notes over and over again in an impossible effort to keep its historical characters straight. Alex Woloch has observed that novelistic characters are the product of a literary dialectic between structure and reference. Structurally, the novel depends on a character system that distributes readers' attention among the novel's many different characters, but to maintain mimetic fidelity, the novel must make its presentation of each character seem to refer to a convincingly lifelike individual.[23] In *Romola,* we might say, the character system becomes so taxing on the reader's powers of attention that the referential functions of character get short-circuited. Like the thieves in the *One Thousand and One Nights,* the would-be reader of *Romola* encounters marks, supposed to enable her to differentiate one thing from another, that proliferate until it becomes impossible to tell things apart. Denotation multiplies distinctions until it undoes itself.

Occasionally, *Romola* itself tacitly signals that the designatory power of reference is being overtaxed by the novel's huge cast of historical figures. In an especially surreal moment, the novel describes an assembly that brings together all the "Florentines of high name" as wax effigies (140). Left as votive offerings in the Basilica della Santissima Annunziatta, the effigies serve the novel primarily as an ironic commentary on the "mimic marriage" of Tito and Tessa by the conjurer Vaiano during the city's celebration of the Nativity of the Virgin (285). But there's more than enough irony to go around, and the effigies also comment on the novel's own efforts to "conjure up a world" for its readers (318). As in historical memory, so in wax: the fortunes of each individual effigy vary widely, some of them retaining their figural integrity, others dwindling down into detached limbs or torsos as the wax has degraded, the least fortunate disintegrating completely, leaving only a gap in the assembly's record. "It was," Eliot writes in what could double as an epigram on *Romola*, "a perfect resurrection-swarm of remote mortals and fragments of mortals" (140).

But *Romola*'s most extended meditation on its failure to be read lies in its depiction of illiteracy, in particular the illiteracy of Tito's abandoned father, Baldassare, who haunts the world of the novel as the figure of readerly failure. Like us, Baldassare is a stranger to quattrocento Florence, and he experiences a bewilderment in navigating the city that should provoke a twinge of readerly recognition. *Romola*, moreover, goes to great lengths to establish parallels between his confused travails through Florence and his inability to read. At the crisis of his public accusation against Tito in the Rucellai Gardens, it is a literacy test that the Florentine leaders put to him to decide the truth of his claims. Or consider his exulting response when his failed attempt to stab Tito temporarily restores his mental powers.

The first move Baldassare makes after he realizes that his mind has cleared is to reach for the nearest book, which happens to be Pausanias's *Description of Greece*, a multivolume effort to systematically describe the cities of second-century Greece that J. G. Frazer called "the ancient equivalent of our modern . . . *Baedekers*."[24] Baldassare flips open the book and reads not a passage or a line but simply a place-name at the heading of a page: "Messenia." The letters making up this name have, by themselves, become "once more the magic signs that conjure up a world . . . rais[ing] Messenia before him," and this restoration of the power of names ensures that Baldassare will (temporarily) be able to orient himself in Florence (318).

During his brief moment of lucidity, Baldassare models for us the kind of reading most of *Romola*'s would-be readers have been unable to perform. When Baldassare tests his powers again with Pausanias the following morning, he knows he hasn't lost his mental acuity overnight when he is able to read thus: "He saw a name, and the images of deeds rose with it; he saw the mention of a deed, and he linked it with a name" (319–20). This model of reference uncannily resembles what Kripke calls "famous deeds" descriptivism. Kripke polemically suggests that descriptivist theories of language (the ones resembling Mill's account of connotative names) gained a certain amount of plausibility by turning insistently for their examples of reference to the names of historical persons, persons who could only be known via textual descriptions. John Searle's "Proper Names," for instance, takes Aristotle (among the most often recurring illustrations in the philosophy of language) as its exemplary case of reference.[25] When asked to identify a historical figure like Aristotle, since we cannot point to the man himself or even any visual representation of him, we seem to resort naturally to definite descriptions of his well-known acts: student of Plato, teacher of Alexander the Great, author of the *Nicomachean Ethics,* and so on. Like Baldassare, in other words, we see the name, and images of famous deeds rise with it.

While Baldassare's famous-deeds reading of *Description of Greece* illustrates the kind of reading required by the names of historical persons that swarm through *Romola,* the illiteracy that dogs Baldassare through Florence outside this brief moment of clarity illustrates the bafflement that is a more common response to the novel. After a relapse into his former condition, Baldassare spends the remainder of the novel lost in the labyrinth of Florence, not least because his illiteracy is accompanied by the radical diminishment of his powers of memory, historical and otherwise. In place of the mastery of reference that effortlessly conjures up worlds from names, Baldassare finds only a "blank in his mind—[a] past that f[alls] away continually" (259). Baldassare's amnesia culminates in illiteracy because it strikes squarely at his capacity for knowledge by description, the kind of knowledge that is exclusively propositional. Nicholas Dames has observed that Baldassare exemplifies a wider tendency for "the very presentness of the body . . . continually [to overtake] the power of memory in the novel . . . whereby what is not available to bodily sensation, bodily imagination, bodily perception—in general, texts, cultural memory, historical fact—becomes ever more difficult for characters in the novel to access."[26] Baldassare, we might say, embodies *Romola*'s missing readers as limited almost exclusively to knowledge by acquaintance.

Lost in Florence: Spatial Perception in Nineteenth-Century Optics

The key formal difficulty of the historical novel is the challenge of using description to conjure up a world of which the novel's readers can have no direct experience. This difficulty is especially acute in *Romola* because of the remoteness of its quattrocento Florentine setting for its Victorian readers. In the illiteracy of Baldassare, the novel figures this formal problem in terms that fit squarely within the categories of knowledge by description and knowledge by acquaintance, categories that John Grote was then on the verge of introducing. Although *Romola* finished publication in 1863, two years before Grote's *Exploratio Philosophica* appeared, its formal problems led Eliot to think about how the historical novel enables readers to know the past in ways very similar to Grote.

After the publication of *Exploratio Philosophica,* Grote's categories found their most appreciative audience in philosophers and scientists working on sensory perception. In the same way, *Romola*'s parables of reading verge quickly onto questions about the nature of perception. So, for example, the success of Baldassare's famous-deeds reading of *Description of Greece* hinges on his ability to imagine the deeds that belong to a given name. When he loses the power to correctly identify the reference of a name, Baldassare also loses the power of images; after his relapse, "his power of imagining facts needed to be reinforced continually by the senses" (409). With what he can know limited to whatever he has encountered with his senses recently, Baldassare's capacity to generate mental images of whatever he hasn't sensed lately suffers the same fate as his capacity to read.

Imagination isn't just for idle daydreaming, moreover; as a capacity to retain and spontaneously recall memory images, it also seems to guide the way Baldassare perceives whatever is right in front of him. Here is how the novel describes Baldassare's brief moment of triumph following the sudden but temporary restoration of his mental powers: "[Florence], which had been a weary labyrinth, was material that he could subdue to his purposes now. . . . He was once more a man who knew cities, whose keen sense of vision was instructed with large experience, and who felt the keen delight of holding all things in the grasp of language. Names! Images!—his mind rushed through its wealth without pausing, like one who enters on a great inheritance" (318). Baldassare's great inheritance includes names and images, but also a "large experience" that instructs his sense of vision in a way that promises to make it possible for him to navigate the labyrinth of Florence. Eliot here draws a parallel between how that large experience instructs the senses and the capacity of language to apprehend things. Like the epigraph from *Daniel Deronda* with which we began, Baldassare's neurological impairment unsettles firm distinctions between verbally mediated knowledge and direct sense experience, since the same kind of textual knowledge that permits him to read Pausanias, it seems, also enables him to recognize whatever he is looking at well enough to find his way around.

Here, too, the inquiry into the nature of reading Eliot undertook in *Romola* dramatizes the fortunes of description and acquaintance as epistemological categories in the later nineteenth century and afterward. For Victorian scientists and philosophers, there were two ways of taking Grote's distinction between acquaintance and description. In the strong interpretation (exemplified by G. H. Lewes and Hermann von Helmholtz), Grote's distinction categorically differentiated between sense perception and linguistically mediated knowledge. In contrast, adherents to the weak interpretation, such as Russell and James, applied the distinction *within* sense perception itself, using acquaintance and description to distinguish sensations from the kind of perceptual interpretations that, as Eliot puts it above, instruct the senses with a large experience. In this section, I account for the larger experience that permits Baldassare to orient himself by reading his travails through Florence in light of how nineteenth-century optics understood the visual perception of space. The theory of how we come to localize our visual sensations worked out by Hermann Lotze and Hermann von Helmholtz, I suggest, can help us understand why Baldassare's illiteracy—the loss of his capacity for knowledge by description—gets him lost in Florence.

Knowing one's way around is, fundamentally, a problem of sequence, of knowing what will come into view following a given series of movements. In that regard, the visual perception of space actually requires something like vision in its larger, prophetic sense. Visions and prophecy are a recurring concern throughout Eliot's work, of course, but where Eliot takes up prophecy in connection with sympathetic ethics in "The Lifted Veil" and physiological inheritance in *Daniel Deronda*, prophecy in *Romola* appears as a problem of visual reference. Eliot noted in her journals that she had been reading Emil du Bois-Reymond's biography of Johannes Müller, the German scientist whose encyclopedic *Elements of Physiology* (1833–40) became a key text for British physiology after being translated into English between 1837 and 1843.[27] Eliot's interest, however, lay in Müller's earlier work on visual hallucinations, which he published alongside a treatise on the comparative physiology of vision in 1826.

Müller's *On the Fantastic Apparitions of Vision* participated in a broader scientific shift toward treating hallucinations as objects for scientific study, displacing older traditions, like those often debated in *Romola*'s Florence, that understood visions as (at least potentially) mystical revelations. Among the new scientific works on visions, Müller's is distinctive for declining to regard hallucinations as purely illusory phenomena. Müller maintained that hallucinatory visions are just as real as any other visual sensations. The problem with visions, he argued, is not that they are unreal but that they are easily misinterpreted.

For Müller, all interpretations of visual sensations, whether mistaken or not, are the product of the imagination. Müller had himself experienced hallucinations regularly since childhood. In 1828, two years after *On the Fantastic Apparitions of Vision* appeared, he and Johann Wolfgang von Goethe met and compared notes on their recurring hallucinations. Modestly enough, Müller diagnoses the visions they suffered from as the symptoms of a rich interiority whose imagination has become too powerful for its own good: "The more active the inner life, the less efficient is the capture of the external. Complete and wondrous images can be formed in response to incomplete and defective external impressions (*Sindrücken*). A heater will become a priest, the furniture of a room will become an assembly of people, a busy market, a dramatic representation."[28] These images are disproportionate to their external stimuli, but the imagination is otherwise acting here just as it does in normal perception.

The key to Müller's understanding of hallucinations lies in his famous concept of the law of specific nerve energies. In his physiological texts, Müller elaborated on the theoretical implications of experiments first conducted by Charles Bell in which Bell excited visual sensations in the absence of visible light by mechanically stimulating the optic nerve. Such experiments demonstrated, Müller thought, that while the function of the senses is to register certain kinds of stimuli (electrical, mechanical, chemical, and so on), the qualities of sensations that result are the product of the energies of the specific nerve pathways stimulated rather than any intrinsic property in the stimuli themselves. What we take to be the objects making up the world, in this account, are really our own internal feelings, which we refer outward. The imagination is the faculty responsible for that projection, so transforming our visual sensations that "this sense [vision] appears to us to have an action exterior to our body, and in place of the images depicted on the surface of the retina, the imagination conceives the idea of real objects."[29] Consequently, whenever we see anything, whether pink rats or the most prosaic objects of everyday life, it is always the case that "by imagination . . . a mere sensation is interpreted as something quite different" (2:1068). The imagination in effect learns to read sensations by performing an act of reference: "We refer . . . the sensations in the nerves to the objects themselves" (2:1079). The difference between visions and sight is that for visions those external objects aren't really there; the mind is doubly misled if it refers those sensations outside the body because they are the product of causes internal to the brain or nervous system.

Müller's work on vision laid the foundation for later theories of perception by joining together an account of how we learn to read sensations and an account of how we learn to navigate space. In *Elements of Physiology,* Müller recounts the genesis of perceptual reference in a hypothetical infant, who by finding that her field of vision changes when she moves her body gradually learns how to estimate distances (to see with depth perception, in other words) based on visual sensations. Seeing objects arranged in space thus depends on a kind of localization—learning to orient ourselves in space is how we learn to perform the alchemy of interpretation that transforms internal sensations into a world of external objects. While Müller held that some parts of the visual perception of space are learned (depth perception and apparent size), he also maintained the nativist position that two-dimensional shape and directional position are the result of the anatomical organization of the eye itself and not of perceptual learning.

In the 1850s, the physiologist and philosopher Hermann Lotze and Müller's student Hermann von Helmholtz developed Müller's work into a fully empirical (and nonnativist) theory of spatial perception. At the heart of this account was the theory of local signs.[30] Lotze and Helmholtz argued that in addition to the quality of sensation produced by a stimulus acting on the eye's specific nerve energies—the sensation of a blue patch, for instance—there is a separate feeling specific to the place on the retina that is stimulated (importantly, this is not to say that this sensation is a spatial one, just that its specific quality is due to its location).[31] If we see a blue object in our peripheral vision and rotate our eyes and head in order to bring it into focus, the blue object moves across the retina triggering a series of localized visual sensations accompanied by localized sensations of muscular exertion (sensations produced by the so-called muscle sense).[32] The combination of localized sensations and muscular adjustments together constitute what Lotze and Helmholtz call local signs—a battery of sense data whose interpretation allows us to orient ourselves within, by making our way through, the world around us.

For the empiricist Helmholtz, our capacity to pick up from experience how to perform the complex mental operations involved in perceiving space testified to the rigor of perceptual knowledge. Helmholtz was an early adopter of Grote's epistemological categories of acquaintance and description, using them in his 1868 lecture course later published as "Recent Progress in the Theory of Vision." Helmholtz, though, adhered to the strong interpretation of these categories, maintaining an absolute distinction between empirical and propositional knowledge. What seems to have appealed to Helmholtz here is the tacit parity between these two categories of knowledge, the suggestion in their juxtaposition that acquaintance (*Kennen*) "may attain the highest possible degree of precision and certainty, and is so far not inferior to any knowledge

(*Wissen*) which can be expressed in words."[33] Not inferior, and not so different either. According to his own theory of spatial perception, knowledge by acquaintance operates on signs just as much as knowledge by description does.

As we saw in chapter 1, Helmholtz understood perception as the product of unconscious logical processes, and he thus goes on to suggest that knowledge by acquaintance has its own propositional logic:

> If I know that a particular way of looking, for which I have learnt how to employ exactly the right kind of innervation, is necessary in order to bring into direct vision a point two feet off and so many feet to the right, this also is a universal proposition which applies to every case in which I have fixed a given point at that distance before, or may do so hereafter. . . . It may any moment become the *major* premiss of a syllogism, whenever . . . I fix a point in the supposed position and feel that I do so by looking as that major proposition states. This perception of what I am doing is my *minor* proposition, and the "*conclusion*" is that the object I am looking for will be found at the spot in question. (199)

Given that both kinds of knowledge share a basic propositional logic in this way, the only real difference Helmholtz points to between acquaintance and description is that knowledge by description is communicable in words, whereas knowledge by acquaintance can only be communicated if you can present the perceptual object in question or represent its sensory effects "as by drawing the portrait of a man instead of producing the man himself" (198). The only real difference between knowledge by acquaintance and knowledge by description, in other words, is that to have the former you just have to be there.

In Britain, G. H. Lewes took the theory of local signs as the key to knowledge by description and knowledge by acquaintance. Adapting these two epistemological categories into what he calls the logic of feelings and the logic of signs, Lewes makes them central components of his groundwork for the *Problems of Life and Mind* series published between 1874 and 1878. Like Russell after him, Lewes erects the logic of signs on the foundation of direct acquaintance. "All interpretation" of signs, he writes, "must finally be a reduction into terms of Feeling, all the symbols must signify sensations."[34] Signs can be cashed out as sensations, in Lewes's account, because of how he understands logic. Drawing from Max Müller's etymological discussion of logos and the function of names in *Lectures on the Science of Language,* which Lewes read together with Eliot as she was beginning to write *Romola,* Lewes characterizes these logical interpretive processes as an activity of gathering and condensing: "In succession we feel that a thing is visible, tangible, resistant, etc., and such successions are condensed into a single perception. Any one element of this group becomes the *sign* of all the rest" (314).[35]

While the logic of feelings gathers up sensations into a perception, the logic of signs gathers up perceptions into an abstraction. Perceptual signs, for Lewes, are read ostensively. The interpretation of perceptual signs, that is, unconsciously calls up sense memories of a lifetime's worth of experiences with certain kinds of objects—for instance, "all the sensations we have had of [a certain kind of animal or flower] in relation to our several senses"—but perceptual signs nonetheless always directly denote the object actually present before us: "*this* animal or *this* flower" (126). In contrast, the logic of signs functions descriptively. For Lewes, signs per se do not deictically denote an object present to direct acquaintance but rather describe abstract conditions that can only be instantiated by such directly present objects. By the means of these descriptive signs "detaching the mind more and more from sensible observation . . . facts are condensed into laws, and direct vision is multiplied and magnified by remote pre-vision" (158). Acquaintance and description both yield knowledge through the interpretation of signs, but the perceptual signs denote what is present (or could be quickly made present with the right movements) whereas signs proper *represent* what is absent but might, under certain conditions, be made be present.

All signs, though, are local signs for Lewes. Lewes in fact elevates Lotze and Helmholtz's (uncredited) theory of local signs into the second of his three psychological laws, which he calls the law of signature: "Every feeling . . . has its particular signature, or mark in Consciousness, in consequence of which it acquires its objective Localization, i.e., its place in the organism or in the cosmos" (112). Feelings here are localized within two dimensions—the body and the world it inhabits. Lewes understood the nervous system as much more plastic than did Helmholtz or Johannes Müller, in effect conceiving of neural impulses in terms of Newtonian mechanics combined with Spencerian evolution. Any previously unexperienced nervous stimulation at first distributes its force diffusively, like a rush of water without a riverbed to follow. Hence, for an infant, "all impressions must at first be irradiated, and produce a chaos of vague sentience," but over time neural impulses carve out pathways within the nervous system and with this more precise localization within the body comes a corresponding precision in feeling (133). Localization within the nervous system transforms sensations into local signs that orient the body in space:

> All sensitive reactions have their *Signatures*. In proportion as their intensity and massiveness decrease they become more and more *Signs*, and thus become fitted to enter into intellectual operations which are purely symbolical. The least *sensible* of the Senses . . . is Sight, and therefore . . . it is the most *impersonal*,—that which draws with it the least amount of feeling. In looking at an object, it is the object out of us which most calls upon the attention. . . . On the other hand, a more subjective feeling, say of sound or taste, becomes objective so soon as it is connected with a sight. (121; italics in original)

The primacy accorded sight here underscores the origins of Lewes's version of the theory local signs in the physiological optics of Lotze and Helmholtz. Lewes, however, is leveraging an account of visual signs into a theory of signs in general, and so he very quickly corrects himself and cites the "definite *localization*" and reduced "massiveness and diffusiveness" of the sensations produced by any sensory mode as the reason that they are "fitted to become *signs*" (123; italics in original). For Lewes, localization simply is signification.

While *Problems of Life and Mind* would not begin publication until a decade after *Romola* finished its run in *Cornhill*, Eliot already seems in *Romola* to be thinking through what will become Lewes's argument. Hence the neurological impairment that renders Baldassare illiterate also results in his persistent spatial disorientation. Even before his malady struck, Baldassare's distinctive brand of scholarship was to interpret classical texts in light of their settings. A sort of anticipation of Heinrich Schliemann, the archaeologist who later in the 1860s would help discover the site of Troy based in part on close study of the *Iliad*, Baldassare practiced a site-driven classical scholarship closer to archaeology than textual criticism, and it was these efforts that led to his capture and enslavement in Ottoman Greece just before the narrative begins. As Tito explains to Bardo, Baldassare believed in "a new and more glorious era [that] would open for learning when men should begin to look for their commentaries on the ancient writers in the remains of cities and temples, nay, in the paths of the rivers, and on the face of the valleys and mountains" (63). For Baldassare, places, locations, were themselves interpretations.

Once he is illiterate and lost in Florence, the novel describes Baldassare's predicament using the hydraulic metaphors in whose terms Lewes would later figure the development of the nervous system. Where, for Lewes, localization occurs as the currents of nervous impulses first overflow and then carve out channels, the afflicted Baldassare's impressions wash over him. He picks up the volume of Pausanias in the hope that he might "by striving get a firm grasp somewhere, and lift himself above these waters that flowed over him" (261). In the novel's most striking figure for his memory loss, Baldassare wonders whether all his extensive reading was "utterly and for ever gone from him, like the waters from an urn lost in the wide ocean? Or was it still within him, imprisoned by some obstruction that might one day break asunder?" (254). The more optimistic second scenario (which turns out to be correct, if only temporarily) here rehearses the blind Bardo's trope for his own loss of literacy when he explains to Romola that "blindness acts like a dam, sending the streams of thought backward along the already-traveled channels" (50). Eliot thus compares Baldassare's condition to a visual impairment. While confusedly following Tessa through Florence with the vague hope of finding a means to revenge himself on Tito, Baldassare's "mind was dwelling upon her and her circumstances as feeble eyes dwell on lines and colours, trying to interpret them into consistent significance" (404). Baldassare, then, is like someone who has lost the ability to read local signs.

Character References: Perceiving Fictional Characters in the Philosophy of Language

Eliot's fiction consistently troubles the firm distinctions between empirical and propositional knowledge maintained by Helmholtz and Lewes. For both of these scientific figures, knowledge by acquaintance relies on propositional logic just as much as knowledge by description, but there remains a key difference: the objects of knowledge by acquaintance are present to the body, while the objects of descriptive knowledge are not. Eliot, however, would have had good reason to demure from this way of carving up what we know, because one of the aims of the novel as she understood it was to present empirically what might otherwise be inaccessible to its readers. She announces as much in "The Natural History of German Life," when she declares that fiction "is a mode of amplifying experience and extending our contact with our fellow-men beyond our personal lot."[36] Taking Eliot's claim that the novel amplifies our experience of other people seriously, in this section I sketch an account of what fiction seems to make present for us. That is, I aim here to lay out an ontology of fictional characters proper to Eliot's fiction. To that end, I follow the history of knowledge by description and knowledge by acquaintance a little further by attending to how these categories have shaped the philosophy of language. Ultimately, I suggest, the fortunes of these categories in twentieth-century philosophy can help explain why twenty-first-century literary critics are embracing description as a method that seeks, like Eliot, to make reading more like firsthand experience.

The prevailing Victorian understanding of sensory perception in terms of propositional logic made the distinction between description and acquaintance difficult to draw and maintain. For the same reason, the descriptivist accounts of linguistic reference that emerged at the turn of the century were persistently drawn into comparisons with sensory perception. One of the aims of Frege's 1892 essay "On Sense and Reference" is thus to assert a clear distinction between perception and linguistic reference. For Frege, all names have (or at least should have) a reference—an object they designate—as well as a sense, which he defines as "the mode of presentation" through which the name points to its reference.[37] So, for Frege, the sense of the name "Aristotle" would be something like "the pupil of Plato and the teacher of Alexander the Great" (37n). In both its definition and its etymology (the German *Sinn* is in this regard very similar to the English "sense"), Frege's sense would seem to trade implicitly on an analogy between names and sensation.

Frege, however, pointedly distinguishes his notion of sense from sense impressions (which he calls associated ideas). Sense impressions, Frege thinks, are subject to wild variations based on the quirks of individual bodies and the accidents of prior individual experiences. To illustrate the difference between sense and sensation, Frege asks us to imagine someone observing the moon through a telescope as having three components: the moon (reference), the telescopic image (sense), and the observer's retinal image (sensation). Where the retinal image varies with the eye shape of different observers, the "real image" presented by the telescope remains constant for each one (39). In the same way, the verbal technology of sense functions as a stable description that presents the object of reference in the same way to everyone. Sense is "the common property of many and therefore is not a part or a mode of the individual mind" (39). Its being held in common in this way safely insulates sense from the vagaries of sensory acquaintance.

Frege identifies sense, but also sensation, as the material on which literature operates. "Poetic eloquence," he suggests, seeks to give the sensational qualities of "colouring and shading" to the sense of words (40). For this reason, literature is indifferent to the truth value of the propositions it contains, since a proposition's truth value is a function of its reference—of whether it accurately describes a real state of affairs in the world: "In hearing an epic poem . . . we are interested only in the sense of the sentences and the images and feelings thereby aroused. The question of truth would cause us to abandon aesthetic delight for an attitude of scientific investigation. Hence it is a matter of no concern to us whether the name 'Odysseus' . . . has reference, so long as we accept the poem as a work of art. It is the striving for truth that drives us always to advance from the sense to the reference" (42). Sense and reference, Frege contends, thus divide literature and science between themselves. Frege's argument on fictional characters here is flatly wrong, as I'll go on to explain, but it was his claim that reference determines a proposition's truthfulness that gave Russell the opening he needed to formulate his own descriptivist account of reference.

Sense and reference, Russell claimed, could not explain how we assess the truthfulness of propositions with empty references. Russell's famous example of this kind of sentence is the proposition "The King of France is bald."[38] Given the law of the excluded middle, either that sentence or its negation must be true. But since there is no king of France, neither "the King of France is bald" nor "the King of France is not bald" can be true. Frege could only account for the specific kind of falsity at issue here by supplying the absent reference with a null class.[39] Russell thought he had a better solution, and it turned on description and acquaintance.

Russell defines denotation as a form of descriptive knowledge. Denoting phrases, he explains, describe states of affairs with which we have no direct acquaintance. Russell suggests that the most primitive form of denoting phrases are the words "everything," "nothing," and "something," each of which crucially involve quantities—every, none, some (480). Recasting sentences into the language of symbolic logic, Russell analyzes names and definite descriptions (like "the King of France" or "the teacher of Alexander") into these primitive phrases, which allows him to treat names and definite descriptions as, in essence, phrases stipulating quantities. Thus "The King of France is bald" becomes "There is exactly one man who is now King of France, and that man is bald." Given this sentence's new form, he can satisfy the law of the excluded middle by stating, "It is false that there is exactly one man who is now King of France, and that man is bald."

Rejecting Frege's efforts to lift sense and reference above the accidents of sense experience, Russell contends that denoting phrases describe the world in terms of knowledge by acquaintance. Under his version of descriptivism, we assess the truth of sentences by first resolving them into a set of properties (kingness, Frenchness, baldness), and then determining whether there is an object that would be able to instantiate them. Russell's descriptivism here recalls Mill's account of general names, in which acts of reference likewise begin with a set of connoted attributes ("man" connotes corporeity, rationality, a human form, etc.) and then proceed by asking whether a candidate for that name possesses them (this thing must be a man). For Russell, though, these connoted attributes must be reducible to things we know by acquaintance. Thus, he declares, "The fundamental principle in the analysis of propositions containing descriptions is this: *Every proposition which we can understand must be composed wholly of constituents with which we are acquainted.*"[40] Acquaintance in this way provides us with the elements of description, making it possible for us to know things that are inaccessible to our direct acquaintance. Oddly enough, other people are Russell's favorite example of things we cannot be acquainted with. No matter how often they are presented to us, what we can know of others is only that "'So-and-so has a mind which has such and such properties' . . . [and] in such a case, we know the properties of a thing without having acquaintance with the thing itself" ("On Denoting," 493).

The same is true, Russell suggests, of the objects we perceive. We can know directly, he explains, the sense data that together make up the appearance of a table, "its colour, shape, hardness, smoothness, etc.," but to infer from these sensations the presence of a physical object, the table itself, is to pass into knowledge of a more indirect kind (*Problems of Philosophy,* 46). To propose that "the table is 'the physical object which causes such-and-such sense-data' . . . *describes* the table by means of the sense-data" and is therefore properly knowledge by description (47). Russell in effect disaggregates Lewes's logic of feelings back into their component sensations. He does so to secure knowledge by acquaintance against Cartesian skepticism. Since sense data are precisely that—data, givens—they are not subject to the kind of doubt that can be levied against perceptual interpretations. For Russell, even in dreams and hallucinations we are on safe epistemological ground—as long as we do not infer the presence of physical objects from what we are seeing.

Russell thus adheres to what I've called the weak interpretation of Grote's categories, classifying sensations as acquaintance and perceptions as descriptions. In this regard, he follows James, but Russell falls into an error of misplaced concreteness here that James sidesteps. James understood sensations and perceptions as abstractions. In experience, sensations and perceptions arrive fused together and we can only distinguish them retrospectively through further experience. We simply do not experience the visual sensation of an oblong brown patch that we then infer to be a table. James, along with Eliot, Lewes, and Helmholtz, was well aware that it is virtually impossible to see without seeing objects.[41] Alfred North Whitehead wrote to Russell criticizing his argument in *The Problems of Philosophy* on just these grounds.[42] Even if it were possible, however, this kind of knowledge of pure sensations would be a knowledge sanded down to such a vanishingly fine grain as to be hardly worthy of being called knowledge at all.

Perhaps this is why knowledge by acquaintance virtually disappears as an explicit epistemological category after the mid-twentieth century (although it has recently seen something of a revival in the philosophy of mind).[43] One of the peculiar consequences of this disappearance, I want to suggest, was a new capaciousness in the category of description as it absorbed the empirical knowledge formerly belonging to acquaintance. Its subsequent epistemological flexibility, I think, is what has allowed description to serve as the pivot for two descriptive turns in opposite directions. In *The Interpretation of Cultures* (1973), published during the ascendancy of structuralism and linguistics, Clifford Geertz turned to thick description in the service of a semiotic conception of culture that pushed the observational social science of anthropology closer to literary criticism. Now, in our STEAM-driven era when the humanities count it a victory to insert a single letter (A is for Art) into the Science-Technology-Engineering-Mathematics education policy acronym, literary criticism is looking for new energy by using description to turn back toward the observational sciences.

Much of this work has drawn from Bruno Latour's sociology of science, which discerns the promise of a renewed empiricism in the effort to "just describe the state of affairs at hand," but perhaps the most rigorous methodological statement about what description can offer literary criticism has come from Heather Love, whose work with thin description reveals the parallels between close reading and the observational practices of the social sciences.[44] Taking full advantage of the epistemological flexibility of description, Love toggles between Nathanael West's *Miss Lonelyhearts* and social psychology case studies, giving fictional representations equal priority with firsthand accounts in her own descriptions of social realities. For her warrant, she points to the precedent set by social scientists themselves (the sociologist Erving Goffman included passages from West's novel among the case studies he analyzes in *Stigma*) as well as to the meticulous attention to observable reality within literary realism, all of which undergirds her bracing contention that with thin description "one might undertake rigorously empirical analyses of objects that do not exist" ("Close Reading and Thin Description," 429). This is a pretty startling sentence when you think about it, but it highlights the fact that description can be at once a written account that attempts to accurately convey empirical observations—the direct observations made by a social scientist or a novelist—and an object that can itself be empirically encountered and analyzed. Put another way, description blurs the distinction between presentations and representations.

All of this should lead us to ask what it is that fiction makes present for us. Here we might find help from Saul Kripke. In a series of lectures delivered in 1973 but only published forty years later as *Reference and Existence* (2013), Kripke takes up the problem of fictional names—names referring to objects that are usually said not to exist. Unusually, Kripke says that the objects of fictional names do exist, and his lectures lay out what he calls an "ontology of fictional characters."[45] In naming a character, any fiction pretends that the name functions normally—that all the criteria for successful reference are fulfilled—even as it also, in declaring itself a work of fiction, likewise declares that it is just pretending and that its characters do not really exist outside the story world. But when we make statements about a character from a work of fiction after we've read it, we are not pretending to refer anymore. When we state that Grandcourt is a sadist, for instance, we refer to the fictional character as he is stipulated to be in *Daniel Deronda* (and also secondarily, I would argue, as he is stipulated to be in the wider paratexts of secondary criticism, television adaptations, and so on). Kripke points out that it would be impossible to discuss characters—to dispute whether Hamlet is mad or just pretending or whether Dorothea's second marriage is a moral victory or a waste of her intellectual force—without granting them a sort of second-order existence in this way. Fictional characters begin life as pretenses, but they are made real through our reading practices.

In this respect, Kripke suggests, they have something in common with nonveridical perceptions—cases when what we see differs markedly from what we know the object we are seeing to be like (stars, for example, or hallucinations). Like fictional characters, the objects of nonveridical perceptions are strangely liminal entities. Grandcourt is and is not a collection of words on the pages of a book, just as the bright speck we call the Pole Star is and is not the multistar system Alpha Ursae Minoris. This peculiar kind of identity reflects the fact that fictional characters and illusions share a second-order ontology: "One can attribute to language—when and if it extends the use of the verb 'see' to allow an object even when there is no physical object there—the recognition of a special kind of thing called 'the hallucinatory object.' . . . The DTs patient who sees pink rats sees some hallucinatory objects. They can be described as pink rats, even though they are not real animals, by the same sort of convention that one can predicate of a fictional character its attributes in the story" (94). As the otherworldy inhabitants of what Kripke calls "an extended realm of entities," fictional characters and hallucinations are somehow present even as they are also not exactly there (100).

Of course, such phantasmal entities are not present in experience as fully as the objects of veridical perceptions. Perceptual realists distinguish perception proper from illusions and hallucinations by pointing to the kinds of dynamic, sensorimotor interactions with the environment that constitute perceptual consciousness.[46] We recognize the object of veridical perception when it varies predictably in continuity with our own movements. To perceive something, on this account, is quite literally to know one's way around it. The objects of nonveridical perceptions do not respond to us in the same way. Stars, for instance, are too far away for our own bodily movements to make them perceptibly shift positions, which should be our first clue that they might look very different up close. Something very similar is the case with fictional characters. Thus, Elaine Auyoung has recently suggested that we should think of the relationship between readers and fictional characters in terms of parasocial interaction—the kind of comparably one-sided relationship that mass-media spectators enjoy with movie stars.[47] Such impassivity places hard limits on the possibilities for empirical exploration in literary criticism.

Nevertheless, nonveridical perceptions involve us in the world in ways that open up possibilities for rigorous, even if constrained, empirical analysis. As Alva Noë observes, most nonveridical perceptions are in fact "cases of *merely partial* nonveridicality . . . [since] the world *is* at hand, and is present . . . as a partner in the experience" (73; italics in original).[48] While the possibilities for sensorimotor interactions with stars are necessarily limited, for instance, astronomers have been able to learn quite a bit about what they are actually like simply by modulating their positions and cross-checking results with other observers.[49] Anna Henchman has described how the complex semiveridical status of sensory perceptions within astronomical observations gave rise in nineteenth-century literary culture to "contradictory impulses to represent sense-based perceptions and to erase the distortions of embodied subject-positions."[50] More broadly, fiction has of course long traded on its merely partial nonveridicality, leveraging its status as a chronicling of imaginary events into claims that it can therefore convey larger truths about the world. The world enjoys a strange kind of presence in both phantoms and fictional characters.

Eliot often meditates in her novels on the true illusions of fiction. Here is how she opens her first novel, *Adam Bede:* "With a single drop of ink for a mirror, the Egyptian sorcerer undertakes to reveal to any chance comer far-reaching visions of the past. That is what I undertake to do for you, reader. With this drop of ink at the end of my pen, I will show you the roomy workshop of Mr. Jonathan Burge, carpenter and builder, in the village of Hayslope, as it appeared on the eighteenth of June, in the year of our Lord 1799."[51] The novel, Eliot promises here, will combine the fictive with the veridical in a way instantiated by its setting—neither Hayslope nor Jonathan Burge's workshop exist but the hyperprecision of showing them to us on the exact date of June 18, 1799, declares (a little drily) Eliot's intention to make the novel's imaginary places reflect historical reality as closely as possible. The model for the novel's semiveridicality, Eliot suggests, is a conjurer's trick. The novel and the conjurer's trick are both attempts to reveal visions—illusions—that have the truthfulness of a mirror.

One crucial element in the conjurer's trick of the novel is a certain distortion of scale. Here a drop of ink is made to yield far-reaching visions in the same way that the rural community of Hayslope will be made to yield far-reaching understanding of nineteenth-century Britain and the wider world. Eliot had an abiding interest in the way that fictions of provincial life could (and could not) scale up in significance in this way, but scale jumping from the particular to the general and back also underwrites the logic of fictional characters. Because early British novels seemed newly veridical, Catherine Gallagher notes, eighteenth-century novelists needed to fend off potential charges of libel stemming from the resemblance of their characters to particular individuals. So novelists claimed that the referents of their characters were not individuals but types, abstractions drawn from multiple persons, and thus presented general truths in the form of particular fictional characters. Fictional characters are supposed to be taken not as truthful descriptions of how existing individual persons have behaved but rather as truthful descriptions of how people in general would behave; they are not to be believed in so much as to be believable. In this regard, fictional characters embody what Gallagher identifies as the paradox of fictionality: literary fictions are "believable stories that [do] not solicit belief."[52]

At the same time, in order to make her characters fully believable, the novelist has to ensure that they exceed their types, since the mark of real individuals is that they are not reducible to such abstract categories. To become fully realized, fictional characters thus have to pry themselves loose from the types they refer to. Eliot often makes this tension between reference and realization the engine of her plots, so that realization forms the horizon toward which the arcs of her characters' lives bend. In Eliot's novels, the logic of fictional characters thus precipitates what Gallagher calls "a *desire* to be real."[53] Eliot's characters pulse with that desire in time with her readers, because the readers are the ones who must realize the characters by imaginatively embodying them. Thus, for *Middlemarch,* "to enliven is not so much to inspirit as to embody [and] Eliot makes us imagine, not an independently living and breathing Dorothea, but instead an idea called Dorothea requiring that we conceive her bodily sensations to make her real" (73). The pleasures of reading Eliot, Gallagher suggests, lie in the way she makes us want to experience fictional characters with all the intensity and immediacy of hallucinations.

Romola, a historical novel peopled by fictional versions of individual persons who actually existed, torques the logic of fictional characters at work in Eliot's other novels. The referent of a historical character like Savonarola isn't a type; it is the historical individual Savonarola. Like all historical novels, *Romola* renders its historical individuals in a fictional way, giving us access to thoughts for which no historical evidence exists and showing them interacting with its fictional protagonists (such as Romola herself).[54] What underwrites such narrative license, however, is the historical novel's aim of convincing readers that its presentation of those historical individuals can best help us grasp what they were really like. As Devin Griffiths puts it, the historical novel is "*truthy*"; it asks us to discriminate historical fiction from historical fact only to put that difference under erasure, so that we ascribe necessity to what is in essence a "psychological construct."[55] The historical novel, that is, cannot just be believable. Even as we know better, it also has to be, in a sense, believed.[56]

Believing in *Romola*

The historical novel, then, sits along the frontier between belief and doubt, and this, as it happens, is just where Eliot sets *Romola.* Florence under the Medicis was on the frontlines of what Jacob Burckhardt, the Swiss historian whose *Civilization of the Renaissance in Italy* Eliot consulted during her research for *Romola,* characterized as the "general disintegration of belief."[57] As emergent Renaissance Humanism made increasingly assertive claims to autonomy and Savonarola launched a reformist attack on the authority of Rome, Florence during the 1490s heralded the advent of atheism as well as the fragmentation of belief into different denominations as a result of the Reformation. Belief and unbelief coexisted uneasily, often in the same person. Burckhardt cites the example of Pierpaolo Boscoli, a devotee of Savonarola who later abandoned his faith out of an enthusiasm for the stern civic virtues of classical Rome only to make a dramatic return to the fold just before he was beheaded for attempting to go Brutus two better by assassinating three different members of the Medici family at the same time in 1512 (542–43).

In the "Proem" to *Romola,* Eliot imagines a similarly vexed coexistence of faith and skepticism in the figure of the fifteenth-century Shade she resurrects to return to modern Florence. Essentially a prosperous bourgeois, the returning Shade is an inheritor of quattrocento Florence's "strange web of belief and unbelief" (8). An enthusiastic collector of classical manuscripts and marbles—the fetish objects of the new Humanism—he still prays to the saints and tithes to the Frati, whose superstition he ridicules, "for the Unseen Powers were mighty. Who knew—who was sure—that there was *any* name given to them behind which there was no angry force to be appeased, no intercessory pity to be won?" (7; italics in original). Eliot here frames the contradictory effects of the disintegration of belief in terms of the powers, or lack thereof, belonging to names. The names of the unseen powers here are not the empty names of fictional characters waiting for readers to make them real. Instead, they belong to canonized saints, and what is doubtful about them is not the historical existence of their objects so much as whether they can be invoked effectively in the present. In this regard, the Shade's doubtful belief in the unseen powers of names instantiates the response the historical novel aims to elicit in its readers.

Such doubtful belief in the power of *Romola*'s names, however, has often been hard to come by. The sheer profusion of those names, combined with their unfamiliarity and the historical distance from the objects they designate, have made it especially difficult for the novel to give its would-be readers what such credence requires: a sense of acquaintance with the world it describes. For the historical novel as well as for empiricism, belief (even doubtful belief) is secured by the feeling that something is present, and *Romola*'s historical Florence has felt too distant, too purely descriptive, to many of its readers. Eliot writes that formal difficulty into the plot of the novel, which turns on the way names can lose their grasp on things.

Mary Ann Evans, Marian Evans, Marian Evans Lewes, George Eliot—George Eliot's many names attest her keen sense of the power of names to shape expectations about their objects' behavior. As she was preparing to write *Romola,* Eliot had new occasion to appreciate that power when Margaret Oliphant began anonymously publishing *The Chronicles of*

Carlingford in *Blackwood's* and persistent rumors kept attributing Oliphant's work to her. Eliot vented her frustration in a letter to Sara Hennell:

> A little reflection might, one would think, suggest that when a *name* is precisely the highest-priced thing in literature, any one who has a name will not, except when there is some strong motive for mystification, throw away the advantages of that name. I wrote anonymously while I was an unknown author, but I shall never, I believe, write anonymously again . . . [on ground of] the desire only to be responsible for views and feelings that one really shares, and again, to prevent others from being made responsible for one's own doings,—quite apart from any monetary reasons.[58]

Eliot's letter softens pecuniary self-interest with a principled appeal to ethical responsibility, but the financial advantages of her name derive from the same source as ethical reputation: the expectations a name engenders that the object it designates will behave or write in a certain way. Having just been offered a small fortune in advance for a novel that departs considerably from the successful formula of her first four books, Eliot would likely have known intimately how compelling the expectations attached to even the highest-priced name can be.[59]

In *Romola,* the binding power of names—"that force of outward symbols by which our active life is knit together so as to make an inexorable external identity for us"—creates the erotic and ethical conflicts that drive the plot (304). So when Romola, disguised as a nun, makes her first attempt to escape from Florence and Tito, she is stopped on the path outside the city when she hears, out of nowhere, the voice of Savonarola pronouncing her name: "You are Romola de'Bardi, the wife of Tito Melema" (338). Against Romola's feeling that she is justified in leaving Tito to begin a new life after his betrayal of her father, Savonarola goes on to urge her to return to shoulder "the obligations of her place and name" (344). As a member of the Florentine Bardi family, he suggests, it is her duty to aid the city; as the wife of Tito, it is her duty to remain faithful to the marital bond. The problem for Romola, though, is that conflicting duties are attached to her name.

The plot events of the novel intolerably aggravate those conflicts. Ultimately, remaining with Tito would require acquiescing in his betrayal of her father, Bardo, and her godfather, Bernardo del Nero; remaining in Florence under Savonarola would require acquiescing in the city's beheading of her godfather in contravention of the Law of Appeal Savonarola's government had passed. "Why should she care," Romola thus asks herself, "about being called by her own name? She despaired of finding any consistent duty belonging to that name" (471). Resolving to abandon her name, Romola goes on to suggest that the connotations of Savonarola's name have also failed to bind him to an ethical course of action. Disillusioned over Savonarola's refusal to protest the city's clear violation of the Law of Appeal in executing Bernardo del Nero, Romola bitterly concludes that "his striving after the renovation for the Church and the world was a striving after a mere name which told no more than the title of a book" (472). In short, Savonarola becomes all name, while Romola becomes nameless. While the unmanageable number of historical persons it features overtaxes the denotative capacity of names in *Romola,* the plot subjects names' connotative powers to a similar strain.[60]

Vagueness is consequently a key problem both in and for the novel. For Nicholas Dames, it takes the form of what he calls "nostalgic vagueness," a nineteenth-century narrative mode that smooths away the particularities of the past—the kind of details that the novel initially gives such lavish descriptive specification to—and thus submerges history in personal memory.[61] The tension here between the personal and the social is in fact the hallmark of Eliot's approach to the problem of vagueness. In the slipperiness of ordinary language's grasp on the world, Daniel Wright argues, Eliot saw the crucial difficulty involved in explaining oneself and one's desires to others and vice versa. Grappling with vagueness, Wright thus suggests, is the way ethical and erotic knowledge in particular are obtained in Eliot's fiction.[62] The ethical and erotic crises precipitated by vagueness in *Romola* are framed in just these terms. Thus the novel describes Romola's break with Savonarola as originating in "a conflict between the demands of the outward law which she recognized as a widely ramifying obligation, and the demands of inner moral facts which were becoming more and more peremptory" (441). Vagueness, then, straddles the line dividing the internal and the external, self and world, which is the same indeterminate zone where we experience visions.

In Victorian science, visions were understood as a kind of vagueness in sensory perception. After Johannes Müller, the scientific consensus held that visions arise from the off-kilter interplay of external physical forces and the internal energies of the nervous system. The challenge of understanding visions rightly was thus seen to lie in discriminating what in them comes from the exterior world and what from the interior self, while their powerful hold on us was supposed to come from their capacity to make us mistake the purely imaginary for the world's real presence.

Romola struggles with this same difficulty as she tries to resolve the conflicting demands of the outward law and her inner moral facts. Panged by Tito's betrayal of her father's last wishes, Romola's disillusionment with her husband leads ironically to intense sensory illusions. Dwelling obsessively on her dying brother Dino's dream, which he recounted to her as a divine vision auguring disaster from her prospective marriage, Romola starts to find "these inward images and voices" assuming such intensity that they "pressed upon her almost with the imperious force of sensations . . . rous[ing her mind] to resistance of impressions that, from being obvious phantoms, seemed to be getting solid in the daylight" (308). Still an unbeliever at the time, Romola here experiences the vision of a vision, and as she does so she begins to absorb Dino's faith in the veracity of his vision as well as her own.

Belief in *Romola* hinges on the vagueness of visions. Romola resists belief in Dino's dream by reasoning that she would rather have married unhappily "than be a creature led by phantoms and disjointed whispers in a world where there was the large music of reasonable speech, and the warm grasp of living hands" (308–9). Romola's judgment echoes the narrator's earlier verdict that Dino's attempt to warn his sister failed because "the prevision that [his] words had imparted to Romola had been such as comes from the shadowy region where human souls seek wisdom apart from the human sympathies which are the very life and substance of our wisdom" (155). Eliot casts the critique of Dino's visionary monasticism in the terms she learned from translating Ludwig Feuerbach's *Essence of Christianity,* which likewise argues that divinities are really aspects of ourselves that we project outward in order to come to know. "In the perceptions of the senses consciousness of the object is distinguishable from consciousness of self," the argument runs, "but in religion, consciousness of the object and self-consciousness coincide. The object of the senses is out of man, the religious object is within him."[63] Christianity is something like the hallucinatory stage in the development of the *Weltgeist*, a world-historical case of mistaken reference when we confuse what is within for what is without.

But in *Romola*'s visions, as in the objects of sense perception itself, it is no easy task to disentangle what is actually present and what is virtually present, or what we must believe in from what we might doubt.[64] So in spite of Romola's retrospective self-justification that she was right to prefer the touch of living hands to Dino's shadowy world of visions, she marries Tito because she too erroneously believes in the reality of a phantom. Her erotic desire for Tito condenses itself around what she believes are his feelings, but "a girl of eighteen imagines the feelings behind the face that has moved her . . . as easily as primitive people imagined the humours of the gods in fair weather: what is she to believe in, if not in this vision woven from within?" (66) While the narrator puts that question with an apparently rueful irony here, the novel takes it seriously because the desire such visions help us articulate is necessary for ethical actions toward others. Thus the narrator subsequently observes, "That supremely hallowed motive which men call duty . . . can have no inward constraining existence save through some form of believing love" (471). Precisely because it is so difficult to distinguish in them what comes from the world and what comes from us, visions provide an experiential space for *Romola*'s characters to negotiate the porous boundary between the personal and the social that defines their ethical and erotic lives.

In the ways that visions involve us unpredictably in the world, they also provide Eliot with a kind of theory of the historical novel. That theory becomes clearest in the episode of *Romola* that itself has the most dreamy vagueness in the novel. Once she has given up her name in despair of acting in accordance with it, Romola enacts her own variation on what comes closest to a primal scene in Eliot's fiction by getting into a boat and casting off to drift aimlessly, departing not just Florence as she floats in the Mediterranean but the symbolic order and its localizations entirely so as to "repose in mere sensation" (473). Several chapters later, Romola emerges from the "Lethe . . . of subtle indefinite sensation" when she washes up on the shore of an unnamed coastal village, where in the course of nursing the inhabitants through a plague epidemic she experiences "a new baptism" (527). The new village name she acquires is "the blessed Lady who came over the sea," a definite description that also rather obviously echoes Mary, our Lady, the Star of the Sea (527). Eliot has already encouraged readers to make just this identification in a pair of chapters following Romola's first return to Florence under the guidance of Savonarola. The first, chapter 63, "The Unseen Madonna," details the procession of the Madonna dell'Impruneta, a historical icon of the Holy Mother and child supposed to have been painted by Saint Luke, which is carried through the streets of Florence enclosed in a tabernacle (and thus unseen). The following chapter, narrating Romola's charitable visits to Florentine children suffering from the plague, is then titled "The Visible Madonna." Romola here, the novel suggests, makes a historical figure visible, present to the senses in a way that it cannot be without her.

Of course, Eliot often characterizes her protagonists as modern versions of a mythic or historical figure. Thus we could say that Romola is like Mary in the same way that Dorothea is like Saint Theresa—a belated, diminished version whose banality in comparison with the original reveals the difference in social conditions between a mythic past and a prosaic present and at the same time makes the diminished modern version mythic in her own right because her very commonplaceness makes her widely representative.[65] In other words, we could read such identifications in *Romola* as purely metaphorical. In *Romola*, though, Eliot employs this figurative technique in a curiously literal way. No one in *Middlemarch* actually mistakes Dorothea for an apparition of Saint Theresa. That novel's rueful characterization of its protagonist as "a Saint Theresa, foundress of nothing" remains at the extradiegetic level of narration.[66] Romola, in contrast, directly embodies Mary in the story world. On her way into the village, she picks up the orphaned child of a Jewish family killed by the plague on its outskirts before heading to the well where she meets her first villager, Jacopo:

> Romola certainly presented a sight which, at that moment and in that place, could hardly have been seen without some pausing and palpitation. With her gaze fixed intently on the distant slope, the long lines of her thick grey garment giving a gliding character to her rapid walk, her hair rolling backward and illuminated on the left side by the sun-rays, the little olive baby on her right arm now looking out with jet-black eyes, she might well startle that youth of fifteen, accustomed to swing the censer in the presence of a Madonna less fair and marvelous than this. (522)

Romola here fully incarnates the iconography of the Holy Mother, all the way down to the aureole and the Jewish baby. That is to say, she brings an image to life, transforming a representation into a presentation. She is, in a word, a vision.

When Romola incarnates Mary, she likewise embodies the aim of the historical novel writ small—to make the past real, to make us feel somehow directly acquainted with what can only be made known by description. *Romola* has had mixed success in giving its readers that kind of access to the world it describes. Nonetheless, in its searching attention to what is present for us in fiction, the novel asks us to get reacquainted with how the world does and does not show up for us in our descriptions.

3

Reading in the Dark

SENSORY OBSCURITY IN *THE RETURN OF THE NATIVE*

> Let a person enter his room in the dark and grope among the objects there. The touch of the matches will instantaneously recall their appearance. If his hand comes in contact with an orange on the table, the golden yellow of the fruit, its savor and perfume will forthwith shoot through his mind. In passing the hand over the sideboard or in jogging the coal-scuttle with the foot, the large glossy dark shape of the one and the irregular blackness of the other awaken like a flash and constitute what we call the recognition of the objects. The voice of the violin faintly echoes through the mind as the hand is laid upon it in the dark, and the feeling of the garments or draperies which may hang about the room is not understood till the look correlative to the feeling has in each case been resuscitated.
>
> —William James, *The Principles of Psychology*

When Thomas Hardy decided to stop writing novels in the 1890s, he blamed his readers. Reflecting on the notorious charges made by Mowbray Morris in the *Quarterly Review* that *Tess of the D'Urbervilles* (1891) was a "clumsy sordid tale of boorish brutality and lust," Hardy remarked in a private note: "How strange that one may write a book without knowing what one puts into it—or rather, the reader reads into it! Well, if this sort of thing continues no more novel-writing for me. A man must be a fool to deliberately stand up to be shot at."[1] This note has helped shape a pervasive critical narrative in which Hardy, a liberal crusader against unjust social conventions, is hounded out of fiction writing by the hypocritically prurient overinterpretations of late Victorian readers.[2]

Among other things, this critical narrative obscures the fact that both long before and long after the scandals occasioned by *Tess* and *Jude the Obscure* (1894–95), Hardy's writings betray a persistent unease about reading, often representing it as a solipsistic and even dangerous act. This is especially true of Hardy's 1878 novel, *The Return of the Native*. Consider, for example, the disastrous mésalliances that comprise the plot of that novel. Bad marriages are thoroughly typical in Hardy's fiction, but in *The Return of the Native* they are directly precipitated by acts of reading. Characters in that novel read each other, each regarding the other's face "not as a picture, but . . . as a page," and in doing so they misread each other, with catastrophic results.[3] The novel treats these acts of reading as instances of prosopopoeia—literally, to make a face. Hardy himself later felt that he had been victimized in just this way during the furor over *Jude the Obscure,* when "he underwent the strange experience of beholding a sinister lay figure of himself constructed by [readers and reviewers], which had no sort of resemblance to him as he was" (*Life and Work*, 288).[4] Yet *The Return of the Native* also suggests that the capacity for acts of prosopopoeia, for transforming phenomena into figures, is the defining characteristic of "the more thinking among mankind," a group in which Hardy, naturally, included himself (11).

The Return of the Native thus depicts reading as at once an empowering practice of understanding and a solipsistic practice of misinterpreting others. The novel's most emblematic reader in this regard is Clym, whose combination of insight and fatal misunderstanding is literalized, in Hardy's terms, when he goes blind from reading too much. For Hardy, reading and blindness imply one another, but not strictly as cause and effect. Hardy's novel suggests that blindness is the effect of the inevitably partial character of reading and, at the same time, the state that makes possible its interpretive activities.[5] In *The Return of the Native,* reading is a narrowly focalized mode of perception. Its concentrated cognitive activity depends on the subject's ability to block out a larger field of stimuli.

Hardy understands this inattention required by reading as a state of curtailed sensory responsiveness whose most emblematic form is blindness. Hence, Clym's blindness is not only the consequence of reading but also its precondition. Clym blinds himself not just by reading per se but also, quite specifically, by reading in the dark.

The blindness of reading in *The Return of the Native* signals Hardy's debt to Victorian sciences of mind, particularly to associationist psychology, a branch of psychology influential in Britain following the publication of David Hartley's *Observations on Man* in 1749 until the end of the nineteenth century.[6] The fundamental tenet of the school was that any given idea or sensation automatically recalls to the mind other ideas and sensations connected to it by similarity and temporal or spatial contiguity. Association thus served as the cognitive function responsible for transforming sensations (in James's example, the waxy, textured roundness your hand feels on the table) into perceptions of objects (the orange in all its citric glory) (James, *The Principles of Psychology,* 1:555–56). In this way, associationism provided psychologists and philosophers an account of how what John Locke called simple ideas generate complex ones. Associationists held that all objects are bundles of contiguously experienced sensations and that each sensation in the bundle, if experienced in isolation, stimulates the memory of its partners.

Sensations, psychologists insisted, were in this regard analogous to signs, and perception itself to reading.[7] In the epigraph to this chapter, for example, William James illustrates the principle that any given sensation serves as a sign for its associates. The recognitions James describes there are instances of contiguous association—the recollection of the sensations that are usually experienced alongside the signifying sensation. Because they were chiefly concerned with accounting for the cognitive mechanisms involved in perceiving objects, early associationists such as Hartley and James Mill tended to emphasize contiguous association to the exclusion of association via similarity. In the late Victorian period, however, James and other theorists of association shifted focus back to association via similarity as the basis for a concept of agency responsive to the theories of mind that were being advanced in the burgeoning fields of sensory physiology and experimental psychology.

Operating through unpredictable leaps from the signifying sensation to others with which that sensation is less routinely linked, association via similarity became the means of an interpretive reenvisioning of experience, a way of breaking up and transfiguring the routinized perceptions of contiguous association.

Hardy's novels and critical essays demonstrate an intense interest in these late Victorian theories of perception and an abiding investment in a similar model of cognitive agency. *The Return of the Native* suggests that blindness—or any other condition that obscures the sensations by which objects are routinely perceived—can stimulate the imaginative reinterpretation of experience that late Victorian associationists identified with association via similarity. In his essays and notes, Hardy claims that this mode of associative cognition provides a model for the kind of widely interpretive perception—the "imaginative sense of fact"—that drives his own artistic practice.[8] For both author and reader, Hardy suggests, associative interpretation is an embodied version of Matthew Arnold's ideal of criticism: the spontaneous play of consciousness on stock notions and habits. Like Arnold's critical ideal, Hardy's model of what we might term critical perception is a form of aesthetic agency in the fullest sense, through which we imaginatively construct the world at the level of sensory perception. If association thus makes authorship possible, however, Hardy suggests that it does so by licensing a peculiar form of solipsism. Moreover, Hardy's writings evince a fear that, by investing such transformative agency in the act of interpretation, association also empowers the reader to displace the author—a misgiving that looks forward to twentieth-century accounts of the death of the author.

This chapter explores the theory of critical perception elaborated in Hardy's essays and in *The Return of the Native.* I argue that reading for Hardy is a broadly aesthetic and affective act, encompassing modes of associative perception that operate on the full range of bodily sensations. In doing so, I aim to correct the tendency in much scholarly work on Hardy to ascribe too much importance to the faculty of vision. In addition, I hope to reorient recent lines of inquiry on embodiment in Hardy's writing toward his fascination with theories of sensory perception.[9] It is ultimately this fascination, I argue, that gives rise to Hardy's lasting ambivalence toward reading and shapes his indignant response to the critical attacks on his later novels.

The Associationist Aesthetics of Buildings and Books

In his 1888 essay "The Profitable Reading of Fiction," Hardy claims that in addition to judging a novel's "regularity" of character and plot, "the appreciative, perspicacious reader . . . will see what his author is aiming at, and by affording full scope to his own insight, catch the vision which the writer has in his eye, and is endeavoring to project upon the paper, even while it half eludes him."[10] Hardy here suggests that reading is an act of collaboration, in which the reader supplements the text by reconstructing the author's intentions despite his imperfect expression of them. This collaborative dynamic defines Hardy's ideal reading scenario; he repeatedly, if implicitly, invokes it in his remarks on the reading of his work.[11] If this ideal reading scenario assumes a fairly generous reader, it also assumes that the reader is encountering a text with gaps or opacities, that the author's vision has in fact "half elude[d] him." Indeed, it implies that the best kind of reading—"appreciative, perspicacious" reading—can only be called forth by an imperfect piece of literature. The reader's perspicacity can only exist in proportion to the text's imperfection.

Hardy in fact expects his reader to do for the text what Hardy himself had done for decaying buildings when he worked as an architect. During the ten years Hardy spent as a practicing architect before he turned to novel writing full time, the bulk of his work lay in restoring churches. Hardy was the beneficiary of an unprecedented campaign of church restorations during the mid-Victorian period. Altogether, Hardy and his professional colleagues restored some seven thousand churches (about 80 percent of the total number existing) in England and Wales in the years between 1840 and 1875.[12] The restorations generally followed the principles laid down by the Cambridge Camden Society, a gothic revivalist group founded by Cambridge students in 1839. "To restore," the CCS wrote in its journal the *Ecclesiologist*, "is to recover the original appearance which has been lost by decay, accident, or illjudged alteration. The method of the restoration depends on the idea of the original which the architect may form."[13] Looking back at his career as a church restorer in his 1906 essay "Memories of Church Restoration," Hardy confirms that he was guided by this notion of restoration. Victorian church restorers, he suggests, aimed to grasp the formal beauty of buildings, which inheres not in the particular materials making up a given church but in its "insubstantial" outline. Architectural form is an "aesthetic phantom without solidity," freed from the contingencies of its concrete manifestation as long as its ideal outline can be discerned.[14] Just as the reader restores the imperfect text by completing the vision that has half eluded its author, the restoring architect sees through the dilapidated church to the ideal form it approximates.

Victorian church restoration involved the architect in a relationship to the past that was combative as well as collaborative. British gothic churches hadn't simply been built as complete forms and left to stand unaltered but for decay until they passed under the hands of the restorers. Instead, their forms had continuously evolved as each subsequent historical period deposited its own additions and alterations made in its own styles. Consequently, Victorian church restoration was haunted by a contradiction that E. A. Freeman noted in his 1846 tract, *Principles of Church Restoration.* While church restorations were motivated by a new, distinctly Victorian "reverence for . . . [the] historical associations" of buildings, in practice the "one hard, unswerving law" of restoration dictated that the accretions of history had to be stripped away in order to bring the building back to its supposed original state.[15]

This contradiction between motive and methods attracted criticism from figures like John Ruskin and eventually provoked organized opposition to church restorations. The Society for the Protection of Ancient Buildings, which still does preservation work in the United Kingdom, formed in the 1870s with the mission of protecting churches from restoration (Hardy himself was an early supporter and began working with the SPAB as a speaker and consultant in 1881). On March 22, 1877, the year before *The Return of the Native* began publication, William Morris and other Pre-Raphaelites convened a public meeting in Bloomsbury to inaugurate the SPAB.[16] In the lecture he delivered as a manifesto for the organization, Morris attacks the fundamental aim of restoration as arbitrary and capricious. "While professing to bring back a building to the best time of its history," he claims, restorers "have no guide but each his own individual whim to point out to them what is admirable and what contemptible; while the very nature of their task compels them to destroy something and to supply the gap by imagining what the earlier builders should or might have done."[17] Restorers thus do not grasp the original builder's intention so much as they willfully extrapolate from it in ways that transform buildings beyond recognition.

Hardy's own work had already been singled out for similar criticism. In 1870, he had been tasked with the restoration of the parish church in St. Juliot, Cornwall (it was while conducting this restoration that Hardy met Emma Gifford, then living nearby in Bodmin, whom he married in 1874). Completed in 1872, Hardy's restoration was given a very mixed review in the *Royal Cornwall Gazette*. While the paper conceded that the restoration had been well done "from a builder's point of view," it complained that several features of the church were "now destroyed and swept away forever, adding another unmistakable specimen of Vandalism to what has already taken place [at neighboring churches]."[18] Although he does not mention this church or the newspaper review of it specifically, Hardy does offer a kind of public apology for his work in "Memories of Church Restoration." Architects who had participated in church restorations had, he there admits, privileged formal beauty over the more valuable impressions elicited by association—the memories clinging to the materials in which the buildings' forms are embodied. Hardy suggests that this associative sense both depends on and fosters historical continuity and social cohesiveness insofar as it values the traces of human activities and histories left on the materials composing the church and the ad hoc alterations to its form—the very things, in other words, that were stripped away in the process of restoration.[19]

Written long after Victorian church restorations had fallen into public disrepute, "Memories of Church Restoration" elaborates on ideas that Hardy had in fact developed in the 1870s when the controversy over restoration was still a live issue. I want to claim here that *The Return of the Native* was a key site where Hardy worked out his own response to the aesthetic dilemmas involved in church restoration. He suggests as much himself in an 1878 note reflecting on landscapes by Giovanni Boldini and Meindert Hobbema. Here is how Hardy describes these painters' signature techniques: "'The method of Boldini . . . [and] Hobbema . . . is that of infusing emotion into the baldest external objects . . . by the mark of some human connection with them. This accords with my feeling about, say, Heidelberg and Baden *versus* Scheveningen—as I wrote at the beginning of *The Return of the Native*—that the beauty of association is entirely superior to the beauty of aspect, and a beloved relative's old battered tankard to the finest Greek vase. Paradoxically put, it is to see the beauty in ugliness'" (*Life and Work*, 124). Initially, it is hard to know what to make of the way Hardy glosses the beginning of *The Return of the Native* here, since the famous description of Egdon Heath with which Hardy opens that novel suggests that the mark of human connection is just what that landscape lacks. "A Face on which Time makes but little Impression," Egdon is impervious to the marks of human activity over time on which historical associations fasten (9). But that very lack of distinguishing features is what Egdon shares with the landscapes of Boldini and Hobbema in Hardy's description—Egdon and those landscapes are made up of "the baldest external objects," and that is what invests them with the beauty of association.

Nineteenth-century philosophers and critics believed that the beauty of association became particularly intense when the objects possessing it were most scanty. This line of thinking about the aesthetics of association originates in Archibald Alison's *Essay on the Nature and Principles of Taste* (1790). The first major attempt to apply associationist theories of mind to aesthetics, Alison's book enjoyed continuing popularity in the Victorian period (new editions were issued as late as the 1850s). In contrast to the physiological aesthetic theories that predominated in eighteenth-century Britain, Alison classes beauty and sublimity as emotions inhering in the trains of thought elicited by objects instead of in the sensory experience comprising their "simple perception."[20] Indeed, Alison claimed that attention to an object's sensory qualities actively interfered with aesthetic appreciation. Supposedly, we only feel the beauty and sublimity of an art object when we relax our focus on it and "lose ourselves amid the number of images that pass before our minds" (21). Alison thought that critics were therefore the least capable of the aesthetic appreciation they aimed at. By paying minute attention to a painting or a text, as we do in close reading, critics resist the very thing that would allow them to appreciate it—"yielding [themselves] to its suggestions" (23). For Alison, the more the actual sensory presence of an art object recedes, the more intense the aesthetic experience.

Alison's identification of aesthetic experience with reverie leads him to identify the beautiful with association by resemblance in particular. Nineteenth-century psychologists identified association by contiguity as the associative mode most typically at work in perception, as we have seen. Contiguous association was the cognitive process that bundles the sensations frequently experienced alongside each other into discrete objects of perception; after these bundles have become sufficiently tied in the mind, whenever one sensation bound up in them is experienced, "it serves as a sign or cue for the idea of the others to arise" (James, *Principles of Psychology,* 1:555). Operating according to the rhetorical logic of synecdoche, this process of generating a complete perception out of a fragment was termed redintegration by Victorian psychologists. Contiguous association was thus supposed to be the cognitive function responsible for "simple perception," and Alison therefore saw it as at odds with association as an aesthetic experience. For Alison, the beauty of association lay instead in resemblance, "the relation of all others, the most loose and general, and which affords the greatest range of thought for our imagination to pursue" (25). Following the substitutive logic of metaphor, Alison's beauty of association leads the mind away from the clear perception of objects.

It was Alison's identification of aesthetics with this kind of dreamy distraction that put him in Ruskin's critical sights. Ruskin had a certain affinity for the beauty of association. He too departed from the eighteenth-century notion of beauty as fundamentally a form of sense experience—in volume 2 of *Modern Painters* (1846) Ruskin argues that beauty should be reclassified from a species of *Aesthesis* (sense perception) to a species of *Theoria* (contemplation). For Ruskin, though, *Theoria* was above all disinterested, and consequently judgments of the beautiful made claim to the universality and objectivity of disinterested judgments more broadly. The beauty of association, in contrast, had all the contingency and sheer randomness of any given train of thought. The second volume of *Modern Painters* thus works vigorously to distance Ruskin's notion of the beautiful from association, which it subdivides into two different modes: rational association, under which he classed the historical associations belonging to objects and places linked to events in history; and accidental association, which comprises the private memories that happen to get linked to material things through individual experience.[21] Categorically distinct from the associative vagaries of both history and individual perceptual experience, beauty for Ruskin is the divinely ordered apprehension of the beautiful object's essential form.

And yet, as many critics have noticed, Ruskin's work contained irreducible associationist elements.[22] Rachel Teukolsky thus observes that in spite of its attack on Alison, *Modern Painters* describes visual artworks using "associative flights of language [that] work against [Ruskin's] object-centered ideas of beauty; the use of metaphor itself . . . creat[es] a chain of substitutions particular to the author's own mind."[23] The tensions in Ruskin's thinking about beauty and association become most aggravated, however, when he turns from paintings to churches. Like the later Hardy, Ruskin prefers his buildings with formal imperfections. In his case, this preference derives from the moral imperative Ruskin famously elaborates in "The Nature of Gothic" (1853), where he declares that formal imperfection in Gothic architectural ornaments indexes the mental freedom of the Gothic craftsman. The perfect regularity of modern, mass-produced ornament, in contrast, signifies the mechanized thralldom of the alienated industrial worker stuck forever churning out identical commodities. Ruskin begins staking this argument out four years earlier in *The Seven Lamps of Architecture* (1849), which contrasts "the abstract beauty of [architectural] forms, which . . . we will suppose to be the same whether they come from the hand or the machine" with the beauty arising from "the sense of human labour and care spent upon [them]."[24] Vying with the beauty of a building's formal outlines, this latter, more ethical sense of beauty depends on the associative links connecting the building's less rigidly regular form with the greater freedom of its builders.

Ruskin uses this associative sense of beauty to attack church restorations in "The Lamp of Memory." Apart from the technical challenges involved in determining a church's original form, the effort to restore is doomed from the start because "the spirit of the dead workman cannot be summoned up and commanded to direct other hands, and other thoughts" (194–95). Even if we could raise the dead, Ruskin suggests that the spirit would have to direct the contemporary worker's hands and thoughts and thus take away in the current generation of laborers the very freedom whose expression is being aimed at. Restoring churches, Ruskin thought, works against the capacity of architecture to preserve the associative beauty of memory, but that preservation itself inheres in the ruination of the church's sensible form. So much becomes clear in the qualified defense "The Lamp of Memory" mounts for the architectural picturesque. Ruskin argues that the picturesque depends on accidental features that actively obscure the essential beauty of architectural form—broken lines, fractures, weather stains, plants that seep out of or burst from or drape themselves over the walls. Yet despite the way the picturesque obscures form, Ruskin claims that it "is an exponent of age, of that in which . . . the greatest glory of the building consists; and therefore, the external signs of this glory, having power and purpose greater than . . . mere sensible beauty, may be considered as . . . pure and essential characters" (193). As Ruskin appreciates architecture more associatively, its sensible presence recedes as its significations (its builders' working conditions, the unimaginable touch of time) are brought forward.

Hardy's retrospective views on his work as an architect clearly draw from Ruskin's associative architectural aesthetics, but Hardy also held a similar understanding of the work he did in his second career as an author. Hardy suggests that the logic of redintegration defines the authorial "art of observation . . . [which] consists in this: the seeing of great things in little things, the whole in the part—even the infinitesimal part" (*Life and Work*, 262). Similarly, in Hardy's 1891 essay "The Science of Fiction," he distinguishes between the external observations of the mere imitator and the artist's apprehension of subtle qualities through "the mental tactility that comes from a sympathetic appreciativeness of life in all its manifestations." The "intuitive power" that the artist gains through sympathy, he claims, is the redintegrative ability "to see in half and quarter views the whole picture, to catch from a few bars the whole tune."[25] Hardy's artist does not interpret these fragments according to their contiguous associates, as we typically do when perceiving things. Rather, he transfigures the objects he encounters, and it is the capacity to do so that separates the artist from the "mere imitator," who only reflexively transcribes his routinized perceptions and thus turns the novel into "a spasmodic inventory of items" (*Life and Work*, 309). Hardy's artist sees the unexpected connections of things, which is to say, he perceives them according to association by similarity.

What Hardy characterizes as the artist's gift for association via similarity reflects a wider shift in Victorian psychologists' thinking about association. This shift began with Alexander Bain's *The Senses and the Intellect* (1855), which identified association by resemblance as the mental operation at work in abstract reasoning. Resemblance, Bain argues, allows us to abstract the similar qualities of different objects (thus making classification possible) and to identify the common elements in separate events or instances (thus making inferential propositions possible).[26] Bain's account thus treats association by similarity as the mechanism underlying more strenuous, higher-order thinking. At the same time, as contiguous association became identified with the routine functioning of perception, psychologists and physiologists came to think of it as functioning automatically and unconsciously, like a more complex version of the reflex arc (indeed, many Victorian scientists proposed that there was a physiological mechanism underlying contiguous association—pathways inscribed in the nervous system by repeated experiences).[27] Association by similarity thus gradually came to seem more volitional as well as more sophisticated.

No other text celebrates association by similarity with as much enthusiasm as James's *Principles of Psychology* (1890), which goes so far as to make this capacity the signature of not only genius but even the human itself.[28] The metaphorical logic of association via resemblance is the key to what James calls the "selective agency of interested attention" (1:578). James locates this associative agency squarely within the movement from the metonymic chains of contiguity to the leaps of metaphor: interested attention first decomposes a perceptual object by focusing on one of its component sensory qualities and then interprets it as a synecdoche for a different object sharing that quality.[29] It is this capacity to analyze objects of perception and generate new wholes from the parts thus isolated that "separates the man of genius from the prosaic creature[s] of habit and routine thinking," those who, "by the general flatness and poverty of their aesthetic nature, are kept for ever rotating among the literal sequences of their local and personal history" (*Principles of Psychology* 1:583, 582). Association thus has two interpretive modes: the literal or metonymic (contiguity) and the metaphorical (similarity). Indeed, the theory of association played a crucial role in shaping our current critical understandings of metaphorical and metonymic modes of interpretation. Roman Jakobson's influential account of metaphor and metonymy as occurring along, respectively, a vertical axis of substitution and a horizontal axis of combination in fact drew from Sigmund Freud's concepts of displacement and symbolism in *The Interpretation of Dreams* (1900), which Freud developed by reworking theories of association by contiguity and similarity.[30]

As is usually the case, the flights of genius inspired by similarity are liable to slip into reverie and dream. Such a liability dogged association by contiguity as well, since the arbitrary and overlapping connections between sensations mean that, however automatic they are, the paths tracked by the mind will always be indeterminate and aleatory. So while James maintains that association is redeemed from "perfect indeterminism" because it is guided by identifiable principles, he admits that those principles seem to yield little predictive power in any given case.

"It must still be confessed," James wrote, "that an immense number of terms in the linked chain of our representations fall outside of all assignable rule.... It thus remains true that to a certain extent... which associate of the interesting item shall emerge [in any train of thought] must be called largely a matter of accident—accident, that is, for our intelligence. No doubt it is determined by cerebral causes, but they are too subtile and shifting for our analysis" (*Principles of Psychology* 1:577).

James here confronts the peculiarly unpredictable predictability of metonymy. As Elaine Freedgood observes in a different context, "Metonymy is both routine and random, an invitation to cliché that comes packaged with the threat of contingency."[31] Nonetheless, Victorian psychologists like James speculated that metonymic association operated not only through habit but through what were effectively reflex arcs created by habit, and for this reason they held that even the relative unpredictability of metonymic association pales before the sublime freedom of association by similarity. Hence the metaphorical logic of association by resemblance retains a certain Dionysian cast in *Principles of Psychology,* as when James refers to "the lawless revelry of similarity" (1:582–83).

Hardy understands authorship as requiring just this kind of association by similarity. In this 1887 note, Hardy distinguishes his preferred mode of artistic practice from realism on the basis of an associative transformation of perceptions that closely resembles James's "selective agency of interested attention":

> I feel that Nature is played out as a Beauty, but not as a Mystery. I do not want to see landscapes, i.e., scenic paintings of them, because I do not want to see the original realities—as optical effects, that is . . . the exact truth as to material fact ceases to be of importance in art—it is a student's style—the style of a period when the mind is serene and unawakened to the tragical mysteries of life; when it does not bring anything to the object that coalesces with and translates the qualities that are already there—half hidden, it may be—and the two united are depicted as the All. (*Life and Work,* 192)

As in his earlier note on landscapes, in which Hardy identifies with artists who do not imitate but rather transform external objects by infusing them with emotion, the mature artist here projects part of himself into the objects he represents. Further, Hardy signals in this note that mature style is the product of associative perception by invoking the progress narrative of aesthetic transformation that opens *The Return of the Native,* a progress narrative that asserts the superiority of the beauty of association over the beauty of aspect.[32]

Sensory Obscurity in *The Return of the Native*

In the description of Egdon Heath that famously opens *The Return of the Native,* Hardy contrasts "orthodox beauty" with the "chastened sublimity" of Egdon, which, appealing "to a more recently learnt emotion," will become the aesthetic preference of "the more thinking among mankind" (10–11). Hardy identifies orthodox beauty with the southern, Hellenic ideals of beauty that are sensual, serene, and self-contained.[33] Egdon Heath, on the other hand, possesses a chastened sublimity in common with the other gaunt wastes of the North.[34] Hardy suggests that this peculiar preference is emerging because the mournful sublimity of these gaunt wastes accords with the feelings of those who have grasped the dim prospects for human happiness in a world governed by the defective laws of an indifferent Creation. In contrast, the gardens of southern Europe and "smiling champaigns of fruit and flowers" (10) painfully jar the moods of the more thinking among mankind because, like other instances of orthodox beauty, they express a "Hellenic idea of life" that Hardy identifies with the "old-fashioned reveling in the general situation" (167). The beauty of association that Hardy defines as finding beauty in ugliness here seems to consist of morose northern Europeans finding pleasure in landscapes whose austerity echoes back to them their own gloominess. As it continues, however, the description of Egdon suggests that the beauty of association comprises a certain form of relation between the subject and the objects of experience, and not merely the affective content of any such encounter.

Egdon is defined by gloom not as a mood of despondency but as a state of darkness. The heath attains to its most active and characteristic state "during winter darkness, tempests, and mists. Then Egdon was aroused to reciprocity. The storm was its lover; and the wind was its friend" (11). A "near relation of night," Egdon engages in affective reciprocity with other forces of obscurity—night, storm, mist, and so forth (10). While the novel opens with a description of how the approaching twilight underscores the division between the darkening heath and the still daylit sky, this dividing line is attenuated as the heath rises to meet the atmospheric elements of obscurity sympathetically, "in a black fraternisation towards which each advanced half-way" (10). This reciprocal relation between night and heath parallels the harmony between the heath and its observer, a harmony that is likewise called forth by obscurity, for Egdon "could best be felt when it could not clearly be seen" (9).

The Return of the Native is replete with such instances of perception through or despite sensory obscurity. Mrs. Yeobright and Thomasin discern the invisible reeds along the bank of the stream behind the Quiet Woman Inn from the "sounds as of a congregation praying humbly, produced by their rubbing against each other in the slow wind" (44). Though the dried heath bells cannot be seen in the dark, the listener "inwardly" sees them when hearing the wind rustle hundreds of them at once. This dry, papery sound, which Hardy calls the "linguistic peculiarity of the heath," brushes "so distinctly across the ear that, by the accustomed, the material minutiae in which it originated could be realised as by touch" (56). At Eustacia and Wildeve's midnight meeting on the heath after the Guy Fawkes fires have been extinguished, "compound utterances addressed themselves to their senses and it was possible to view by ear the features of the neighborhood. Acoustic pictures were returned from the darkened scenery . . . for [the] differing features [of the heath] had their voices no less than their shapes and colours" (87). While the emphasis in many of these examples is primarily on acoustic pictures, the sense of seeing somehow given through the sense of hearing, Hardy is not focused exclusively on the relation of these two senses. In addition to the claim that one could realize "as by touch" the dry heath bells from their sound, Hardy draws a parallel between acoustic pictures and the relation between touch and hearing when describing Eustacia's pursuit of Clym and his family along the darkened heath. Eustacia's sense, while listening intently to their movement and conversation, that "her ears were performing the functions of seeing as well as hearing" is, according to the narrator, an impression homologous with that of John Kitto, who, having gone deaf at age twelve, claimed that his body had subsequently become "so sensitive to vibrations that he had gained the power of perceiving by it as by ears" (116).

These recurring instances of synesthesia implicitly invoke the theory of association, according to which any sensation tends to call to mind its associates, but they are also insistently described as moments of sensory obscurity analogous, for Hardy, to sensory disability. This analogy appears most forcefully in the narrator's account of how Mrs. Yeobright developed a "comprehensiveness of . . . view" despite her removed and isolated social position living on the heath as a woman with a class status above those of the other heath dwellers:

> There are instances of persons who, without clear ideas of the things they criticize, have yet had clear ideas of the relations of those things. Blacklock, a poet blind from his birth, could describe visual objects with accuracy; Professor Sanderson, who was also blind, gave excellent lectures on colour, and taught others the theory of ideas which they had and he had not.[35] In the social sphere these gifted ones are mostly women; they can watch a world which they never saw, and estimate forces of which they have only heard. We call it intuition. (188)

Hardy here invokes common Victorian discussions of the epistemologies of disability to describe Mrs. Yeobright's comprehensiveness of view in spite of her limited knowledge.[36] Hardy's Professor Sanderson, who features saliently in those discussions as well, is in fact Nicholas Saunderson, a friend and expositor of Isaac Newton who became blind as a child and went on to hold the Lucasian Chair of Mathematics at Cambridge and serve as the inspiration for Denis Diderot's *Letter on the Blind* (1749).[37] His work explicating Newton's optics, in particular, made him a key example for Diderot and others of the way the disabled could come to understand aspects of the world without experiencing them directly. Saunderson in this regard provided the Victorians with a signal instance of knowledge by description—propositional knowledge supplementing the direct experience comprising knowledge by acquaintance.

Saunderson, moreover, was popularly supposed to have come by his descriptive knowledge of color through a kind of metaphorical reasoning. From the end of the eighteenth century onward, he was popularly (but erroneously) identified as the "studious blind man" in an endlessly recycled anecdote told by John Locke in *An Essay Concerning Human Understanding.* In Locke's anecdote, the studious blind man explains to a friend that after having extensively studied descriptions of the color scarlet he finally understands that it is "like the Sound of a Trumpet."[38] For Locke, the blind man's answer demonstrates the impossibility of grasping so-called simple ideas (elemental sensations) without direct experience. The metaphor, apt as it is, indicates that the blind man can at best grasp scarlet as a complex idea (a perceptual concept) containing multiple simple ones. As the anecdote gets retold by subsequent writers, though, the aptness of the metaphor comes to displace the subtle epistemological distinction it pointed to for Locke. So the writer of an essay on the blind in *Cornhill* retails Locke's anecdote (without attributing it to him) and breathlessly remarks, "How striking is this answer. One feels that he had realized the essential meaning of the colour, and translated it from the known to the unknown language."[39] Hardy seems to follow Locke—Saunderson does not have the ideas of color, but he has grasped the theory of them by understanding their relations. And yet he seems thereby to have attained to the kind of comprehensive view that Hardy elsewhere identifies as the signature of the artist, who likewise translates the optical effects of things into a more associative, unitary vision of the world. Saunderson's literal and Mrs. Yeobright's figurative blindness seem to prompt the more comprehensive views that Hardy claims to strive for as an author.

Sensory obscurity stimulates comprehension for certain characters in *The Return of the Native* insofar as it elicits the conscious mental effort of perceptual interpretation. As I have argued above, associationist theories of perception became particularly important in the nineteenth century because they helped account for how the mind constructs and cognizes a stable world of objects on the basis of often fragmentary and imperfect sensory input. Victorian psychologists conceptualized association as the perceptual supplementing and interpretation of sensations acting as signs. Similarly, in *The Return of the Native,* sensations denote perceptual objects. Eustacia's undressing in the dark is "denoted" by the rustling sounds of her clothes and her movements (67). The presence of reeds along the stream bank behind the Quiet Woman is "denoted" by the sounds of the wind rubbing them together (44). The contours of the landscape lying below the Guy Fawkes revelers on Blackbarrow are "denoted" by masses of shade (19). And so on. Sensory obscurity calls attention to the denotative nature of these perceptions (at least for the novel's narrator), but for Mrs. Yeobright, Clym, and Eustacia, the three characters who are each in their own way alienated from the heath and its customs, sensory obscurity also makes possible a mode of association that transforms such denotative perceptions. Just as James's selective agency of interested attention proceeds by isolating sensuous qualities in a given object so that the mind can leap from them to objects sharing those or similar qualities, in *The Return of the Native* the absence of the full set of sensations composing an object allows wider latitude in the perceptual interpretation of the remaining sensations. Sensory obscurity for Hardy is thus equivalent to the narrow focalization preliminary to the metaphoric leaps that bring different objects or ideas into relation with one another, and in this way, as the narrator remarks in *Tess*, "The defective can be more than the entire."[40]

While Hardy often valorizes this mode of associative perception when it is applied to landscapes, *The Return of the Native* registers a deep anxiety that, when applied to other subjects, it raises difficult ethical, erotic, and epistemological questions. These questions are foregrounded in the novel's description of Clym's face. Whereas Egdon Heath is a type of the beautiful landscapes of the future, Clym's face is identified as "the typical countenance of the future," a status his face owes to its embodiment of the strain of thought (167). Though its original physical beauty is still apparent when Clym first returns to Egdon, the "outer symmetry" of his face is already breaking down under "a wearing habit of meditation" (137). Clym's pensiveness is prompted by "a full recognition of the coil of things," the same perception, that is, of the "defects of natural laws" that allows the observer to perceive the beauty of association in the face of the heath: "The lineaments which will get embodied in ideals based upon this new recognition will probably be akin to those of Yeobright. The observer's eye was arrested, not by his face as a picture, but by his face as a page; not by what it was, but by what it recorded. His features were attractive in the light of symbols, as sounds intrinsically common become attractive in language, and as shapes intrinsically simple become interesting in writing" (167–68). As Clym's recognition of the coil of things allows him to perceive the face of the heath as associatively significant, his own face becomes a text signifying this recognition to another observer. However, the associative perception that makes such significations possible also introduces an uncertainty about their provenance. The text of Clym's face is written by the "inner strenuousness" of his "unfold[ing]" thought: "[His] face was well-shaped, even excellently. But the mind within was beginning to use it as a mere waste tablet whereon to trace its idiosyncrasies as they developed themselves" (137). At the same time, Clym's face as a text requires a reader, who may, via association, project meanings of her own onto it: "People who began by beholding him ended by perusing him. His countenance was overlaid with legible meanings" (137). The adjective "overlaid" here suggests not that the face's legible meanings are expressions of the mind within but rather that they are superimposed by those perusing it.

The dilemma hinted at in this description of Clym's face—in reading a face, does one project meaning onto it or discover the meanings expressed by its owner?—plays out in the novel's plot through the courtship and marriage of Clym and Eustacia. Clym and Eustacia begin their mutual fascination without being able to see each other's face. Eustacia's interest in Clym is sparked just before his return to Egdon when she overhears two furze cutters remark on what a suitable match he might be for her, or as the narrator puts it, "on the harmony between the unknown and herself" (110). When Eustacia first comes into contact with Clym in person, as he is walking with his family on the heath at evening, she is conspicuously denied a glimpse of his face. Instead, as she surreptitiously follows him, she attends closely to his voice, but not to the words it is speaking. His voice becomes the object of an act of association—it is at this moment that the narrator invokes Dr. Kitto to explain Eustacia's sense that her ears are seeing as well as hearing—that proceeds independently of whatever feelings or ideas Clym is attempting to express. For Eustacia, Clym thus serves, as Wildeve did before him, as "the single object within her horizon on which dreams might crystallize" (95).

Similarly, Clym is unable to see Eustacia's face when he meets her, after the brief encounter on the darkened heath, at the Yeobrights' Christmas party. Eustacia attends the party as the Turkish Knight in the mummers' play, and her costume includes ribbons draped over and disguising her face. Although Clym is still "arrested" by her presence and guesses her gender despite the costume, Eustacia bemoans the limits imposed on her beauty by the circumstances: "The power of her face all lost, the charm of her emotions all disguised, the fascinations of her coquetry denied existence, nothing but a voice left to her; she had a sense of the doom of Echo" (143). Eustacia's "doom" here mirrors her meeting with Clym on the heath, when he likewise appears to her only as an "awakening voice" (120). Insofar as they are at first only voices to each other, both she and Clym share the fate of Echo, the nymph who fell into unrequited love with Narcissus and pined away until only her voice remained. In addition to "fate" or "end," however, "doom" also denotes "judgment" or "punishment." Before she fell in love with Narcissus, Echo distracted Juno with stories to keep her from discovering the other nymphs in the act of sex with Jove. When Juno discovered the trick, she punished Echo by rendering her mute except to repeat others' words. The doom of Echo is thus to be unable to speak for herself, to speak only the speech of others. Hardy's allusion hints at the broader question at issue in Eustacia's and Clym's misreadings of each other and in *The Return of the Native* generally: Is the transformative mode of perception aimed at by Hardy as an author inevitably an act of prosopopoeia, of narcissistically apprehending any object, whether animate or inanimate, as a text that merely echoes oneself?

Prosopopoeia is a pervasive rhetorical device in *The Return of the Native*. The heath is frequently subject to acts of prosopopoeic ventriloquism by both the narrator and the novel's characters. After his separation from Eustacia, for instance, Clym perceives her presence in all the sounds of the surrounding heath: "A bird searching for worms in the mould of the flower-beds sounded like her hand on the latch of the gate; and at dusk, when soft, strange ventriloquisms came from holes in the ground, hollow stalks, curled dead leaves, and other crannies wherein breezes, worms, and insects can work their will, he fancied that they were Eustacia, standing without and breathing wishes of reconciliation" (336). The heath here is given voice through a double ventriloquism: first its inanimate features are figured as being spoken through by breezes and insects, but then this speech is transformed in Clym's hearing into the sounds of his estranged wife.

The ventriloquism of the heath in this passage echoes the earlier description of the sounds—made by the wind through the dried heath bells—that accompany Eustacia's vigil on Blackbarrow. There, the narrator's associative recognition of the dead heath bells triggered by the sound of their rustling is immediately followed by a meditation on the phrase "the spirit moved them." "A meaning of the phrase forced itself upon the attention," he observes, "and an emotional listener's fetichistic mood might have ended in one of more advanced quality. It was not, after all, that the left-hand expanse of old blooms spoke, or the right-hand, or those of the slope in front; but it was the single person of something else speaking through each at once" (56–57). What the narrator describes here is a relay of perceptual agency. The passive listener has a phrase and its meaning forced on her by the sound of the heath bells, which is in fact the voice of the wind speaking through them, a "voice" that is in turn bestowed by the "fetichistic" emotional listener in the prosopopoeic act of figuring the wind as a speaking "single person."

Ultimately, this relay of ventriloquism expands to include Eustacia herself. "The bluffs, and the bushes, and the heather-bells had broken silence," the narrator remarks, "at last, so did the woman; and her articulation was but as another phrase of the same discourse as theirs. . . . What she uttered was a lengthened sighing . . . [and] there was a spasmodic abandonment about it as if, in allowing herself to utter the sound the woman's brain had authorized what it could not regulate" (57). Eustacia's dubious self-control here—allowing a spasmodic abandonment, authorizing an action she cannot regulate—suggests that her voice is not her own so much as an expression of a more encompassing force around her. This moment thus seems to anticipate *The Dynasts,* in which human thought and action are almost totally determined by the combination of relentlessly unfolding natural and social logics that Hardy calls the Will. And yet to read Eustacia as spoken through by something like the Will in the same way that Napoleon and the Duke of Wellington are acted through by the Will in *The Dynasts* is to elide the fact that the description of her in this passage is *already* a reading, an interpretation of her utterance. The description is an instance of free indirect discourse focalized through the same hypothetical "emotional listener" who has just prosopopoeically composed a single person speaking a discourse from the varied sounds of the heath (56).[41] Eustacia is spoken through by the emotional listener, who perceives her utterance as a spasmodic abandonment that picks up and extends the discourse of the heath; Eustacia is here simply one more link in the relay of perceptual agency. The inclusion of Eustacia within this prosopopoeic circuit takes us back to the question of what it means to read others in *The Return of the Native,* but this circuit hints at a broader question underlying this one.

The Affects of Critical Reading

What does it mean to read *The Return of the Native?* The relay of perceptual agency in the passage above provides a partial answer to this question because it is a figure for critical reading. As we have seen, for Hardy an author by definition engages in the kind of emotional listening above because he must associatively transform the objects of his perception. In "The Profitable Reading of Fiction," it is implicitly on the basis of this transfigured perception that Hardy equates the results of his own literary activity, which he calls "representation[s] of life," with the "criticism of life" that, according to Matthew Arnold, constitutes poetry.[42] Authorship, Hardy suggests, requires something like the spontaneous play of consciousness on stock notions and habits comprising Arnold's ideal of criticism.[43] In other words, an author is a sort of critic.

Arnold in fact maintains a quietly insistent presence in *The Return of the Native.* His *Culture and Anarchy* (1869) features as the inspiration (anachronistic, since the novel is set in the 1840s) for Clym's quixotic "culture scheme," which seems to consist of providing an informal liberal arts education to the furze cutters and peasants of Egdon and which he pursues with a more complete disregard for all practical concerns than Arnold could have dreamed of (245). Clym's "modern perceptiveness," cultivated through his time spent abroad in Paris, likewise closely resembles Arnold's vision of detached, reflective criticism. In this regard, Clym serves in the novel as a kind of surrogate for Hardy himself, the native of Dorset who was also, as Mark Ford puts it, half a Londoner.[44] Like Hardy, Clym is also an author of sorts; in Clym's case the text is his face, composed of "marks derived from a perception of his surroundings" (137). While Hardy and Clym, as returning natives, enjoy the kind of detached perspectives on their places of origin that Arnold advocated, in another way their perceptions are not detached at all. Arnold pressed claims for the objectivity of criticism even further than Ruskin—the critic, he famously argues in "The Function of Criticism at the Present Time" (1865), endeavors "to see the object in itself as it really is."[45] Hardy and Clym, on the other hand, transform the objects they perceive by investing them with emotions and even, in the case of Clym's reading of Eustacia, with eroticism.[46] The detachment characterizing Clym and Hardy's critical perspectives comes paired with a tendency to perceive things in terms of their attachments to them.

In this regard, *The Return of the Native* looks forward to the vexed questions around the relationship of affect to critical reading for twentieth- and twenty-first-century literary studies. In their essay on the "affective fallacy," W. K. Wimsatt and Monroe Beardsley categorically reject affective response as a legitimate mode of reading because, like the associative readings of faces in *The Return of the Native,* it licenses a form of "impressionism and relativism" that interpolates the text so that the text, "as an object of specifically critical judgment, tends to disappear."[47] Affective response returns with a vengeance, however, in Roland Barthes's pyrotechnic poststructuralist analysis of reading, *S/Z*. Barthes there divides reading into two modes: the readerly and the writerly. Like the student's style of seeing Hardy disparaged as realism, readerly reading is passive and unfree. A consumer rather than a producer of literature, the readerly reader is "plunged into a kind of idleness—he is intransitive. . . . Instead of functioning himself, instead of gaining access to the magic of the signifier, to the pleasure of writing, he is left with no more than the poor freedom either to accept or to reject the text."[48] Readerly reading is constrained by the metonymic, unidirectional logico-temporal order of the hermeneutic and proairetic codes that bind it according to conventional notions of truth. Over and against the readerly, the writerly reader is an active agent who produces the text's multivalence, its plurality, by playfully moving between codes and thus achieving jouissance. Writerly reading, Barthes was happy to declare, renders the author not only irrelevant but dead. In spite of such radicalism, though, Barthes's two modes of reading were easily assimilated to the opposition between critical and uncritical reading that has historically served literary studies as its disciplinary rationale. As Michael Warner suggests, literary studies' apparently anodyne commitment to the practice and teaching of critical (as opposed to uncritical) reading signals the discipline's ongoing participation in the same Enlightenment project of liberal self-making that Arnold advocated.[49]

If literary studies' commitment to critical reading has come to seem strangely doubtful, this is in no small part because of a widespread disenchantment with what has come to be seen as the feeling of critique. As both a method and a pedagogy, critical reading in practice seems to many critics less an exercise in Arnoldian liberal detachment or Barthesian autoeroticism than an episode of paranoia. Over the past several decades, the story runs, literary criticism absorbed the interpretive protocols of the so-called hermeneutics of suspicion, in the process transmuting critical detachment into the paranoia of critique. Paranoia, though, bears a cousinly resemblance to detachment insofar as it is, in Eve Sedgwick's words, a theory of negative affects: a strategy to avoid unpleasurable feelings so all-consuming that it tends to exclude the seeking of pleasurable ones.[50] In the classroom, suspicion is now frequently singled out as the culprit behind critical reading's long-standing capacity to anaesthetize students' pleasures in literature by forbidding their naïve attachments to characters, plots, national traditions, the genius of particular authors, and so on.[51]

But notwithstanding its antipathy to such attachments and its tendency to prefer avoiding pain to seeking pleasure, critical suspicion does offer readers what Rita Felski describes as a "ludic delight . . . in creating complex designs out of textual fragments."[52] Here again, though, we come back to the question of whether those complex designs are reconstructions (in this case, of the repressed forces really at work in a text) or reimaginings that force the textual fragment into a pattern purely of the critic's own making. Contending that symptomatic reading pursues the latter path, several critics have recently proposed a raft of alternatives to suspicious reading—reparative reading, just reading, surface reading, postcritical reading—that instead stake out reading as a reconstructive project that strives to ground the reader's relation to the text in ethical care and attachments.[53] Our understanding of these attachments is more likely to be drawn from cybernetics than associationist psychology (the approach favored in this book is Jamesian radical empiricism, which is probably closer to cybernetics than to the associationism of *Principles of Psychology*), but what we share with Hardy is an interest in reading as an affective, sensuous, perceptual practice. Regardless of theoretical framework, any approach to reading as a perceptual practice must contend with the fundamental question involved in understanding perception: On what terms do the perceiving subject and the perceived world partner in experience?

Whether we assign it the most generous or the stingiest, most fragmentary terms in that partnership, the world necessarily includes other people.[54] While other people may not loom large in the landscape of Egdon, buildings and books are another matter. The critical attacks on the alleged impropriety of his later novels merely intensified the concerns Hardy already developed during his career as an architect over just how much deference to the builder should weigh in the aesthetic judgment of a church. In *The Return of the Native*, the beauty of association allows the reader two possible relations to the author. One can defer to the author by reading the text in terms of the conventional, relatively stable contiguous associations that Hardy identifies with realism. Or one can read a text critically, by bringing something to it that coalesces with and translates the qualities that are already there. In this case, both the critical reader and the author take their parts in the kind of relay of perceptual agency we saw with Eustacia on the heath, in which the reader prosopopoeically composes an authorial consciousness out of a curious amalgam of the reading author and the writing reader.

Hardy embodies the two modes of critical and uncritical reading in *The Return of the Native*'s variation on the paired stock figures of the dark lady and the fair lady. The novel's most troubling critical reader is found in the complex figure of Eustacia. Eustacia seems an unlikely choice to exemplify the critical reading identified by Hardy as the aesthetic mode of the future, since the novel opens by opposing this modernizing aesthetic mode to the appreciation of the refined southern beauty of her type. She is thoroughly identified with the southern, "Hellenic idea of life" (167). Hence she fails to appreciate the modern, northern beauty of Egdon. But Eustacia's Hellenism comprises both a refractory, antimodern sensualism and a form of perception strikingly similar to Hardy's version of critical reading.[55] Despite her classical features, Eustacia's beauty is in fact similar to that of the heath; both demand a "trained" eye because both are characterized by "a certain obscurity" (92). Hardy, playing on the full range of meanings of dark/fair, thus opposes Eustacia to Thomasin, her fair rival, whose features are more ingenuously "transparent . . . as if the flow of her existence could be seen passing within" (41).

Thomasin exemplifies the more conventional mode of perception that follows contiguous associations. Unlike Eustacia, Thomasin ventures out on the heath at night in the rain without fear because "to her there were not, as to Eustacia, demons in the air, and malice in every bush and bough. The drops which lashed her face were not scorpions, but prosy rain; Egdon in the mass was no monster whatever, but impersonal open ground. . . . It was in her view a windy, wet place, in which a person might experience much discomfort, lose the path without care, and possibly catch cold" (355). For Thomasin, the heath is as transparent as her own subjectivity, but for that very reason she does not transform its features through metaphoric association. Its features are too clear and self-enclosed—too prosy—to her. She is capable of a certain kind of moderate appreciation for the beauty of association, remarking of Egdon that "I admire its grim, old face" (340). But she does not aspire to reimagine what she sees. Hardy signals her deference to authority in this regard by christening her Thomasin, the feminine version of his own name. Like James's creature of habit and routine thinking, Thomasin reads the heath literally, passively accepting its elements as givens, and thus for her they remain bereft of the emotional significance that would transform them, little more than mere bald, external objects. She is the fair lady—obedient to convention, and thus destined for a happy marriage. For that reason, however, her psychic life is, in the novel's terms, both transparent and shallow.

The rebellious dark lady Eustacia, on the other hand, experiences the heath through metaphorical associations; the raindrops that lash her face are not merely raindrops but scorpions. By thus charging the commonplace phenomena of the heath with significance, Eustacia treats those features as signs in accord with the novel's own definition of what makes up writing: "shapes intrinsically simple" that become "interesting" when invested with meaning (168). Eustacia invests the phenomena of the heath with meaning through the pathetic fallacy—reading it as a reflection of her own emotional condition—and in doing so she practices something like the technique that Hardy himself embraced as constituting "the beauty of association": "the method . . . of infusing emotion into the baldest external objects . . . by the mark of some human connection with them" (*Life and Work*, 124). This mode of perceiving the heath recalls the narrator's account of why Eustacia became involved with Wildeve: because he was "the single object within her horizon on which dreams might crystallize" (95). The narrator confirms this resemblance in an aside that brings marital discord and Eustacia's perception of Egdon into explicit parallel: "To dwell on a heath without studying its meanings was like wedding a foreigner without learning his tongue. The subtle beauties of the heath were lost to Eustacia; she only caught its vapours" (73). The intrinsic meanings of Egdon are incomprehensible to Eustacia because she perceives the heath as echoing her own feelings, a voice through which she speaks to herself. The form of critical perception practiced by Eustacia on the heath is identical to her misreading of Clym's face. And this mode of perception thus leads ineluctably to tragedy: to her disastrous liaisons with Wildeve; to her fatal marriage with Clym; and, finally, to her death from drowning while, in an echo of Narcissus, being rolled by currents along the "gashed and puckered mirror" that is the surface of the weir (361).

Eustacia's associative perception and its narrative consequences seem to rehearse Ruskin's claim, in his discussion of the pathetic fallacy, that "when we are under the influence of emotion or contemplative fancy" we often succumb to "false appearances [that are] entirely unconnected with any real power or character in the object, and only imputed to it by us."[56] In *The Return of the Native*, to perceive another subject critically, as Eustacia does Clym, is to compose a text that necessarily distorts the original text produced by the unfolding of that person's own reflective subjectivity through that same process of critical perception. Hence the double significance of blindness in the novel: the obscurity that restricts one's apprehension of an object, as in the case of Mrs. Yeobright or the blind or deaf poets and scholars invoked by Hardy, can incite a more strenuous form of perception that treats the sensations making up the object as multivalent signs and thus grasps the object and its relations more comprehensively; but as consciousness thus interprets the obscured object, it is liable to be, in Ruskin's phrase, "over-dazzled by emotion," and so lose its comprehensiveness of view after all.[57] Clym's blindness from reading in the dark crystallizes the tendency of the empowerment in critical perception to undermine itself.

The possibility of such a reversal also haunts Hardy as the author of *The Return of the Native*. In displacing the most striking instances of critical misreading from Clym onto Eustacia, who, as the dark lady, is defined by her refusal to abide by the established social order, Hardy underscores his discomfort with the potential of critical reading to appropriate authorial authority. As we have seen, Hardy's critical perception—an active mode of interpretation analogous to reading through which the artist translates objects by infusing them with emotional significance in the act of perception—is the source of that imaginative sense of fact that constitutes a properly artistic style for Hardy. As he practices this mode of perception, the author produces a text that Hardy, articulating his own aesthetics with Arnold's writing on poetry, calls a criticism of life. However, just as metaphoric association both preserves agency and licenses a form of mental play so Dionysian and unregulated that James refers to it as "the lawless revelry of similarity," critical reading opens up its texts to a degree of indeterminacy that Hardy finds both exhilarating and unsettling (*Principles of Psychology* 1:582–83). The plot of *The Return of the Native*—as well as its obsession with prosopopoeia—is driven by this ambivalence. If the critical reader cultivates agency by transforming her text, by prosopopoeically composing an authorial consciousness out of an amalgam of both the author and herself, then Hardy's repeatedly invoked ideal of perspicacious reading—in which the reader faithfully reconstitutes author and intentions in the act of reading—paradoxically leaves no room for critical reading at all. Critical reading, then, lays both the author and his texts open to exactly the kind of misreadings that so infuriated Hardy over the course of his professional life. In an irony of the kind Hardy himself so often made use of in his novels, the same form of critical reading that made authorship possible for him also ensured his own death as an author.

4

Tagging the Vatican Museum with Vernon Lee

DESCRIPTION AND THE AESTHETIC MOVEMENT

> Galleries are necessary things, to save pictures and statues (or the little remaining of them) from candle smoke, sacristans' ladders, damp, worms, and street boys, but they are evil necessities; and the sense of a sort of negative vandalism always clings to them, specially to the galleries of statues, so uninhabited, so utterly sepulchral. Going to a gallery of sculpture, we must be prepared to isolate what we wish to enjoy, to make for it a fitting habitation in our fancy.
>
> —Vernon Lee, "The Child in the Vatican"

IN ROME, ONE WOULD naturally expect to encounter vandals. The material record of the Vandals' sacking of the city in 455 helped make Rome what it was for the Victorians, "the city of visible history," a vast wreck, at once alluring and disturbing, of "gigantic broken revelations."[1] While the Vandals are famous for breaking the city, in a very literal instance of Walter Benjamin's aphorism about civilization and barbarism, their plundering of Rome has also played a key role in its conservation. In a series of reports to the French National Convention in 1794, the Abbé Henri Grégoire described the iconoclastic destruction of public monuments in the aftermath of the French Revolution as a kind of reenactment of the 455 sack of Rome, thus coining the modern term "vandalism."[2] The origins of our notion of vandalism, then, lie in the revolutionary crucible from which the public museum itself emerged; vandalism and the museum are the twin products of the popular and legislative ambivalence toward the extensive monuments and art collections the revolutionaries expropriated from the nobility and the church. Vandalism has ever since accompanied the museum as its shadow, necessitating its preservationist and educational missions.[3]

Vernon Lee suggests this much in the epigraph, taken from her essay "The Child in the Vatican," a jaundiced love letter to Rome as a museum. By placing art objects in the protective space of the museum, we preserve them from the slow cumulative damage entailed by neglect (smoke, worms, damp) as well as the more abrupt breakages of accidental (sacristans' ladders) and deliberate vandalism (street boys) that they are vulnerable to when situated in unsupervised public space. And yet Lee characterizes the preservationist work of the museum as itself a kind of vandalism. Rehearsing a common criticism of the museum, Lee suggests that removing art objects from their original settings in church, square, or temple constitutes a violent wrenching of them from their context in everyday life. The museum, in this line of thinking, negates vandalism but is also vandalism's negative, its reverse image or impression. As such, the museum necessitates a further preservationist effort in a kind of doubling or displacement of the first: just as the museum isolates art objects to preserve them from vandalism by housing them in its protective space, the museumgoer must isolate them all over again to preserve them from the museum's own negative vandalism by rehousing them in a fitting habitation in her fancy, a kind of museum of the mind.

It was only within a similar space, Lee thought, that her own aestheticist essays could properly be read. Like the art objects isolated in the museum, the essays that, along with "The Child in the Vatican," make up her 1881 collection, *Belcaro,* had each been abstracted from its origins in what Lee calls a real setting: "a real, living, shimmering setting of tones and looks, and jests and passion, and anecdote and illustration, and irrelevant streakings and veinings of description and story; a setting too of place and time and personality."[4] Not the least important presence within these real settings was that of art objects themselves. *Belcaro* evangelizes for the Aesthetic Movement, in particular for its vision of a direct, sensuous relation with art objects that bypasses the discursive mediations of historical or theoretical knowledge. Stefano Evangelista thus notes that for her fellow travelers in the Aesthetic Movement, "Lee's authority as critic . . . does not rest on bookish knowledge but on a greatly preferable experience of art that is based on immediacy of sensation, actual physical contact with the object, and emotional investment in it."[5] In *Belcaro,* Lee accordingly disclaims the historical expertise she accrued as the author of *Studies of the Eighteenth Century in Italy* (1880); these essays, she declares, are not expert or systematic explications but rather the sketchy, disorganized notes made by a humble student of aesthetics with the "strong feeling that art questions should always be discussed in the presence of some definite work of art" (8). But that stipulation, of course, is just what is impossible for the discussion of art questions in *Belcaro* to fulfill. In order to become essays, the ideas and impressions originally developed in the presence of definite works of art had "to be removed out of all this living frame-work . . . to be made quite lifeless and inorganic, and dry and stiff, like some stuffed animal or bird," like, we might say, an art object in a gallery display (7). As a book, then, *Belcaro* is itself a kind of museum space, necessarily committing its own negative vandalism.

Hence, like the Vatican's sculptures, *Belcaro*'s essays require what Lee calls "resetting" (6). Resetting does not, however, signify a quixotic effort to imaginatively restore the idea or the statue to its original environment. The fitting habitation in the fancy that Lee gives sculptures in "The Child in the Vatican" relocates them instead to what is best described as an abstract conceptual space, similar to the museum itself, against which their formal presence acquires maximum clarity. Jonah Siegel has suggested that Lee's essay instantiates this process of semiabstraction through its own shifts of location.[6] The sculptures she discusses most extensively are the Niobe group, which are located not in the Vatican but the Uffizi Gallery in Florence, and even then Lee isn't happy with their arrangement there and asks her reader to instead refer to a terracotta and wood model of the group for the purposes of her discussion. As she resets the Niobe group by rescaling and even reembodying them in different material, Lee aims to make the sculptures present as a set of formal relations rather than a set of material objects. She does so, moreover, to abstract those formal relations from another kind of matter—the subject of the sculptures. Resetting the Niobe group, Siegel argues, is the first step in Lee's painstaking effort to make "a tragic vision of a family destroyed by the cruel jealousy of divinity into a formal, not a representational, object of perception."[7]

Her resetting of the essays in *Belcaro* seems, initially at least, to follow suit. The new, artificial setting she aims to provide for her aesthetic notes, she claims, will bear the same schematic, scale-model relation to their original setting as a landscaped garden does to the landscapes one can travel through. But the parallel with her resetting of the sculptures breaks down when she goes on to clarify how she has reset her essays. "In putting together these notes," she writes, "[I have always] had a vision of pictures or statues, had a sound of music in my mind, or a page of a book in my memory; I have always thought, in arranging these discussions, of the real individuals with whom I should most willingly have them: I have always felt that someone else was by my side to whom I was showing, explaining, answering" (8). While pictures, statues, music, and even a page of a book might become formal objects of perception, the real individuals Lee has in mind necessarily have a different kind of imagined perceptual presence. To see what kind, we need look no further than the title of the book itself. As Lee explains in the preface, the title, *Belcaro,* tells us nothing about the book itself, which does not at any point specifically discuss the cinquecento villa Castello di Belcaro from which she took the name. The name Belcaro nevertheless has "a meaning of association" (2). Its associative meaning, she explains, derives from Lee's visit to the Castello di Belcaro along with Mary F. Robinson, the close friend to whom she dedicated the book and with whom Lee was then passionately in love. As she wrote these essays, Lee found herself haunted by memories of that day because, she speculates, it must have been then that she conceived the "vague first desire to put together . . . the helter-skelter contents of the notes over which we had been looking, and give it you [Mary] in some intelligible shape" (3). Here, then, we have the master resetting of Lee's essays along with her imaginary interlocutor made present as associative, rather than formal, objects of perception. Through such associative perception, Belcaro and Mary Robinson do not reveal form so much as they reveal what Lee suggests is a desire for form.

This chapter follows Lee through the museum and other settings in order to trace the relations between associative and formal perception within the Aesthetic Movement. Lee's writings on aesthetics reflect an especially intensive interest in and involvement with the nineteenth-century sciences of perception. The unusual rigor and explicitness of Lee's engagement with psychology and physiology make her writings especially important as documents of the way that the sciences of perception helped shape the Aesthetic Movement. In taking Lee's scientific aestheticism as its main object of inquiry, this chapter aims to contribute to the ongoing major reassessment of Vernon Lee, which has transformed her from a relatively minor figure in the Aesthetic Movement—perhaps best known for the dismissive, homophobic and misogynist attacks on her by modernists and New Critics—into the subject of critical monographs, essay collections, and a literary biography.[8] Paying special attention to her involvement with perception science, Nicholas Dames and Benjamin Morgan have each identified Lee as a theorist of reading who played a key, if neglected, role within the history of literary criticism—for Dames, Lee is a transitional figure leading from Victorian to twentieth-century theories of novel form, while Morgan recuperates her quantitative conception of literary form as an unacknowledged progenitor of the distant reading practiced by contemporary digital humanists.[9] My reading of Lee here builds on this work while departing from it in two ways. First, I trace Lee's accounts of reading and form in in *The Beautiful* (1913) and *The Handling of Words* (1923) back to her earliest aesthetic essays in *Belcaro* and her novel about the Aesthetic Movement, *Miss Brown* (1884). In doing so, I additionally aim to reveal the crucial role the intimate distances of knowledge by description played within the perceptual ontologies of form that Dames and Morgan uncover in Lee's work.

The priority accorded the direct experience of beautiful objects by the Aesthetic Movement entailed a corresponding demotion in status for the kinds of descriptive, classificatory knowledge of art history that organized the museum. But while aesthetes insisted that critical judgments be grounded in the direct perceptual presence of art objects, they were divided when it came to just what exactly was present to the critic thus seeing, hearing, or reading them. The point of contention was whether artworks were rightly perceived as a set of formal relations or, in contrast, as suggestive—as transitively making another, different object present to the mind. In the nineteenth century, perceptual suggestiveness was both an aesthetic quality and a scientific concept, identified with association as well as knowledge by description. The Aesthetic Movement's ambivalence toward description, this chapter argues, crystallized around perceptual suggestion because suggestiveness in fact licensed the lush, finely crafted description of beautiful objects that is the signature rhetorical mode of aestheticist writings. But at the same time, suggestiveness seemed to lead the aesthete's attention away from the artwork's actually present form to what that artwork made virtually present. The account of formal aesthetic perception that Lee spent her life developing sets itself in explicit opposition to perceptual suggestiveness and its attendant modes of descriptive knowledge, which Lee characterizes as species of vandalism. And yet, as Lee knew well, where there is vandalism, the museum cannot be far behind. For Lee, I show, the descriptive contexts and suggested presences do not get in the way of the formal encounter with the artwork—instead, like the museum, and like Belcaro itself, they lead us onto or into the art object. They give us, Lee suggests, a desire for form.

Tagging the Vatican in *Belcaro:* Descriptive Knowledge in the Museum

"The Child in the Vatican" begins, aptly, with a barbarian invasion. The Vatican has been overrun, Lee tells us, with "a lot of children": "small barbarians scarce out of the nursery, who should have been at home" (17). Lee opens *Belcaro* with these barbarian children because the essays collectively attempt to justify a childlike relation to art, one that is innocent of theory and history and therefore perceptually simple and direct. In pointing to these children as barbarians, though, Lee tacitly signals that they are, ostensibly at least, in the Vatican to be civilized. In other words, *Belcaro*'s barbarian invasion invokes the primal scene of the museum's educational and civilizing mission.

Here, though, that mission does not seem to be going very well. Bored, distracted, rambunctious, the kids as Lee imagines them act the way that children generally did in museums. Children were at once a pervasive and a controversial presence in nineteenth-century museums. The British Museum did not admit children under the age of eight. Debates about whether this was good policy occurred frequently, as critics and visitors often complained of parents sending their children to museums on wet days to run around the galleries instead of attending to exhibits.[10] In Lee's essay, likewise, the statues displayed in the Vatican initially fail to attract the interest of the visiting children, for whom the museum is just "a dismal scientific piece of ostentation . . . where art is arranged and ticketed and made lifeless" (18). Lee suggests, however, that the reason the Vatican and its statues so oppress these barbarian children is that ultimately they aren't uncivilized enough.

These children have already been educated out of the simple, direct perceptual relation to art that would have made it possible to enjoy the Vatican's sculptures. The problem, Lee explains, is that they have been brought up on pictures. Here, Lee tacitly appeals to G. W. F. Hegel's famous account of painting (along with music) as the characteristic art medium of modernity.[11] The Vatican's statuary is silent to the "modern child" because pictures have taught her imagination to understand only the language of modernity, "of colour, of movement, of sound, of suggestion, of all the broken words of modern thought and feeling: and the statue has none of these" (20). The child's mind itself reflects this fragmentation under pictorial modernity. Lee describes it as a "soul mass, made up of tightly-pressed, crushed odds and ends of impression; broken, confused, pounded bits of the sights and sounds and emotions of . . . childhood" (22). Lee's turn to something like neurophysiology here suggests that pictures contribute to the fragmentation so characteristic of modernity by training us to perceive representationally, to reflexively call up prior sense impressions in order to fill out and complete our sensations.

That modernized perceptual mode, moreover, scales up to the historicizing habits of mind that undergirded the nineteenth century's own sense of its modernity, of its containing in itself all previous historical epochs. Learning to perceive by supplementing fragmented sensations as children prepares us to regard each art work as "an historic fossil, by study of which, as with the bone of a pterodactyl or an ichthyosaurus, we can amuse ourselves reconstructing the appearance and habits of a long dead, once living civilisation" (23).[12] A central aim in the educational mission of the museum was to train visitors to bring that historicizing gaze to bear on its likewise often fragmentary objects—such as the classical sculptures that had been chipped and broken or removed from the architectural structures of which they were originally part. In a sense, then, the Vatican's statues fail to speak to the modern child because the museum has already succeeded too well in training her to perceive art objects in terms of historical categories.

The provision of such an education in historicism appears again and again in nineteenth-century debates as one major function of the museum. However, proponents of this approach had to contend with competing organizational principles and educational aims (such as providing exemplary models of design) that privileged judgments of a work's aesthetic value over its historical representativeness.[13] Classical sculpture, in particular, aggravated the tensions between these organizing pedagogical principles, since they were celebrated as at once high points of artistic achievement and as embodiments of antiquity. With the founding of the National Gallery in 1824, the British state's public collection of paintings split off from the classical sculptures that remained with the antiquities in the British Museum, but the midcentury parliamentary committee on the National Gallery debated whether this was a mistake and considered joining the classical sculptures with the paintings in the National Gallery under the category of fine arts.[14] Even where such historicist arrangements were more clear cut and feasible, by virtue of combining in a small space the artifacts of schools and periods widely separated in time the museum retained an irreducible element of randomness and accident.

In "The Use and Abuse of Museums" (1883), the economist and logician W. Stanley Jevons drew an unfavorable parallel between the variety of forms displayed in museums and the churches whose similarly eclectic combination of historical forms together in one space had become the target of restoration architects (including, as we saw in chapter 3, Thomas Hardy). Jevons in fact believed that the historical incongruity on display in museums made them ill-suited for children, whose capacity for sustained concentration would be undermined by "glancing at a great multitude of diverse things."[15] Because it contained such diverse multitudes, each object displayed in a museum was necessarily "associated with incongruous objects . . . [and therefore] to realise the true meaning and beauty of an object the spectator must possess a previous knowledge of its historical bearings" (286). Children themselves could not be expected to possess such previous knowledge, but then neither could most of the adults who visited public museums. In lieu of that previous knowledge, museums relied on the next best thing: catalogs.

Catalogs became widespread in the eighteenth century as an indispensable aid to the democratization of art. Ranging from long descriptive paragraphs (the norm in France, naturally) to compact summaries of the most basic identifying information, catalogs made it possible for spectators to identify what they were seeing at auctions, salons, and other public viewings.[16] This public educational function of catalogs became explicit in the nineteenth century. The British Museum and the National Gallery accordingly drew up extensive catalogs of their holdings and sold them as guides to the public. In Britain, Parliament took an active interest in museum catalogs, grilling museum officials on their cost and organization.[17] Ultimately, these concerns helped lead the descriptions contained in the catalogs to become affixed to the museum's walls. In Britain, for example, a parliamentary committee on arts and manufactures in 1836 concluded that laboring museum visitors were likely to be too pressed for time to hunt through the catalog for identifying information. The committee accordingly recommended that each art work should be have placed below it a label specifying its school along with the name and biography of the artist.[18] We can glimpse here nearing completion the process, documented by Ruth Bernard Yeazell, through which catalog descriptions of originally untitled art works transform into the picture titles we now take for granted on the walls in museums and galleries. The migration of such descriptions from a supplementary text to a permanent space adjacent to the art object seemed to make the description itself part of the exhibit.

The increasing prominence of descriptions within the museum, whether affixed to the walls or not, raised questions for Victorian critics and curators about just what kind of education the museum was suited to provide. Despite his reservations about children in museums, Jevons saw museums as embodying a superior approach to learning that made him look forward to a future in which each school contained a museum:

> The Museum represents that real instruction, that knowledge of things as they are which is obtained by the glance of the eye and touch of the fingers. The time ought to have arrived when the senseless verbal teaching formerly . . . predominant in schools should be abandoned. A child should hardly be allowed to read about anything unless a specimen or model, or at any rate, a picture of the thing can be placed before it. Words come thus to be, as they should be, the handles to ideas, instead of being empty sounds. . . . The purpose of a true Museum is to enable the student to see the things and realize sensually the qualities described in lessons or lectures; in short, to learn what cannot be learnt by words. (290–91)

The unfortunate echoes of Lagado's Academy of Projectors in *Gulliver's Travels* aside, Jevons here lays out an almost millenarian vision of children of the future getting an instruction in the real no less than real instruction—the museum will teach them the knowledge of things as they are by providing them with knowledge by acquaintance. Verbal knowledge, on the other hand, occupies the ancillary role of providing a handle, a way to pick up, as it were, the objects on display. Other Victorian critics make very clear, however, that verbal knowledge could not be easily confined to such a subsidiary role in the museum.

The modern museum is in fact defined by a constitutive tension between description and acquaintance. George Brown Goode, then assistant secretary at the Smithsonian, opens his own 1889 lecture, "The Museums of the Future," by characterizing the museum as ideally suited to a modern age when "the eye is used more and more . . . [and] descriptive writing is set aside for pictures, and pictures in their turn are replaced by actual objects."[19] But Goode then went on to recommend that all objects in display should bear a label with a description exhaustive enough to answer all probable questions in advance, and that books of reference and trained specialists should be kept close at hand to provide more detail. Goode so emphasizes the importance of descriptive knowledge of this kind that it eventually displaces the objects it is supposed to supplement, as when Goode is lead to declare that "*an efficient educational museum may be described as a collection of instructive labels, each illustrated by a well-selected specimen.*"[20] Ultimately, the only meaningful difference between a museum and a library that Goode can point to is that where individual readers must take turns with library books, multiple visitors can read the same label at the same time in a museum.

The same tension between description and acquaintance that defines the museum likewise runs through the Aesthetic Movement. The movement's democratizing insistence on the primacy of the direct encounter between aesthete and art object led its apostles to disdain the kind of mediation by expertise that is perfectly distilled in Goode's proposal to have reference books and specialists always at hand in the museum. The encounter with an art object, Walter Pater writes in the preface to *The Renaissance* (1873), prompts the aesthetic critic to ask "What is this song or picture . . . to *me?* What effect does it really produce on me? Does it give me pleasure? and if so, what sort or degree of pleasure? How is my nature modified by its presence and under its influence?"[21] The answers to these questions require neither reference guides nor trained specialists. At the same time, though, the movement's writers specialized in the kind of ekphrastic description of art objects that Pater models elsewhere in *The Renaissance* when he describes Leonardo Da Vinci's *Mona Lisa* as the vampiric embodiment of aesthetic history. While no reference guide would have cross-listed the *Mona Lisa* with vampires (at least not before Pater), Pater's rhapsodic description of the painting enacts a verbal displacement of the painting itself that bears a clear kinship to the way Goode's labels displace the objects of display that they describe by transforming them from exhibits to illustrations. Pater was one of the strongest influences on Lee's aesthetic criticism, so much so that she was often referred to derisively as "Walter Pater's disciple."[22] In *Belcaro,* though, Lee leverages Pater's principles of aesthetic criticism into a polemic against the kind of descriptive techniques embodied by his account of the *Mona Lisa.*

The thrust of Lee's attack on aesthetic description arrives in *Belcaro*'s second essay, "Orpheus and Eurydice." The essay opens with a panegyric on the Orpheus myth, which Lee, adopting the methods of Victorian comparative mythology, reads as a figurative narrative about the emergence of dawn out of night and its inevitable loss under the glare of day. Lee situates the Orpheus myth within a virtuous circle where it bestows its beauty on its various formal embodiments in poetry, sculpture, and music, which in turn add beauty of their own to the myth, collectively forming what Lee suggests is a kind of mythic *Gesamtkunstwerk*. The essay relates how Lee herself had one day taken a relief sculpture in the Villa Albani for a depiction of Orpheus and Eurydice, a link in that virtuous circle. Gazing at it, she composes a narrative description of the relief by matching its features to lines from Virgil's rendering of the Orpheus myth in the *Georgics*. But then in the midst of her reverie, her eye is caught by the "scrap of paper pasted at the bottom of it, a wretched, unsightly, scarce legible rag, such as insult some of the antiques in this gallery, and on it is written . . . , 'Antiope urging her sons, Amphion and Zethus, to avenge her by the murder of Dirce'" (53). Lee's anecdote presents two apparently different species of descriptive error that the rest of the essay goes on to analyze.

First, Lee attacks the practice of supplying titles, even when they are accurate, for leading the spectator to neglect the art object they designate. To begin with, titles prompt us to regard art works as representations, but doing so requires that we already know what they are representing. Titles and catalog descriptions of the relief sculpture are in this regard, she claims, not much different from writing "'This is a lion,' [or] 'This is a horse'" below each figure. But while those designations merely require our "previous . . . acquaintance with a live horse or live lion," no one could have had such acquaintance with mythological persons like Zethus or Amphion (59). The relief sculpture's title, therefore, requires the kind of descriptive knowledge to be found in classical dictionaries and the reference guides that Goode wanted to stock museums with. Incredulous, Lee scoffs, "Is the meaning of a work of Art to depend on Lempriere [*sic*] and Dr. William Smith?" (58–59). Lee poses her own formalism as an explicit alternative to such a possibility: "The clear, unmistakable language of lines and curves . . . [is] a language needing no interpreters, no dictionaries" (61).

Lee's initial description of the relief as Orpheus and Eurydice is in more obvious error. Here, though, what is obvious about that error follows not so much from the way that description refers to classical dictionaries to understand the sculpture as from the way it refers the sculpture to other art forms. Hence, the *Gesamtkunstwerk* within which Lee enrolls the sculptures has the lyrical indifference to factual accuracy of Pater's *Mona Lisa.* But factual and aestheticist descriptive modes share a deeper error, Lee argues, insofar as they both derive from an act of perceptual reference. A spectator identifying a sculpture incorrectly as Orpheus or correctly as Amphion in either case perceives it associatively as an illustration of the story called up by the name. Lee's aestheticist description of the relief, for example, depends on the way it initially "suggest[s] Virgil's lines" (62). The artwork's perceptual suggestiveness thus licenses the aesthete to take it up as part of a *Gesamtkunstwerk.* Such a descriptive synthesis, Lee charges, in effect creates a new artwork, "and having created it . . . you will henceforward perceive your creation and not the original work" (64). In her description of the relief as Orpheus and Eurydice, Lee cannily identifies the phenomenon that Yeazell calls a virtual painting. Once a title has been bestowed, she explains, it generates readings of the work it designates that continue to circulate (often accompanied by a visual reproduction) even after art historians demonstrate conclusively that the title is erroneous. The result is "a virtual painting: not exactly a material object, nor merely a creation of words, but a combination of title and image whose hold on us proves stubbornly resistant to debunking."[23] For Lee, the aestheticist descriptions that create such virtual work and the titling practices that facilitate it treat the art work itself as "a meaningless thing, to which we have willfully attached a meaning that is not part or parcel of it—a blank sheet of paper on which we write what comes into our head, and which itself can tell us nothing" (60). Description, here, is a kind of graffiti.

Suggestive Forms and Formal Masochism: *Miss Brown*

In *Belcaro,* Lee thus champions a conception of the art object's formal autonomy that cuts against the grain of the perceptual suggestiveness that nineteenth-century writers, art critics, and aesthetes had long taken as a hallmark of aesthetics. Suggestion, Noel Jackson observes, was a concept in broad use within psychology, physiology, and aesthetics at the turn of the nineteenth century, when it became integral to the Romantic understanding of aesthetic form inherited by the Aesthetic Movement. Suggestion, Jackson writes, "principally signified the process by which one makes inferences on the basis of sensation," and thus, like association, it became an idiom for the intentionality of perception, the way that sensory stimuli bring to mind perceptual objects.[24] But where association specified the functions involved in that process, suggestion left those functions vaguely defined. Hence Reid, who denied that there could be any convincing account of the causal mechanisms linking together stimulus, sensation, and perception, described that mysterious process as occurring through suggestion.[25] Nonetheless, Victorian associationists like Alexander Bain picked up suggestion as a synonym for association.[26] James even adopted suggestion as a term for both perceptual and linguistic reference in *Principles of Psychology:* "Language is a system of *signs*," he wrote, "different from the things signified, but able to suggest them" (2:356). In aesthetics, Jackson argues, suggestion was adopted in Romantic poetry as a model for the poetic form-giving activity of what Wordsworth called "the language of the sense" (134). The perceptual suggestiveness that enabled the mind to form its experience of the object world out of the chaotic welter of sensations gave poets a rhetoric to account for how the artist gives form to the unpredictable, contingent impressions of history. From Wordsworth and perception science, in consequence, the Aesthetic Movement inherited a conception of aesthetic form as the product of "the poet's capacity for suggestive verbal representation."[27]

The Aesthetic Movement disdained the idea of viewing art works representationally, a tendency it identified with the moralistic popular art criticism that appraised paintings primarily in terms of the didactic value of their subjects. But whereas theories of representation took it as axiomatic that the artwork resembled or mimicked what it represented, suggestion required no such similarity between sensations and perceptions or artwork and impression. Aesthetes therefore saw in suggestion a warrant for their own mode of ekphrastic description. "To the critic," Oscar Wilde has Gilbert pronounce in "The Critic as Artist," "the work of art is simply a suggestion for a new work of his own, that need not necessarily bear any obvious resemblance to the thing it criticises."[28] The strange alchemy involved in such a vaguely defined, enigmatic process meant that suggestion retained for the nineteenth century hints of the occult connotations that the term had during the sixteenth and seventeenth centuries, when it signified the insinuations that prompt one to evil acts. In Jackson's account of the Romantic era, those lingering associations are refracted through the charged political atmosphere following the French Revolution, so that the link between sedition and suggestion opened up possibilities of radical and even utopian critique for an aesthetics of suggestiveness. While those were still live possibilities for the Aesthetic Movement, by the late nineteenth century suggestion more readily figured as an erotic rather than a political temptation. Indeed, the familiar meaning of "suggestive" as insinuating "something indecent" dates from just this period (OED). To the Aesthetic Movement, suggestion licensed erotic as well as descriptive responses to artworks.

Lee's aesthetic essays identify suggestion with the descriptive responses to art works exemplified by the title, the expert, and the reference guide. Like James, Lee frequently characterizes the "difference between the thing seen and the thing suggested" in terms of the difference between the sign and what it signifies.[29] *Belcaro* thus sets its model of attention to "the absolutely objectively existing work of art" in opposition to what Lee sees as the modern tendency "to care not for [the artwork] itself, but for what it suggests, nay, most often for the suggestion of the mere name of the work of art" (184, 108). Lee's second series of aesthetic essays, *Juvenilia* (1887), frames the choice between form and suggestion as a choice between "the reality of the work of art" and the hallucinations and fictions called up by acts of mental reference—acts exemplified by the subtly eroticized "languid enjoyment" Lee experienced as the names of towns she passed on a cruise along the Rhine conjured up a "Fata Morgana Rhineland . . . constructed . . . from the random allusions and incoherent descriptions" of a childhood servant.[30] The essays in *Juvenilia* nonetheless go on to mount a qualified defense of those hallucinations because Lee's notion of form itself involves perceptual reference. Sensations, Lee understood from perception science, are bare qualia having no form in themselves. They only become forms by virtue of their arrangement in patterns. Apprehending those patterns requires the mensuration of sensations, and thus at least a minimal amount of the kind of constructive inferences broadly identified with suggestion. Like language, form functions referentially, and Lee's essays urge aesthetes to reject suggestion's "half articulate . . . language of associations" in order to attend to "the clear language of form, which is equally intelligible to all men" (*Belcaro,* 283).

The clear language of form, moreover, possesses an erotic suggestiveness of its own. Lee harbored a deep ambivalence over the relationship between art and eros. Her biographer, Vineta Colby, suggests that Lee "translated" her desire for Mary Robinson into her aestheticism, characterizing erotic and aesthetic response as fundamentally analogous, if not identical, in structure: "The object of love was a work of art; its physical reality was pure form; and it evoked in the lover a pleasure that in itself was neither moral nor immoral."[31] Lee herself, though, often disdained the aesthete's desire as a mistaken response the artwork's suggestiveness rather than its form. Here she is in *Beauty and Ugliness* (1913) elaborating her second principle of aesthetics—the distinction between form and subject—in a note copied from her gallery diary on the sculptures at the Palazzo Massimo alle Terme (now part of the National Roman Museum):

> Of course all form which we recognize as human awakens . . . the various orders of feeling which are awakened by human beings . . . because the act of such recognition means a reference of them to memory impressions. . . . But this emotion is evoked just in proportion as we refer the artistic form to the human reality. . . . The more a statue makes us look at it, the more it holds us by *its* reality, the less *moral* (or immoral) feelings we shall have. These are got largely by substituting the *word* for the *form.* If men have been in love with statues, it is because they have substituted for them the flesh and blood images of their memory. (266)

Lee here situates her formalism against the erotic encounter with classical statues that had persisted as a common topos in queer art writing since Johann Winckelmann, the eighteenth-century art historian whom Walter Pater describes as "finger[ing] those pagan marbles with unsinged hands, with no sense of shame or loss" (*Renaissance,* 177). But that topos nonetheless appears elsewhere in Lee's own writings, especially in "The Child in the Vatican." In the fable that gives that essay its title, the child learns to perceive art formally after the Vatican sculptures slip her a "love potion," planting in her "a sort of invisible winged seed of passion" that (in a tacit parallel with Lee's experience with Mary Robinson at the Castello di Belcaro) blossoms into a desire for form (*Belcaro,* 27, 25). The love of statues here, I argue, brings into view the way that form, for Lee, elicits desire.

The nature of a desire for form, and for the sculptural form in particular, was the subject of her novel, *Miss Brown* (1884). *Miss Brown* recounts the long engagement of Walter Hamlin, a poet-painter obviously modeled on D. G. Rossetti, and Anne Brown, a working-class woman obviously modeled on Jane Morris. Hamlin initially encounters Anne as a nursemaid in Italy, becomes fascinated with her as he sketches and paints her, and ultimately enters into a kind of promissory contract with her. Legally binding himself to marry her whenever she might demand it, he settles a living on her and arranges for her to be educated, after which he brings her to London, introduces her into aestheticist society, and begins, very slowly, to court her. By pretty much all accounts from the Victorian period to our own, *Miss Brown* is a puzzling failure. Narrated primarily from Anne's perspective, the novel subjects the Aesthetic Movement to a mounting series of grim, repetitive denunciations for its evil, lustfulness, and vanity. The sins of the aesthetes stem, in this novel, from their suggestibility, but *Miss Brown* itself is likewise too suggestive for its own good. For one thing, it is a roman à clef featuring barely disguised fictional versions of the prominent figures in the Aesthetic Movement, many of whom were very offended. More troubling for its early reviewers, *Miss Brown* is alive with a queer erotic energy. In part, that energy is generated by the novel's fiery condemnations of the fleshly school of aestheticism, which struck virtually everyone as suspiciously excessive.[32] Beyond such prurience, though, the relationship between the novel's central pair, Hamlin and Anne, is so recognizably kinky that the reviewer for the *Spectator* disgustedly singled it out as "show[ing] an utter perversity."[33] Critical reactions here keyed into the fact that *Miss Brown* is a (questionably successful) experiment with what Claire Jarvis identifies as formal masochism. The novel's formal masochism, I propose, can help us grasp the queer erotics at play in Lee's understanding of form more generally.

Let's begin with "Desire," the sequence of twelve sonnets that Hamlin publishes against Anne's wishes. We do not know much about the sonnet sequence itself because the novel specifies almost nothing about it, but then again that is very much the point. Anne does not object to the sonnets themselves so much as "what they allude to," or, in other words, what they suggest.[34] Tellingly, when Hamlin defensively retorts that there is not a single objectionable word in the sonnets, Anne counters by asking, "What do the words matter? It is the meaning" (194). Anne's reading enacts the erotic displacement of the art object by responding to the poem's suggestiveness. In this, she follows what seems to be the logic of the poem itself. The nature of Hamlin's desire, Anne thinks, is similarly fantasmatic, since "she did not for one instant believe that Hamlin had ever felt the things about which he was writing" (191). In other words, Hamlin has no more experienced the desire he writes about than Anne seems to experience the poem. An ingenue in aestheticist London, Anne is not always the most astute judge of the novel's other characters. In this case, though, her judgment has been corroborated in advance by the narrator. Hamlin's letters to Anne during her education at a school in Coblenz had similarly confessed to being tormented by "mysterious temptations of unspeakable things . . . [that] he never at all specified," and the narrator explains that Anne had then mistakenly believed him because she did not yet understand "how such things will shoot up in the poetic mind as a result of mere reading, and be nurtured there for a day for the sake of their strange color" (111). As he expresses it in his sonnets and letters, at least, Hamlin is in the peculiar position of knowing his own desire purely through description.

Hamlin does experience a different kind of desire, however, one paradoxically bound up with chastity. The novel dwells at length on Hamlin's chaste ideality, not least because it defines his relationship with Anne. Such chastity is enforced by the contract that Hamlin signs at the behest of her cousin Richard, which pledges him to marry her at her request as an insurance policy against the possibility that he might seduce and abandon her. Important though it is, however, the contract simply codifies the already semiplatonic nature of their relationship. Lee signals as much by having the first step in Hamlin's education of Anne occur when he gives her a copy of the *Vita Nuova,* the book in which Dante elaborated his courtly love for Beatrice. Lee had in fact written extensively about the *Vita Nuova* in "Medieval Love," an essay that appeared in 1884 (the same year as *Miss Brown*) in her collection of Renaissance studies, *Euphorion.* There, Lee claims that the chaste passion of the kind Dante and the courtly love poets felt for their beloveds is identical to the "kind of love which is mainly aesthetic."[35] The kind of idealized, aesthetic passion Lee describes in "Medieval Love" struck Lee's friend Irene Cooper Willis as well as her biographer, Vineta Colby, as an illustration of the way Lee sublimated her sexual desires into aesthetic experience.[36] But what is striking about Lee's notion of medieval love is how it aggravates, rather than sublimating, desire. Debarred from expression through genital sexuality, this kind of desire is articulated, and intensified, through forms: "The ideal love of the Tuscan poets was probably none the weaker, but rather the stronger for the desire which they felt to sing such passion. . . . Platonic love was possible, doubly possible, in souls tense with poetic wants" (398–99). In *Miss Brown,* Hamlin's poetic wants are likewise concentrated in an act of form making, but the form he makes is Anne herself.

Hamlin's aesthetic love generates the narrative of Anne's development. Christa Zorn has read *Miss Brown* as a feminist bildungsroman, a novel of development that dramatizes the constraints under which Victorian women labored to achieve the generic hero's twofold end of crafting an identity and obtaining social legitimation for it.[37] One of the two most significant constraints—the other being marriage—is that Anne's development proceeds under the direction of Hamlin. Anne begins the novel as an inverted version of Rossetti's Blessed Damozel—"a mere soulless body," in one character's tart but accurate words (65). Hamlin's attraction to her begins in outright aversion to the interiority she does not have. Hamlin at first wishes "to know only as much as he could see of her," as indifferent to whatever is "behind" her appearance as someone sketching a beautiful vase is to its contents (31, 30). This purely aesthetic response to her seems to succumb to the same kind of logic we saw Anne enacting when he read his sonnets, as he comes to feel that she is "something much more than a mere form; or rather, [that] the form itself was suggestive of something more" (36). His arrangement to settle money on her to be educated and introduced into London society is in effect an attempt to give her that something more. The narrative of Anne's development is thus Lee's reworking of the Pygmalion myth, as Hamlin ensouls the beautiful form of Anne.

Miss Brown, though, is a perverse reworking of the Pygmalion myth. For one thing, where in the myth Venus brings Galatea to life full of a desire that answers Pygmalion's own, Anne concludes her process of ensoulment in what is, for her, a loveless marriage to Hamlin. Indeed, not only does she lack any desire for Hamlin himself, she professes herself incapable of experiencing desire for anyone. Her inability to desire reflects a kink in the process of ensoulment she undergoes, which does not actually seem to endow her with the hidden recesses and depths of psychic interiority. The novel emphasizes this point continuously, noting that Anne, in contrast to the psychic complexity of its other characters, is "a homogenous woman" (159). J. Hillis Miller has taken the Pygmalion myth, which reverses the materializations of desire that conclude the other stories in Ovid's *Metamorphoses,* as a topos exploring "what is at stake when someone becomes infatuated with a statue or a painting or, for that matter, when someone reads or hears a story and thinks of its characters as 'real people.'"[38] Lee of course was acutely sensitive to just this category error. But Hamlin only seems to make this mistake at the novel's end when he marries Anne. For the rest of the novel, Anne functions for him more as a materialization of desire than a beautiful form confused with a real person. The development Anne undergoes at his direction involves not so much a transformation as a solidification. Her education "fill[s] up the magnificent design which already existed in her" (104). That is not to say, though, that she is filled with the variegated odds and ends of impressions making up what Lee called the "soul-mass" in *Belcaro.* She is homogenous, gaining an interior of the same material as her exterior so that at novel's end she is "completely of a piece, a mass of granite" (424). Anne is not a statue that becomes a woman. She is a statue that acquires density.

In an important sense, then, Anne remains an aesthetic object, as she must if she is to remain erotically inaccessible in the novel. Her statuesque impassivity is what keeps Hamlin in suspense, tense with poetic wants. This relationship is best described in terms of what Claire Jarvis calls "exquisite masochism," an erotics of suspense that plays out formally through novelistic scenes of refusal that aggravate desire by denying its gratification—in effect, scenes that sexualize chastity. Exquisite masochism is typically structured around fluid, ongoing negotiations of power in which the woman is the dominant partner, and it is therefore marked by tension with the formal marriage contract in which power, codified in the law, reverts to the man. The bulk of *Miss Brown* narrates just such a dynamic, with Hamlin having bound himself legally while, ostensibly at least, investing Anne with power over him. Jarvis characterizes "formal masochism" as fundamentally a descriptive style. In contrast to the suggestive, metaphorical descriptions of sex with which writers often circumvent strictures on sexual content, formal masochism is free to precisely describe sexual tension because its scenes of refusal do not involve genital sex. As a result, Jarvis suggests, formal masochism reveals "the novel's somatic medium" by "forg[ing] a connection between the realms of aesthetics and the realms of sensation, connecting the keenness of precise description to a different kind of keenness, the needling, sharp remnant of a discomfiting sensory experience."[39] In other words, formal masochism joins a descriptive acuity with an eroto-sensory one and thus trains the reader's attention on the acute bodily experience of reading itself.

Formal masochism, I want to suggest, points us toward an account of Lee's erotics of forms. Consider, for example, *Miss Brown*'s perversion of the Pygmalion myth. By remaining a kind of statue, Anne defies the penetrative logic of suggestion, which seeks what lies behind or inside the aspect of things—the mind behind the face, the contents inside the vase. While statues are three-dimensional and thus, like Anne, have volume, they present to the spectator not a scene in which he can enter but rather a succession of aspects.[40] Like the object of masochistic desire, statues simultaneously elicit and frustrate a certain kind of attention. Inciting us to explore them in all their three-dimensionality, at every turn they arrest our gaze with yet another two-dimensional aspect. In this respect, they dramatize the fundamental principle of aesthetics that Lee later went on to call empathy.

Kinky Empathy: The Intimate Withholding of Art Objects in Lee's Late Work

The theory of aesthetic empathy was Lee's most distinctive and influential contribution to literary criticism and aesthetics. Literally "in-feeling," a feeling of oneself into something, empathy since the mid-twentieth century has been colloquially understood as the vividly imaginative inhabiting of another's position. At the turn of the twentieth century, though, empathy was a technical term in experimental psychology for the projection of one's self or one's feelings into an object of perception.[41] Lee took this concept of empathy as the fundamental principle for the theory of aesthetics elaborated in her late critical work—*Beauty and Ugliness* (1912), *The Beautiful* (1913), and, less explicitly, *The Handling of Words* (1923). The essays in these books are the product of Lee's most rigorous involvement with scientific psychology. During their composition, Lee read psychological literature extensively, corresponded with researchers, kept careful gallery diaries in which she and her lover and collaborator Clementina Anstruther-Thomson recorded their physiological responses to artworks, and even distributed questionnaires to friends and acquaintances asking about their experiences in museums and galleries. If there had been fewer obstacles to women receiving graduate training in the field, Lee might very well have gone on to test her ideas experimentally in laboratory settings. In the absence of such institutional and laboratory access, Lee relied on data produced by technologies of description—by gallery diaries and questionnaires and the counting up of parts of speech in excerpts from literary texts. As Morgan observes, Lee transforms empathy from a scientific theory into "a critical practice that involves writing about what one feels."[42] Lee's writings on aesthetic empathy, then, entailed a reassessment of the place of knowledge by description within aesthetic experience. In this section, I show how Lee's late critical work deploys techniques of description that eschewed perceptual suggestion and psychic interiority and in doing so attempted to resolve the tensions between description and acquaintance that this chapter has been tracking through the museum and the Aesthetic Movement. If empathetic description seemed to Lee to resolve epistemological tensions, however, I suggest that it did so by ratcheting up the tensions of poetic wants. My claim here is that Lee understands empathy as an experience of intimate withholding that intensifies our desire for form.

Lee is distinctive among the turn-of-the-century writers on empathy for her insistence that empathy is a minimally intentional perceptual experience. In "Beauty and Ugliness," the 1897 essay cowritten with Anstruther-Thomson in which she first described aesthetic empathy, Lee drew primarily on three sources: Theodor Lipps's theory of empathy, Karl Groos's theory of inner mimicry, and the James-Lange theory of emotion. "Beauty and Ugliness" did not acknowledge or try to work through the areas of disagreement or incompatibility among these three sources—which Lee apologized for repeatedly when she reissued the essay in the 1912 collection *Beauty and Ugliness*—but as Lee went on to refine her own position by more carefully sifting her sources' arguments, she rejected just those strands of them that attributed a greater degree of perceptual interpretation to aesthetic empathy.

Consider, for example, her criticism of Groos's notion of inner mimicry. For Groos, inner mimicry explains why and how we project our own feelings into the objects we perceive: without our consciously recognizing it, the perception of an object initiates a series of muscular innervations and proprioceptive sensations that imitate the movement that we perceive as being characteristic of the object. In looking at an antique vase, for example, we might imitate its balance by subtly shifting our weight, its apparent lift by expanding our chest, the pour of its lip with a slight downward adjustment of the head, and so on.[43] Typically, such muscular adjustments will be felt without being enacted, the innervations involved being too weak to produce actual movement—hence it remains *inner* mimicry—but Groos stipulates clearly that the process involves real, experienced innervations and sensations. Lee's account of empathy diverges in two key respects. First, she contends that empathy is not produced by motor sensations but by what she calls "motor-images"—a distinction that, I explain below, held significant epistemological consequences. Second, Lee rejects the notion that a kind of bodily mimesis is the basis for empathy. Inner mimicry, she points out, presupposes the very feeling of animation in inanimate objects that it purports to account for, since we must already have a sense that the vase lifts before we could imitate its lifting. Empathy, she claims in *Beauty and Ugliness,* is emphatically not effected by the "suggestion of locomotion . . . in *represented* things"; empathy is rather the product of "*our attention moving* across [motionless shapes] in the acts of measurement and comparison and . . . our tendency to attribute to what we see the modes of our unlocalized activity of seeing" (111; italics in original). By insisting on a hard distinction between empathy and mimicry, then, Lee renders aesthetic empathy consistent with her aesthetic formalism. In contrast to inner mimicry, which deals with objects and representations, Lee's empathy deals purely with formal shape.

In restricting aesthetic empathy to forms, Lee hoped to avoid the epistemological problems that dogged the sensation-based theories of perception this book has been tracking. Lee's formal empathy shares in what Brian Massumi calls the autonomy of affect. Like Massumi's autonomic reflexes, Morgan explains, formal empathy is not fixed by sociolinguistic knowledge: "It consists of affects that are autoreferential (for example, 'I feel energized') rather than emotions that are intersubjective ('I share your sadness')."[44] This gloss on formal empathy strikingly resembles the way that Reid set forth the distinction between sensations, which are likewise autoreferential ("I feel a pain"), and perceptions, which are intentional, referring to objects in the world ("I see a tree").[45]

Aesthetic empathy is not, however, purely sensational. Lee discusses psychology's distinction between sensation and perception in *The Beautiful,* defining empathy as a mode of perception. Pointing to the etymological origins of perception in the act of grasping, Lee writes that empathy is, like all acts of perception, a "*grasping of meaning,* a mental activity involving what are called *attention* and *memory.*"[46] To experience empathy, she explains, we must focus our attention on sensations and hold them in our minds long enough to be able to bring them into relation with each other. The perception of visible shapes, for example, requires us to execute a series of coordinated eye movements that compose separate visual sensations into patterns of line and extension. To see shapes, "we *compare* [various lines]; and comparing we *combine* them in the unity of our intention: thought of together they are thought of as belonging together" (38; italics in original). In effect, we make the forms that we perceive by mentally holding together the sensations of which they are composed. Empathy is a form-giving perceptual process.

Perceiving shapes, though, is different from perceiving things, and Lee develops the distinction between shape and thing at length in *The Beautiful*. Briefly, shapes are the objects of empathic contemplation, whereas things are the objects of practical inferences. Things and shapes thus seem to fall out according to the long-standing opposition between instrumental reason and aesthetic disinterestedness. In *The Beautiful*, though, Lee rings changes on that opposition by applying it within the domain of perception science. In line with Victorian psychology's identification of perception with knowledge by description, Lee characterizes the perception of things as a mode of "discursive thinking" (70).[47] Things, she suggests, are the product of rapid discursive inferences made from shape perception. Shapes and things, Lee implies, are locked into the familiar tension between description and acquaintance: "*All thinking about things is thinking away from the Shapes suggesting those things, since it involves knowledge which the Shapes in themselves do not afford*" (113; italics in original). Set next to William Whewell's discussion of things and thoughts (addressed in chapter 1), Lee's things and shapes indicate just how far thoughts had burrowed down into things during the roughly seventy years of perception science intervening between Whewell's *Philosophy of the Inductive Sciences* and Lee's *The Beautiful*.

The perception of shapes depends on a certain kind of restraint that is absent from the perception of things. Empathy is a dynamic experience in which we merge the directional tensions and activities of our own perceptual movements with the shape they apprehend. In the case of the vase, for example, we perceive its shape as lifting although it is really our gaze that lifts as our eyes trace the vase's lines. The dynamic feelings entering into shape perception are so foundational to turn-of-the-century accounts of empathy that Morgan adopts the term "motional empathy" to distinguish the object-oriented version of empathy from later theories that understood it as a relationship between subjects.[48] In spite of such motional dynamism, however, empathy partakes of the suspended agency that Elisha Cohn has identified as integral to Victorian aesthetic experience insofar as to experience empathy we must keep ourselves from actually moving.[49]

The motionlessness of motional empathy derives from Lee's distinction between things and shapes. Shapes, she insists, occupy only two dimensions, while things have cubic volume. This odd claim derives in part from the theory of local signs. As we saw in chapter 2, local signs—sensations produced by the position of a visual stimulus on the retina—were the foundation of empirical accounts of space in the nineteenth century. By coordinating local signs with the feelings of muscular adjustment accompanying the rotation of our eyes and head and the movement of our bodies, we develop our sense of visual extension and location in space. The upshot of these accounts, as Lee puts it in *The Beautiful,* is that "we do not really *see* three-dimensional objects, but merely *infer* them by connecting visual data with the result of locomotor experience" (86). Local signs, then, are the data for perceptual inferences, which is to say, for the perception of things as opposed to shapes. While Lee does not deny that local signs would be necessary to coordinate the eye movements that compose two-dimensional shapes from visual lines and extensions, she repeatedly insists that the motional experiences recalled by shape perception—the feeling of lifting recalled by the perception of the vase—are themselves not accompanied by local signs. Here is the reason she rejects Karl Groos's suggestion that faint feelings of active muscular adjustment constitute empathic experience. Instead of active movements, Lee claims that empathy inheres in motor images, which she defines as "the residue of motor conditions which have been deprived by repetition of all marks of origin and environment" (*Beauty and Ugliness,* 62). Paradoxically, these sensorimotor abstractions enable the empath to focus her attention on the concretely present visual sensations. Motor sensations localized in the moving body lead us to follow the logic of suggestion, focusing our attention on what we infer to be present behind the two-dimensional surfaces of our visual field. Motor images, in contrast, are abstract and brain based, and for that very reason they do not lead us to project virtual depths onto the shapes that we see, allowing us to attend to our actually present visual sensations.

Motor images likewise allowed Lee to unify her aesthetic with her literary criticism. For Lee, as for other members of the Aesthetic Movement, literature seemed like a problematic exception to the aestheticist rule that art should be directly experienced in a century when reading stood out as the paradigmatic example of mediated contact with the world. In *Belcaro,* for example, Lee epigrammatically defines poetry as "the art which can neither give nor show but only suggest" (114). But in the essays on literature collected in *The Handling of Words,* Lee began experimenting with a reading practice based on empathy. The first principle of Lee's reading method was that literary texts compose dynamic patterns out of the experiences deposited in readers' memories—in other words, out of motor images. Lee tried to analyze these patterns quantitatively, selecting an excerpt from a text at random and counting up its parts of speech with the aim of identifying and explaining the text's peculiar formal dynamism, its stylistic "gesture or gait."[50] As in her studies of aesthetic empathy, Lee's quantitative literary criticism eschewed questions of representation—of what a literary text makes the reader think about—in favor of attention to the pattern of "mental movements" the reader is made to perform (190).

Lee's method of reading by counting words adapted techniques from perception science to literary criticism. Nicholas Dames reads her literary criticism as modeled on the psychophysics of Gustav Fechner.[51] In the same way that Fechner sought to experimentally quantify just noticeable differences—the thresholds of stimulus intensities at which perception begins—Lee sought to quantify the psychological effects of "the minutest elements to which literary style can be reduced, namely, single words and their simplest combinations" (*Handling of Words,* 187). These quantitative methods of reading themselves anticipate major developments in contemporary literary criticism, notably the rise of distant reading and the digital humanities. At the same time, Morgan notes, Lee's efforts to systematize reader response as the basis for an objective literary criticism had more in common with the New Criticism of figures like I. A. Richards than the New Critics themselves generally allowed. Lee simply retained too much of the aestheticist emphasis on the body for any comfortable assimilation of her work to the modernist, analytical literary criticism to which the New Critics aspired in close reading.[52] Morgan ventures that in our own moment Lee's empathic reading might prove especially important in the way it "allows us to imagine . . . forms of interpretation that would not take for granted an opposition between a phenomenological

What if we took the aesthetes at their word by reading Pater's condition of music both as a figure *and* as indicating actual music? This chapter aims to do just that by situating Pater's invocation of music in "The School of Giorgione" as part of the British response to the acoustics of Hermann von Helmholtz. While he never mentions Helmholtz directly in his published writings, Pater's rise to fame as an apostle of the Aesthetic Movement in the 1870s coincided with an explosion of British interest in Helmholtz's scientific work on music in particular.[9] An English translation of Helmholtz's *On the Sensations of Tone as a Physiological Basis for the Theory of Music* appeared in 1875 (his treatise on optics had to wait until 1924), and the vast majority of articles discussing Helmholtz in British periodicals of the 1870s took music as their focus.[10] Pater's turn to music as the ideal art form in "The School of Giorgione" thus occurs at a moment when Helmholtz was celebrated in Britain as the preeminent scientific theorist of music.

Helmholtz's studies of music were only one part of his larger revolutionary work on sensory perception. As I discussed in chapter 1, during the two decades prior to the 1870s, Helmholtz had conducted a groundbreaking series of experiments in physics and neurophysiology, clocking the (surprisingly slow) speed of nervous transmission in 1849, inventing the first ophthalmoscope to peer inside the retina in 1851, and devising the Helmholtz resonator to analyze complex auditory sensations in the mid-1850s. Taken together, Helmholtz's experiments counterintuitively demonstrated that our perceptions—our conscious apprehension of the world around us—are radically underdetermined by the sense data that seem to straightforwardly cause them.

Sensations, Helmholtz found, are belated, fragmentary, and interpolated by the memory traces of earlier experiences, but more than that they are ignored. The perceiving mind pays only enough attention to sensations to infer the presence of familiar objects likely to have caused them. Helmholtz understood this act of inference as fundamentally semiotic: perception reflexively reads sensations as signs for objects. The first step in discriminating our sensations, he therefore suggests, is to bracket the perceptual meaning or reference we are usually only too quick to assign them. This turn away from meaning is a strategy likewise embraced by aesthetes like Pater. Pater thus declares in "The School of Giorgione" that "a great picture has no more definite message for us than an accidental play of sunlight and shadow for a few moments on the wall or floor" (*The Renaissance*, 104). Helmholtz and the aesthetes fretted that when it comes to both art and perception, we pay so much attention to the things being represented that we constantly lose sight of the *way* they are represented. In linguistic terms, reference overwhelms sense.[11]

In giving sense priority over reference in "The School of Giorgione," Pater seems to live down to aestheticism's reputation for pursuing aesthetic effects to the point of indifference, if not outright hostility, to factual accuracy about the object world. In this view, his essay on Giorgione would thus take its place as simply one more moment in Pater's work when, as Denis Donoghue puts it, "ontology is displaced by psychology."[12] In this chapter, I contest this reading of Pater and the Aesthetic Movement as hedonistically pursuing subjective effects in defiance of facts; I suggest here that Pater's attention to sense has something to offer us in a moment when critical interests have shifted toward exploring the continuities between literary texts and the extratextual world of objects. Long banished from serious critical consideration as "reality effects," the denotative references through which the novel precisely renders event and setting have recently reemerged as an archive hidden in plain sight. We can open up that archive through Elaine Freedgood and Cannon Schmitt's literal or nonfigural reading—meticulously following the path of denotative references from literary texts to technical and scientific manuals to the nontextual objects those manuals analyze, describe, and grapple with. Offering the pleasure of precision, such exacting attention to reference can help us grasp what Schmitt calls "the sheer facticity of fictional worlds," in the process transforming our understanding of a text's figurative or ideological dimensions.[13] Here I want to suggest that Pater's aestheticism is not merely consonant with the aims and method of literal reading—it also expands its scope of application beyond denotative language to include the figurative. To do so, I make two claims: that, for Pater, sense rather than reference best reveals the facticity of the figurative and that, paradoxically, Pater suggests that the best way to grasp the sense of a text is to read it literally.

By tracing Pater's response to Helmholtz's scientific theories of perception across Pater's work after *The Renaissance*, this chapter unpacks the rhetorical logic of what Pater identifies as literal metaphors—instances of figurative language or representation whose figurative significance can be grasped only by taking them literally. I identify and attend to several of Pater's literal metaphors—most extensively musical harmony—but their most emblematic form is the Paterian figure, at once human form and trope. Pater's figures, I suggest, reveal some of the erotic possibilities latent in nonfigural reading. For Schmitt, literal reading calls upon us to pay due attention to the way that novels concerned with work and technical knowledge insist on "love for and commitment to the extra-fictional world in all its particularity and intractability."[14] Aestheticism has a well-known aversion to work, but it knows quite a bit about love. In Pater's writing, I argue, love for the figure and love for the nonfigural reciprocally make and motivate each other. Put another way, Pater's writing insists that reading literally is what you do when you are reading as a lover, more especially a kinky one.[15]

Helmholtz's Two Ears: Sense and Reference in Nineteenth-Century Acoustics

Love notwithstanding, Helmholtz's ear was his most famous organ, in Britain at least. Helmholtz envisioned the ear as a kind of massive keyboard. In his 1857 lecture "On the Physiological Causes of Harmony in Music" and his 1862 treatise, *On the Sensations of Tone,* Helmholtz locates this keyboard inside the cochlea, where the organ of Corti teems with bristling, platelike hair-cell receptors, each tuned to resonate sympathetically in response to one frequency across the spectrum of audible sounds. Each of these myriad receptors transmits its vibrations to one nerve, producing its own distinct tonal sensation.[16] This massive array of keys allows the ear to perform astonishing feats of analysis, which Helmholtz illustrates by invoking the kaleidoscopic spectacle of a ballroom awash in sound:

> The air of a concert-hall or ballroom [is] traversed in every direction . . . by a variegated crowd of intersecting wave-systems. From the mouths of the male singers proceed waves of six to twelve feet in length; from the lips of

> the songstresses dart shorter waves, from eighteen to thirty-six inches long. The rustling of silken skirts excites little curls in the air, each instrument in the orchestra emits its peculiar waves, and all these systems expand spherically from their respective centres, dart through each other, are reflected from the walls of the room, and thus rush backwards and forwards until they succumb to the greater force of newly generated tones. Although this spectacle is veiled from the material eye . . . the ear . . . analyses the interdigitation of the waves . . . separates the several tones which compose it, and distinguishes the voices of men and women—nay, even of individuals—the peculiar qualities of tone given out by each instrument, the rustling of the dresses, the footfalls of the walkers, and so on.[17]

Routinely faced with such protean complexity, the keyboard of the ear effortlessly breaks a veritable ocean of activity down into a recognizable soundscape populated by familiar figures.

The analytical power of the ear is rendered even more astonishing by the phenomenon that served as the cornerstone of Helmholtz's theory of music: upper partials. With the exception of tones played by specially designed instruments such as tuning forks, what we take to be simple musical tones are actually compound waves comprising a fundamental tone combined with upper partials—vibrations at frequencies that are integer multiples of the fundamental tone. Figure 1, taken from *On the Sensations of Tone,* illustrates this combination. Wave A represents a simple tone as produced by a tuning fork. Wave B represents another simple tone an octave higher than the wave A, which therefore completes two vibrations (cresting, troughing, and returning to the baseline) in the same time it takes A to complete one (cresting and returning to the baseline). Together, these two simple waves form a compound wave with the same length as the longest simple wave (the fundamental tone), but also with an altered form. Waves C and D each represent versions of this compound wave, with the dotted lines indicating the form of the fundamental tone (wave A) so as to demonstrate the change in form in the compound wave. The degree of synchronicity between the two simple waves further affects the form of their compound. Wave C, with steeply pointed crests and troughs, represents the compound form that results when the beginning

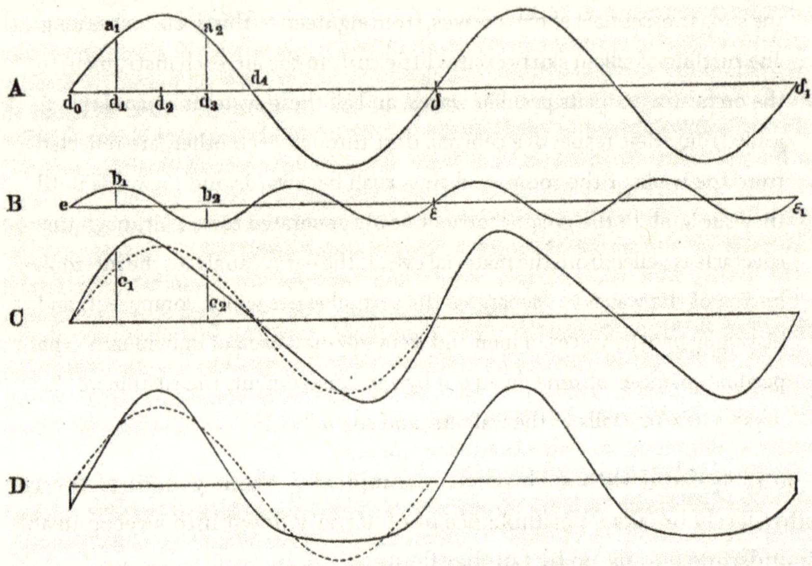

FIGURE 1. Graph of wave forms from Hermann von Helmholtz, *On the Sensations of Tone* (1862)

point of wave B coincides perfectly with the beginning point of wave A, whereas wave D, with pointed crests and flat troughs, represents the compound form that occurs if the deepest point b_2 of the trough in wave B coincides with the initial point d_o of wave A. These small alterations play an outsize role in music because the quality of a tone—its timbre as opposed to its pitch—depends on the form of the soundwave. It is therefore the distribution and intensity of upper partials in a given tone that allow us to recognize just what is producing it: whether it was "generated by the vibrating strings of a piano or violin, the vocal chords of the human larynx, the metal tongues of the harmonium, the reeds of the clarionet, oboe, and bassoon, the trembling lips of the trumpeter, or the air cut by a sharp edge in organ pipes and flutes" (*Science and Culture*, 49). Musical tones we often take to be simple are thus, strictly speaking, harmonic.

Scientific acoustics in the nineteenth century is distinctive for its preoccupation with the exact analysis of such apparently simple tones. Earlier acoustic experiments relied on strings or pipes; tones produced that way were always complex. Nineteenth-century scientists, however, began devising instruments, like sirens or Helmholtz's resonator, to isolate simple tones. Just how such simple elements combined to produce complex tones became a central problem in scientific acoustics. Helmholtz's acoustic studies followed on and attempted to resolve a dispute that played out between August Seebeck and Georg Ohm in the 1840s after Ohm applied Fourier analysis to soundwaves.[18] Seebeck mounted a particularly effective attack on Ohm, partly by pointing to the fact that his theory couldn't explain why we typically hear the fundamental tone as louder than the upper partials. It was just here that Helmholtz's semiotic account of perception proved indispensable. The relative difficulty in hearing upper partials, he argued, is just one more instance of the problem of unconscious sensations, not much different from *mouches volantes*—the fibrous deposits in the eye's vitreous humor that float across our vision—or the retinal blind spot: phenomena that must be constantly present as sensations and yet which we ignore so reflexively as to be utterly unaware of them:

> Whether a violin or a flute, a man or a dog is close by us is a matter of interest for us to know, and our ear takes care to distinguish the peculiarities of their tones with accuracy. The *means* by which we can distinguish them, however, is a matter of perfect indifference. Whether the cry of the dog contains the higher octave or the twelfth of the fundamental tone, has no practical interest for us, and never occupies our attention. The upper partials are consequently thrown into that unanalyzed mass of peculiarities of a tone which we call its *quality*. (*Science and Culture*, 67; italics in original)

The ear, then, both does and does not analyze soundwaves. The reason, Helmholtz suggests, is that there are two kinds of ears: "the material ear of the body" and "the spiritual ear of the mind" (64). Armed with its keyboard of specially tuned receptors, the material ear of the body automatically unpacks each tone into its own distinct assortment of sensations. Meanwhile, the spiritual ear of the mind, concerned first and foremost with navigating the world around it, reflexively ignores those fine discriminations, regarding sensations as "mere symbols" of the type of objects likely to be causing them (66). The split between sensation and perception reconfigures mind/body dualism as a doubling of sense organs.

By identifying sensations as signs, Helmholtz appears to widen the divide between the material world of objects and the world of human meanings. To begin with, signs are not mimetic images. If sensations were images, Helmholtz notes, they would necessarily have "some sort of similarity with the object imaged: from a statue, similarity of form; from a drawing, equality of perspectival projection in the visual field; and from a painting, similarity of colors. A sign, however, need not have any type of similarity with what it is a sign for" (*Science and Culture*, 347). "A system of signs," sensory perceptions "may be more or less perfect and convenient" when dealing with the world of things; they can give us at best a "*practical* truth," not a mimetic one (*Physiological Optics*, 3:24, 19). Helmholtz's *Physiological Optics* thus illustrates the relationship between perceptions and objects with an analogy that appears again and again across his writings: "The idea and the thing conceived belong to two entirely different worlds, which no more admit of being compared with each other . . . than the letters of a book and the sound of the word they denote" (3:19–20). The gap between letters and words in this analogy is found not just between the object and the sensations it effects; the same divide reappears between sensations and the perceptions that reflexively interpret them. Just a few pages earlier, Helmholtz had already pointed to "the connection between the written letters of a word and its sound and meaning" as a key example of just how arbitrarily conventional the relationship between sensations and perceptions can be (3:5). Lost in a book that we take to be the world, we seem twice cut off from the real by signification: once when we sense and then again when we perceive.

Nevertheless, Helmholtz maintained a blithe confidence in the truth of perception owing to what Gary Hatfield terms his classical aesthetics of science. The vocation of the scientist, Helmholtz believed, shares its fundamental aim with perception itself: to edit out the contingent variations of phenomena so as to image the lawlike consistency of the real world. Mimetic images thus sneak in through the backdoor of his epistemology, since even if sensory perceptions cannot represent the real directly, they *do* represent the lawful regularity of the real. Classical art offers us the accomplishment of this aim in its most visually striking form by "giv[ing us] a vivid perception of all the features of an ideal type, whose separate fragments lie scattered in our imagination and overgrown by the wild chaos of accident" (*Science and Culture*, 308).

Music, however, is an exception to Helmholtz's classicism in two key ways. First, we do not listen to music to discern the objects that might be in our environment. Consequently, "music has a more immediate connection with pure sensation than any other of the fine arts, and . . . the theory of the sensations in hearing is [therefore] destined to play a much more important part in musical esthetics than, for example, the theory of *chiaroscuro* or of perspective in painting" (*Sensations of Tone*, 3). More surprisingly, given the objections to Ohm's theory he had to overcome, Helmholtz insists that the spiritual ear of the mind really can discriminate upper partials. Helmholtz designed his special resonator to aid the ear in breaking down harmonic tones into their sensory components, but he claims such devices were not really necessary. All one really needs is to redirect the ear's attention from perceiving "external objects" to "attentively observing itself"—just the kind of redirection of attention, in other words, that occurs in listening to music (61).

The ear's capacity to focalize distinct sensations, Helmholtz argued in his first lecture on music, is unique among the senses. The physiology of the ear, teeming with thousands of resonators that each stimulates its own individual auditory nerve, is in pointed contrast to the eye, which, Helmholtz thought (following Thomas Young), mixes its colors from a palette of just three fundamental color sensations of scarlet red, yellow-green, and blue-violet.[19] "Light, too, has waves of various periodic times of vibration," Helmholtz writes, "but the eye is unable to decompose compound systems of luminous waves, that is, to distinguish compound colours from one another. It experiences from them a single, unanalysable, simple sensation, that of a mixed colour. . . . The eye has no sense of harmony in the same meaning as the ear. There is no music to the eye" (*Science and Culture*, 74). Despite this evocative conclusion, in *On the Sensations of Tone* Helmholtz went on to generalize the ear's power of discrimination. While, he maintains, the eye can only break down compound colors under specially designed experimental conditions, the stereoscope, for example, demonstrated that the perception of a visual depth of field could be reduced to its two component visual images even in ordinary vision. Similarly, we can learn to consciously see our retinal blind spots and *mouches volantes;* gourmands can identify the separate ingredients that together make up the flavor of a dish; careful scrutiny can break down the tactile perception of wetness into the simpler tactile sensations of smoothness and coldness. As trifling as these mental powers of analysis are, Helmholtz points to them in the service of distinguishing between two grades of perception. "The lower grade," he writes, "is that where the influence of [a] sensation . . . makes itself felt only in the conceptions we form of external things and processes, and . . . without needing or indeed being able to ascertain to what particular part of our sensations we owe this or that relation to our perceptions. In this case, we will say that . . . the sensation in question is *perceived synthetically*" (*On the Sensations of Tone,* 62; italics in original). In contrast, he goes on, "the second and higher grade is when we immediately distinguish the sensation in question as an existing part of the sum of the sensations excited in us. We will then say that the sensation is *perceived analytically*" (62; italics in original). Helmholtz thus held up hearing—and especially hearing music, when our attention to sensations of tone is heightened—as the most characteristic and highly developed sensory mode of analytic perception. The highest form of perception, Helmholtz suggests, operates most paradigmatically through what he called a "sense of harmony" (*Science and Culture,* 74).

Literal Metaphors and the Transformations of Myths in *Greek Studies*

Walter Pater's aesthetic criticism aims at just that kind of sense of harmony; it is built on a drive to decompose and analyze impressions. The preface to *The Renaissance* characterizes the basic working method of aesthetic criticism as "analyzing and reducing [the influence of each art object] to its elements" (xx). For this very reason, moreover, Pater's aesthetics share with Helmholtz's ear a vexed relationship to classicism. Classical thought, he writes in "Coleridge" (1866), "sought to arrest every object in an eternal outline"; for modern thought like Pater's own, in contrast, "experience gives us, not the truth of eternal outlines ascertained once for all, but a world of fine gradations and subtly linked conditions, shifting intricately as we ourselves change—and bids us, by a constant clearing of the organs of observation and perfecting of analysis, to make what we can of these."[20] Paterian aestheticism, I want to suggest, is fundamentally musical in Helmholtz's sense.

But let's begin with reference. Pater's essays on myth in the 1870s, later collected in *Greek Studies*, develop an idiosyncratic theory of reference that engages with Helmholtz by way of Hippolyte Taine and Max Müller. The first part of *On Intelligence* consists of an attempt at what Taine calls "psychological chemistry," an effort to systematically analyze the phenomena of mental life and reduce them to their fundamental elements. Taine thus follows the links in what he calls a "chain of substitutions" that works its way back from ideas to images to sensations, finally touching ground in "external fact" (31). A ghostly and impalpable presence in Taine's account, external fact only becomes known to us insofar as it is signified by our sensations. Following Helmholtz's semiotic theory of sensory perception, Taine thus defines a sensation as an "internal sign . . . transcrib[ing] with greater or lesser approximation [the external fact] whose internal substitute it is" (149). Already scanty, external facts are attenuated even further by virtue of the fact that the mind has trouble making out their transcriptions. While empiricism had long taken sensations to be the primary building blocks of the mind, Taine stresses that sensations as we consciously experience them are not simple but compound—they cannot make up the primitive elements of his psychological chemistry. To arrive at this fundamental reduction, Taine turns to Helmholtz's theory of music, arguing that Helmholtz's work on upper partials demonstrates that the sensations of hearing are uniquely susceptible to such an analysis. Just as what we take to be simple tones can be broken down into a set of fundamentals and upper partials, so, Taine claims, all sensations we consciously experience are made up of more elementary microsensations, becoming "more reduced and fragmentary as the nervous action exciting them becomes more simple" until, finally, they dwindle into something like atoms, utterly invisible to the naked eye unless massed together into a qualitatively different entity (186). The compound sensations we consciously experience are further compounded by what Taine calls images—the memories of past sensations that the mind reflexively recalls in order to fill out and complete crude sensory data in the present. The "education of the senses," Taine suggests, lies in building up a repertoire of these images, which then serve as "acquired perceptions" (100, 73).

Taine defines human intelligence as the capacity to abstract general ideas from particular experiences, a capacity that is made possible by names. "What . . . we call a general idea," Taine writes, "is only a name; not the simple sound that vibrates in the air and strikes our ear, or the collection of letters which blacken the paper and attract the eye, not even these letters perceived mentally, or this sound pronounced mentally, but this sound or these letters endued . . . with a double property, that of arousing in us images of individuals belonging to a certain class . . . and the property of reviving when, and only when, an individual of this same class is present to our memory or experience" (13). As the telos of perception, the development of names is the culmination of Taine's education of the senses. "After having come in contact with a series of similar objects," he writes, "we experience spontaneously . . . a tendency which corresponds to what there is in common to these objects; that is to say, to some general character, to some abstract quality, to an extract from the objects, and this tendency results in a gesture, in some mimicry, in some distinct sign, which in maturity becomes a name" (19).

Just as Helmholtz identifies the logic of common perception with the practice of science, Taine sees the development of names as the vernacular expressions of scientific reasoning. Names, he argues, "enable us to . . . seize the order and internal structure of the world" (14). But by a quirk in the logic of perception, habit simultaneously enables us to develop names and tends to make them invisible to us. Just as "when an impression . . . is many times repeated, our attention ends by fixing itself entirely on the interesting and useful part" and neglecting the rest, so when we reflect on our general ideas we tend to ignore the sign itself—the simple sound that vibrates in the air or the collection of letters that blacken the paper—for the sake of the images it calls up (32). In ascending Taine's chain of substitutions, habit teaches us to read sensations by combining them into names for general types of phenomena, but at the cost of blinding us to the names in favor the objects they refer to.

Pater takes up the problem of Taine's names in "The Myth of Demeter and Persephone" and "A Study of Dionysus," two essays that appeared in 1876, the year before the publication of "The School of Giorgione." It is an established critical fact that Pater borrows his approach to his mythic subjects from the comparative mythology of Edward Tylor, Ludwig Preller, and Max Müller.[21] Victorian comparative mythologists held that mythic figures emerged out of folk experience with natural phenomena. So in *The Queen of the Air* (1869), John Ruskin, who preceded Pater in trying his hand at comparative mythology, meticulously unpacks the goddess Athena into the atmospheric elements from which the ancient Greeks created her. This comparative framework treats mythic figures as, essentially, names as Taine understood them: spontaneously emerging signs abstracted from repeated experiences.

In "A Study of Dionysus," Pater traces the god Dionysus back to the experience of Greek peasants toiling in Mediterranean vineyards. Appearing first as "the soul of the individual vine," Dionysus is next transformed by "the higher intelligence" into "the soul of the whole species," before ultimately becoming "not merely the soul of the vine, but of all that life in flowing things of which the vine is the symbol, because its most emphatic example" and only then, at last, being named "for the brightness of the sky and the moisture of the earth" that he has come to stand for.[22] The myth of Dionysus, Pater suggests, embodies the power of the Greek imagination to "harmonise" natural fact in way that instantiates the power of names more generally to grasp and hold together fugitive impressions (29). At the same time, the naming of Dionysus does not adhere faithfully to the trajectory Taine describes, since the name in this case does not denotatively refer to a class of objects. Unlike, say, the word "vines," the name Dionysus is a proper name. It therefore "welds into something like the identity of a human personality the whole range of man's experiences of a given object, or series of objects" (29). Denotative reference, in this case, operates figuratively as it gathers up fugitive impressions into myths.

Pater's Dionysus is a figure in both senses of the word: a human form and a trope. As Carolyn Williams notes, this double notion of figure is integral to Pater's work, allowing him to embody complex social and material histories in representative individual persons—Leonardo,

Winckelmann, Marius, and so on.[23] In "A Study of Dionysus," Pater thus draws a parallel between names and the art of sculpture. Like names, classical sculpture strives to "condense the impressions of natural things into human form; to retain that early mystical sense of water, or wind, or light, in the moulding of eye and brow; to arrest it, or rather, perhaps, to set it free, there, as human expression" (33). This passage evokes his essay on "Coleridge" and its definition of classical thought as seeking to arrest every object in an eternal outline, only to revise it, paradoxically finding something like freedom in the arrest of experience.

The figural logic at work in Pater's account of mythopoetic development draws substantially from Max Müller's *Lectures on the Science of Language*, which likewise identifies the figurative work of naming with the emergence of myth.[24] Metaphor, for Müller, is fundamental to the growth of language, since its transference of a name from one object to another with similar qualities is what allowed the first language users to generate new words from a limited stock of roots. The power of metaphor thus drives the first mythic effort to give a name to every object in the world, a labor that is then done over again in the scientific work of classification, which, much like Adam, aims to throw "a simple tissue of names . . . over the garden of nature."[25]

For both Pater and Müller, metaphor governs the intermediate phase of a three-stage process of development shared by myth and science. In "The Myth of Demeter and Persephone," Pater describes this process as consisting of a mystic phase when primitive impressions of natural phenomena give rise to folk traditions, a literary phase when poets simplify and fix the outlines of those traditions into narratives, and an ethical phase when those narratives are read as "abstract symbols . . . of moral or spiritual conditions" (*Greek Studies*, 91). Steven Connor traces the origins of Pater's tripartite model of mythic development to Ruskin's *Queen of the Air*, which likewise identifies three structural parts of mythic figures:[26] "Now, therefore, in nearly every myth of importance . . . you have to discern these three structural parts—the root and the two branches:—the root, in physical existence, sun, or sky, or cloud, or sea; then the personal incarnation of that; becoming a trusted and companionable deity, with whom you may walk hand in hand, as a child with its brother or its sister;

and lastly, the moral significance of the image, which is in all the great myths eternally and beneficently true."[27]

But both these models of mythic development in fact recapitulate Müller's three stages of scientific development, which include an empirical stage of observing facts; a classificatory stage during which those facts are arranged under names; and a culminating theoretical phase elucidating the laws that underlie those classificatory arrangements. For Müller, however, the metaphorical logic of naming simultaneously drives and disrupts this developmental process. Müller's names, like Taine's, were subject to the same problem that Ian Duncan has recently described as haunting Victorian science more broadly: "Knowledge . . . obliterate[s] the imaginative as well as cognitive labor of its production [as] signs become natural, fitted to the world, [and] we become unconscious of . . . their original, figural strangeness."[28] In Müller's argument, a name is generated by metaphor but it degenerates into a mythology as soon as it becomes so familiar that we forget its figurative nature and thus confound one thing with another—that is, as soon as we take it literally.

Pater's names, though, avoid this danger by inverting Müller's narrative of the decadent slide from metaphor into literalism. We can see the narrative of decadence in play in Pater's description of Phidias's *Olympian Zeus*. In the gold and ivory form of his chryselephantine statue, Phidias embodies the primitive impressions of the sky that Zeus emerged as a name for—the breadth and expanse, the warmth and freshness—features that then in turn "impress" the devotees "who came to sun themselves in the god's presence . . . while all the time . . . consciously apprehend[ing] in the carved image of Zeus none but the personal, and really human, characteristics" (*Greek Studies*, 31). The Zeus at Olympia thus distills into one art object the life cycle of a name, from its formation to its degeneration into mythology: the statue threads together folk impressions of the sky into a human figure that transmits those primitive impressions to later generations whose conscious apprehension mistakes them for the characteristics of the human figure itself.

But if the outlines of folk experience become fixed when myth transforms natural phenomena into human figures, Pater emphasizes that those figures were always liable to revert back into natural phenomena—as they do over and over again in classical myths. Plato, Pater points out in "The Myth of Demeter and Persephone," expelled from his Republic just those kinds of stories—"stories in which, the hard material outline breaking up, the gods lay aside their visible form like a garment, yet remain essentially themselves" (*Greek Studies*, 119). By forbidding these stories, Plato aims to ensure that his republicans read myths in agreement with what Pater describes as their third, ethical phase, during which mythic figures are interpreted as abstract symbols of moral and spiritual conditions. Turning Müller on his head, Pater suggests that it is this highest phase of myth that collapses into mythology—its abstract, symbolical mode of reading disavows the origins of myths in folk impressions of the natural world and disdains the condensed experiences gathered up in them.[29] Before the abstract eye of the ethicist, myths remain arrested, frozen into "mere transparent allegory" (98). To access the richness of arrested experience in myths, "the more delicately trained eye" of the "modern reader" must break them down by putting them back in motion (119). Like Giotto and William Blake in their handling of myths, the modern reader must unite "a certain simplicity, taking all things literally, *au pied de la lettre* . . . to a vivid preoccupation with the aesthetic beauty of the image itself, the *figured* side of figurative expression, the *form* of the metaphor" (98–99; italics in original). Rather than serving as an alternative to figural reading here, the literal creates its possibility—taking names literally ensures attention to them *as* figures.

Kinky Literalism: Reading Plato as a Lover

Names were still on Pater's mind in 1877 when he published "The School of Giorgione" in the *Fortnightly Review.* But in moving from the name of Dionysus to that of Giorgione, Pater turned from the making of a myth to the imploding of one: J. A. Crowe and Giovanni Cavalcaselle's *A History of Painting in Northern Italy* had eviscerated the legend of Giorgione by drastically reducing the number of paintings attributed to him.[30] As Pater put it, Giorgione's "great traditional reputation, woven with so profuse a demand on men's admiration, has been scrutinised thread by thread;

and what remains of the most vivid and stimulating of Venetian masters, a live flame, as it seemed, in those old shadowy times, has been reduced almost to a name by his most recent critics" (*The Renaissance,* 113). If the name of Dionysus emerges out of a plenitude of folk experiences, then Giorgione's name, in contrast, emerges as a remainder—it is all that's left after the threads have unraveled and the flame has burned out. "The School of Giorgione" aims to restore the plenitude of Giorgione's name by arguing for the historical and social significance of the fact that so many paintings were misattributed to him. As Jonah Siegel cannily observes, the revelation that so many of Giorgione's supposed paintings were actually painted by his followers, far from diminishing his significance, in fact only underscores his continuing importance; his school demonstrates "a kind of force of personality" much more clearly than authenticated paintings by themselves could.[31] Hence, Pater writes, "All is not done when the real and the traditional elements in what concerns [Giorgione] have been discriminated; for in what is connected with a great name, much that is not real is often very stimulating" (116). The name "Giorgione" comprises not just authenticated works but also what Pater famously calls the *vraie vérité,* a complex and ongoing social history of representation that exists over and above the real.

"Giorgione," in short, is not just a name; he is a figure, an "impersonation of [cinquecento] Venice itself, its projected reflex or ideal, all that was intense or desirable in it crystallising about the memory of this wonderful young man" (116).[32] In this regard, "The School of Giorgione" instantiates one of the most fundamental critical principles and figurative techniques of Pater's work more broadly: the essay makes knowing *things* into a matter of knowing *persons.*[33] "Giorgione" is one in a long line of what Pater in *Marius the Epicurean* (1885) calls "sensible exponent[s]"—persons rendering visible historical processes that in themselves cannot be made concretely present to sensory experience.[34] Marius's companion Cornelius, for instance, is the sensible exponent of the Christianity that, in the novel's second-century Roman setting, will soon supplant classical Roman civilization; Marius had inferred almost this much from their first meeting, when he instinctively perceived that "every object of [Cornelius's] knightly array . . . seemed like the indication or sign of something far beyond itself" (151). Figures in this sense make possible Pater's historicism, which, as Stephen Arata puts it, aims to "track the movement of the world's energy by assigning it a series of proper names."[35] This figurative historicism, however, seems utterly at odds with the aesthetic principle Pater has laid down just pages earlier in the same essay—that a painting has no more definite message for us than the accidental shimmering of sunlight on the floor. His account of "Giorgione" interpolates this play of light with historical meaning—with the artist's biography, with cinquecento Venetian society, with the development of the *Weltgeist*. The two contradictory arguments of "The School of Giorgione" dramatize the split between two Paters: Pater the apostle of aesthetic democracy, who advocated a direct, sensuous, and individual art experience; and Pater the conservative historicist, who in the late 1870s and 1880s became increasingly interested in the way collective social traditions and practices suffuse individual experience.[36] This apparently irresolvable tension between the real and the historical in Pater's work disappears, however, if we take Pater's figures literally.

Pater notably practices this reading method in *Plato and Platonism* (1893), where he takes figures literally in order to read Plato himself as of the aesthetes' party without knowing it. Pater recuperates the aesthetic Plato by contrasting his diverse world of forms with Parmenides's notion of the Absolute. Whereas Parmenides's Absolute was a frozen, undifferentiated Oneness, Plato repopulates this blank realm of truth with forms that "emerge again from the dead level, the Parmenidean *tabula rasa*, with nothing less than the reality of persons face to face with us . . . as if the firm plastic outlines of the delightful old Greek polytheism had found their way back after all into a repellent monotheism."[37] Comparing Plato's forms to the return of the gods in a climate of frigid monotheism, Pater reads those abstract forms the same way that he reads Dionysus—as figures capable of reverting back to their origins in sensory experience.

In spite of Plato's hostility to myths in which the gods change forms, he himself performs a similar kind of reading in the *Cratylus*, his dialogue on names. Plato argues in the *Cratylus* that names are not the arbitrary products of a system of differences, as linguistics since Saussure has maintained, but rather convey some truth about the objects to which they refer. That truth is not natural and direct, however; it is the joint product of a dialectician, whose inquiries seek to understand the truth of things, and a "nomosthete," a name maker who fashions names out of letters and syllables that express the truths of the dialecticians. Plato suggests that these truths are fallible because they are historically contingent. Improvising bizarre, tongue-in-cheek etymologies for a series of Greek names, Socrates maintains that the ancient nomosthetes and dialecticians who together devised Greek were all Heracliteans; the truths about things embodied in Greek names were thus by no means truths that Plato would have accepted as such. As Benjamin Jowett approvingly remarks in his introduction to the *Cratylus,* Plato suggests that "the lesson which may be gathered from words is not metaphysical or moral, but historical."[38] That historical truth is expressed through the nomosthete's combination of onomatopoeic phonemes and what Plato calls "primary names," elemental names that serve as something like a fundamental set of roots for the nomosthetes. As Socrates explains to his interlocutors, "Our job—if indeed we are to examine all these things with scientific knowledge—is to divide where [the ancient nomosthetes] put together, so as to see whether or not both the primary and derivative names are given in accord with nature."[39] To examine names scientifically, in the *Cratylus,* is to unravel them into their constituent elements.

In *Plato and Platonism,* Pater likewise undertakes to unravel Plato's figures. Plato, Pater writes, "breaks . . . visible color into the very texture of his work: his vocabulary, the very stuff he manipulates, has its delightful aesthetic qualities; almost every word, one might say, its figurative value" (140). Characteristically, Pater uses "figurative value" here literally, as in useful for making a figure. "For a lover [like Plato]," he writes, "the entire visible world, its hues and outline, its attractiveness, its power and bloom, must have associated themselves pre-eminently with the power and bloom of visible living persons. With these, as they made themselves known by word and glance and touch, through the medium of the senses, lay the forces, which, in that inexplicable tyranny of one person over another, shaped the soul" (135). In their primary aspect, persons are just as fundamentally a matter of sensation as art objects—they too seem to be "receptacles of so many powers or forces" (*The Renaissance,* xix)—but here physics' metaphorical language of forces is also made literal: the physical forces registered by the senses *really are* powers, exercising a tyranny that shapes the soul of the perceiver. At the same time, Pater eroticizes that tyranny, sublimating its power dynamics into a kinky form of love akin to pederasty.

Pederastic love was a lifelong preoccupation for Pater, who was keenly aware that love's tyranny over the lover depends, perversely, on the lover's agency. To know his beloved or anyone else, the lover must first of all perform the constructive work of imagining him. As Pater reflects in *Marius*, "One builds up from act and word and expression of the friend actually visible at one's side, an ideal of the spirit within him" (203). We typically build up our ideas of others unconsciously, just as, in Helmholtz's view, we typically build perceptions out of our sensations unconsciously. But loving someone means lingering on the little things we know our beloved by—word or glance or touch—and it is in these, Pater suggests, that the force of the beloved resides.

If Pater makes knowing things a matter of knowing persons, loving persons requires us to attend to the things through which we come to know them. Arata calls this dynamic "impersonal intimacy," an effect Pater achieves in his writing by insisting "that we see [his] fictional characters . . . as aesthetic objects made out of words."[40] For Arata, Pater makes us feel at once intimate and alienated from his characters and from himself, somewhat in the way an extreme close-up photograph distances us from its subject by bringing us unwontedly close to it. Heather Love similarly comments on "the dual movement of solicitation and self-effacement [that] occurs throughout Pater's writing. In his approach to the reader, Pater somehow manages to be both forward and shrinking, both suggestive and withdrawn."[41] In Love's argument, Pater's curiously forward restraint is emblematic of his queerness, but it seems equally plausible to me to identify Pater's idiosyncratic style with his kinkiness. Kink names an erotic satisfaction in being dominated by another but also, literally, a twist or recursive turn backward. Both meanings capture the traffic of the lover's attention from the figure to the nonfigural and back motivated by the kinky fetishizing of the things through which one comes to know one's beloved—the very things, in other words, that tyrannize over us so forcefully. For Pater, that is to say, reading literally is a form of kink, a fetishistic domination of the lover by the sensory elements of a beloved figure.

Pater offers us a model of this kinky literalism in his reading of Plato: "To trace [the] thread of physical colour, entwined throughout, and multiplied sometimes into large tapestried figures, is the business, the enjoyment, of the student of the Dialogues, as he reads them" (141). The reader of the dialogues does two things to Plato's figures at once, both of which are distilled in the verb "trace." By tracing Plato's figures, the reader outlines them but also unravels them, picking apart the tapestried figures so as to discriminate and trace threads back to their origins in sense experience.[42] In *Plato and Platonism,* Pater reads Plato as a lover, which is to say that he reads him by simultaneously weaving and unweaving the literal and the figurative, sense and reference.

Pater's Harmonic Figures: Florian, Marius, Giorgione

A lover of Pater myself, in the remainder of this chapter I trace his strategy of reading as a lover back to the sensory-perceptual experience of harmony. My claim here is that Pater learned to read as a lover partly from Helmholtz's harmonic theory of musical tones. Helmholtz, as we've seen, singled out musical tones as the paradigmatic instance of our perceptual powers of synthesis and analysis: when we listen to a musical tone, the ear mechanically unpacks a compound soundwave into several distinct tonal sensations that the mind, in turn, synthesizes into a simple tone with a recognizable quality. When we listen harmonically, Helmholtz claims, we can thus at once give our attention to the figural quality of a tone, as it were—to whether it sounds like a cello or an oboe or a voice that we know intimately—and to the discrete elements giving it that quality. For Pater, who encountered Helmholtz while reading Taine and Müller and very likely also in the discussions of Helmholtz's work that were prevalent in music theory in the 1870s, harmony served as a model figure for the kinky literalism of erotic reading.

The figure of harmony appears frequently in Pater's work following his elevation of music to the pinnacle of the arts in "The School of Giorgione," beginning with the first of his *Imaginary Portraits,* "The Child in the House" (1878). Recounting its imagined sitter Florian's dream about his childhood home, this portrait "trac[es] back the threads of his complex spiritual habit" to his first "material habitation."[43] In contrast to the "strange, perpetual weaving and unweaving of ourselves" from moment to moment that Pater envisions in the conclusion to *The Renaissance,* Florian's spiritual habit is more durably sewn (188). Florian's childhood home had, "through the law which makes the material objects about them so large an element in children's lives," actually "become a part" of his spiritual habit, "inward and outward being woven through and through each other into one inextricable texture—half, tint and trace and accident of homely colour and form, from the wood and the bricks; half, mere soul-stuff, floated thither from who knows how far" (4). As Florian traces the threads of this inextricable texture back to their origins, Pater plays on three related meanings of habit: as dress or attire, as mental constitution or custom, and as material constitution or habitation. Florian's spiritual habit actually incorporates traces of the material elements of his home—its wood and bricks—into a bodily vesture that is also a spiritual one. The threads of Florian's spiritual habit thus modulate into nerves as he traces the developmental process of "brain-building" that takes place through his interactions with his early sensory environment (4).

Florian's brain building here is fundamentally a perceptual education. "Our susceptibilities, the discovery of our powers, manifold experiences," Pater writes, "belong to this or the other well-remembered place in the material habitation . . . and the early habitation thus gradually becomes a sort of material shrine or sanctuary of sentiment; a system of visible symbolism interweaves itself through all our thoughts and passions; and, irresistibly, little shapes, voices, accidents . . . become parts of the great chain wherewith we are bound" (6). Florian's system of visible symbolism emerges out of the developmental logic of perception described by Taine: Florian's habits abstract stable perceptual concepts out of unstable sensory phenomena so that he gradually learns to make "a constant substitution of the typical for the actual . . . in his thoughts" (16). Florian's habitation thus seems to teach him to do just what Pater warned against five years earlier in *The Renaissance* when he declared that habits lead us to confuse the actual, present objects of our experience with their stereotypes.

Pater's reconsideration of habits in "The Child in the House" stems, in part, from his growing interest in music. *The Renaissance*'s pronouncement that to form habits is to fail in life was in fact a frontal assault on the broad Victorian consensus, shared by Oxford dons and *Self-Help* devotees alike, that habits were the foundation of ethics.[44] As Pater revised his positions in the wake of the scandalized critical attacks on *The Renaissance,* he used music to account for the ethical dimensions of aestheticism. In "The Child in the House," Florian uses music as a figure to imagine the pain of others. After caging a starling away from her nestlings overnight and hearing her anguished cries, he remorsefully marvels at "that great machine in things, constructed so ingeniously to play pain-fugues on the delicate nerve-work of living creatures" (10). This ethical epiphany in fact precedes his aesthetic one; it is only after this episode instructs him in the moral urgency of sensory experience that he determines to "yield . . . himself to [sensible] things, to be played upon by them like a musical instrument" (12).

But crucially, Pater also has recourse to musical figures to describe Florian's ethical relationship with cultural and religious customs. Florian has the "good fortune" of living in a home that is "typically home-like" for an Englishman and thus facilitates his acculturation within the wider space of the nation itself, with the effect that "the sense of harmony between his soul and its physical environment became, for a time at least, like perfectly played music" (7). Pater then employs the same figure to recount Florian's turn to religion, which likewise proceeds through his acquiring a system of visible symbolism, one that allows him to make "the habitual recognition, beside every circumstance and event of life, of its celestial correspondent" (16). Florian figures these celestial correspondents as a "complimentary strain or burden, applied to our every-day existence, whereby the stray snatches of music in it re-set themselves, and fall into the scheme of some higher and more consistent harmony" (15). The aesthetic education of "The Child in the House" culminates in a sense of harmony.

This sense of harmony reappears insistently throughout *Marius the Epicurean,* where it again functions to reconcile a thinly disguised version of Paterian aestheticism with the historicized forms of cultural and religious custom. Cornelius Fronto's public speech on the nature of morals develops the trope extensively in order to defend "right conduct [as] a deference, an 'assent,' entire, habitual, unconscious, to custom[,] to the actual habit . . . of others" from an Epicureanism (like Marius's) so insistent on the primacy of "realised consciousness in the present" that it can imagine such deference as, at best, ironic (164, 99). "Preferences from of old," Fronto proclaims, "become now a weighty tradition as to the way in which things should or should not be done, are like a music, to which the intercourse of life proceeds—such a music as no one who had once caught its harmonies would willingly jar" (165). Fronto here puts the accent on volition—the *willingness* to defer or not to a harmony once caught—but catching is a funny kind of action that can be as passively receptive (I've caught a virus) as it can be actively aggressive (the police have caught the suspect), and catching a music's harmonies could thus suggest the careful discernment of a tune's sonic structure or its insidious burrowing into the ear so that it conforms all stray snatches of music to itself.

Tellingly, Fronto himself seems to have caught this figure from Heraclitus, who in Pater's telling uses harmony to conceive of an order that persists even within the ceaseless flickering of the all-consuming fire. Even amid the perpetual flux of things, Pater writes, Heraclitus identifies "a continuance, if not of their material or spiritual elements, yet of orderly intelligible relationships, like the harmony of musical notes, wrought out in and through the series of their mutations . . . and this harmony in their mutation and opposition, was a principle of sanity and reality in things" (88). Even as the particular water molecules in Heraclitus's famous river change so that you cannot pass through it twice, their configuration into a river persists as something that you might be able to pass through again after all. This kind of continuity is a key concern of the novel, bearing as it does on the very possibility of history as well as the reality of things. The narrator thus criticizes Marius for ignoring this aspect of Heraclitus's philosophy in his initial enthusiastic embrace of Epicureanism. Here as elsewhere, the novel seeks to imagine continuity by turning to harmony as the paradigmatic example of a stable configuration of unstable elements—a set of notes that might change (going up or down an octave, being played by a piano or a bassoon) and still be recognized as the same tune as long as their mathematical relations to each other persist. Harmony itself serves as just such a portable configuration, employed now by Heraclitus to figure ontological duration, now by Fronto to figure historical duration. In short, Pater finds in harmony something like a model for understanding the conditions of possibility for forms.

In reviewing Plato's philosophical antecedents in *Plato and Platonism*, Pater seems to suggest that form is identical to the configuration only and the elements thus organized are a matter of indifference:

> It is hardly an exaggeration to say that in Plato . . . there is nothing absolutely new: or rather, as in many other very original products of human genius, the seemingly new is old also, a palimpsest, a tapestry of which the actual threads have served before, or like the animal frame itself, every particle of which has already lived and died many times over. Nothing but the life-giving principle of cohesion is new; the new perspective, the resultant complexion, the expressiveness which familiar thoughts attain by novel juxtaposition. In other words, the *form* is new. But then . . . in all . . . products of art, *form*, in the full signification of that word, is everything, and the mere matter is nothing. (8; italics in original)

But what is the full signification of "form"? This passage suggests that Pater conceived of artistic form on analogy with organic form. While Pater here claims that form comprises only the configuration of preexisting elements, the figures woven in the tapestry rather than the threads making them up, the next several chapters of *Plato and Platonism* belie this claim through their careful scrutiny of just those threads in tracing Plato's debts to Heraclitus, Parmenides, and Pythagoras. Such scrutiny was a key part of Pater's strategy for apprehending the aesthetic qualities of Plato's forms. The full signification of form, for Pater, is never reducible to pure configuration, the organic "life-giving principle of cohesion" without reference to the elements involved in that coherence. For Pater, I propose, form is harmonic.

Harmonic form in "The School of Giorgione" underwrites both Pater's uncompromising insistence on painting as a radically meaningless sensory event—an accidental play of light—and his reading of Giorgionesque painting as a presentation of Venetian history. The signature of the Giorgionesque, in fact, is a sense of harmony. The school of Giorgione arrests "exquisite pauses in time" from the feverish world of Venice, presenting in their work "profoundly significant and animated instants, a mere gesture, a look, a smile, perhaps—some brief and wholly concrete moment—into which, however, all the motives, all the interests of a long history, have condensed themselves, and which seem to absorb past and future in an intense consciousness of the present" (118). Giorgione's school identifies such exquisite pauses with the moments when Venetians played or listened to music, "the musical intervals in our existence, [when] life itself is conceived as a sort of listening" (119). For Giorgione's contemporaries, these musical intervals were moments of play, snatched in between bouts of labor, that permitted them to relax the "servile, everyday attentiveness" demanded by instrumental reason (119). Giorgione's musical intervals thus very prosaically denote cinquecento Venetians' recreational breaks devoted to music.

But a musical interval also denotes the difference between two musical tones. During the intervals when life itself becomes a kind of listening, the Venetians painted by Giorgione and his school are listening for intervals: in *The Concert*, which Pater takes as the key example of the Giorgionesque, the painting's subjects display "intent faces, as if listening . . . to detect the smallest interval of musical sound" (119). Giorgione's auditors in these musical intervals are, like Helmholtz, striving to apprehend the minute and almost unnoticeable harmonic complexity that gives these exquisite moments their quality, which is to say that they are striving to decompose a formal configuration back into its elements. The Giorgionesque sense of harmony, then, brings into view the peculiar double movement of Paterian aestheticism: the gathering up of reference and the breaking down into sense, the arrest of classical outlines and the modern's analytic flux.

This sense of harmony shapes Pater's description of *The Concert* (figure 2). For Pater, *The Concert* offers us a musical interval both figuratively (it depicts a recreational moment of play with music) and literally (its three musicians are finding the "true interval," which is to say, the tonic, the harmonic center of the piece they are about to play):

FIGURE 2. *The Concert,* Titian, 1510–11. (Gallerie degli Uffizi)

> The *Concert* in the *Pitti* Palace [*sic*], in which a monk, with cowl and tonsure, touches the keys of a harpsichord, while a clerk, placed behind him, grasps the handle of a viol, and a third, with cap and plume, seems to wait upon the true interval for beginning to sing, is undoubtedly Giorgione's. The outline of the lifted finger, the trace of the plume, the very threads of the fine linen, which fasten themselves on the memory, in the moment before they are lost altogether in that calm unearthly glow, the skill which has caught the waves of wandering sound, and fixed them for ever on the lips and hands—these are indeed the master's own. (113)

Giorgione's skillful effort to catch the waves of wandering sound doubles that of the musicians, who are likewise trying to arrange those waves by reconfiguring their wandering into an orderly harmonic development. At the same time, Pater is busy breaking that arrangement back down as his attention wanders along the analytical axis of three key Paterian tropes: the stability of an "outline," even if one of a finger rather than a full figure, gives way to the more insubstantial "trace," which then in turn leads the eye through sheer metonymic force to the "very threads" out of which the larger figures are woven. This fixation of elements, however, then gets "lost," subsumed by a calm, unearthly glow. Should we read this loss only as an uncannily prophetic anticipation of the effects of Giovanni Morelli's later thread-by-thread scrutiny of *The Concert*, which led him to the conclusion that it was painted not by Giorgione but by Titian during his Giorgionesque period?[45] Let's say, rather, that the unearthly glow is the momentary ecstatic forgetfulness that gratified desire can elicit in even the most rigorous critics when they love what they read.

Epilogue

> Perception is not a matter of sensation; it is never a matter of mere feeling. Perceiving is an activity of securing access to the world by cultivating the right critical stance, that is, by cultivating the right understanding.
>
> —Alva Noë, *The Varieties of Presence*

How might Victorian practices of reading with the senses inform literary studies today? The intervening century of disciplinary history has rendered our similarities uncanny. If Walter Pater's kinky literalism bears a strong family resemblance to contemporary methods of literal reading, for example, Pater's criticism displays little of the painstaking attention to precise details of the object world that is the hallmark of those methods. Consider one of Pater's most famous passages, the description of *La Gioconda* in his essay "Leonardo da Vinci":

> She is older than the rocks among which she sits; like the vampire, she has been dead many times, and learned the secrets of the grave; and has been a diver in deep seas, and keeps their fallen day about her; and trafficked for strange webs with Eastern merchants; and, as Leda, was the mother of Helen of Troy, and, as Saint Anne, the mother of Mary; and all this has been to her but as the sound of lyres and flutes, and lives only in the delicacy with

> which it has moulded the changing lineaments, and tinged the eyelids and the hands. (99)

A literal reading of *La Gioconda* today would meticulously examine the rocks among which she sits, moving carefully from the painting's depiction to Leonardo's geological researches and beyond in order to see how they change our understanding of the painting.[1] In contrast, Pater's description is thick, excessively so—it piles layer upon layer of social significance on top of its object in apparent defiance of the actual details of the painting.[2]

Such extravagant thickness is where aestheticism shades into a kind of antirepresentational modernism. As the descriptions in aesthetic criticism like Pater's thickened, they called so much attention to themselves as to displace their objects. Oscar Wilde had this thickening in mind in "The Critic as Artist" (1890) when he pointed to Pater's account of the *Mona Lisa* as an illustration of his principle that criticism is an effort to see the object as in itself it really is not.[3] In this way, aestheticist descriptions point toward what Jacques Rancière characterizes as the modernist paradigm: "the break of every kind of art with the enslavement of representation, which made all art the means of expression of an external referent, and art's concentration, instead, on its own materiality."[4] As this paradigm came to dominance in the early twentieth century, a parallel development played out in literary studies through formalist efforts to define a specifically literary language. Formalists identified the poetic function of language with figurative language, as distinct from referential language in particular. As Roman Jakobson describes it, the poetic function enacts something strikingly like the modernist paradigm: "By promoting the palpability of signs, [the poetic function] deepens the fundamental dichotomy of signs and objects."[5]

In a sense, the rise of an antirepresentational modernism and a formalism that replicates its estrangement from representational or referential objects completes the arc that this book has been tracing. When Thomas Reid identified sensations with signs and perception with their interpretation in the eighteenth century, he was arguing for perception's immediacy, a directness that he thought was grounded in the Book of Nature.

But his version of that direct realism depended on taking as simply given the precise nature of how the physical facts of sensations give rise to the mental phenomena of perceptions. Once that dynamic became the object of scientific inquiry in Victorian physics, physiology, and experimental psychology, the Book of Nature came unbound. Sensory signs and perceptual interpretations untethered over the course of the nineteenth century. Cut loose from strict causal or cognitive relations with objects, sensations became autonomous.[6]

Meanwhile, the salience of reading as the master metaphor for these scientific accounts of sense experience gave Victorian literary writers license to experiment with reading as a technology of perception. George Eliot's hallucinatory descriptivism, Thomas Hardy's tight associationist focalization of signifying sensations, Vernon Lee's dynamically restrained empathic reading, Pater's harmonic literalism—in their different ways, each of these techniques models a reading practice that would be attentive to sensations as such. These Victorian literary practices of reading with the senses thus participated in the intensifying efforts to apprehend autonomous affect that Fredric Jameson identifies as an engine of the development of the nineteenth-century novel.

Looking back at the previous century's literary experiments with perception from the vantage of the early twentieth century, Viktor Shklovsky too saw a principle of formal development intrinsic to art's function as a device for rendering sensory experience. While one strand of Shklovsky's argument emphasizes the way art intimately acquaints us with the objects of experience by reanimating their sensational presence, that strand is entwined with a more strictly formalist argument that the purpose of defamiliarization is "not to draw our understanding closer to that which [the artistic] image stands for" (10). "*Art*," he declares in this vein, "*is a means of experiencing the [perceptual] process of creativity. The artifact itself is quite unimportant*" (6; italics in original).[7] This surprising claim—so at odds with the essay's readings of Tolstoy—reflects the fact that one of the aims in "Art as a Device" was the formalist project of specifying a distinctly literary kind of language, here again explicitly identified with figurative language and distinguished from reference. To the extent that Victorian models of reading with the senses prioritized attention to sensations purely, they promoted the palpability of signs (in Jakobson's evocative phrase) apart from any intentional objects to which they refer. While largely overshadowed by critical attention to developments in linguistics, the history of nineteenth-century perception science thus played a crucial role in the cleaving of language from the world that has been, in various ways, axiomatic for literary studies over the last century.

Looking back at Shklovsky and the original formalist moment from the vantage of the early twenty-first century, it is hard not to feel a small tug of nostalgia. At the outset of literary studies as a modern academic discipline, formalism, for good and ill, defined for the nascent field a specific disciplinary object—figurative language. And it formalized the method of explicating that object—close reading—that subsequently anchored much of literary studies through the many permutations of the field.[8] At that moment of disciplinary formation, the formalists could presume substantial interest in a literature conceived of as palpable signs at a remove from the rest of the world. That no longer seems to be the case. The recent efflorescence of new reading methods and the insistent calls to reimagine the field along interdisciplinary or transhistorical lines reflect a widely shared sense that literary studies (like the humanities more broadly) needs to make a better case for why it matters.[9] We should tread carefully here. An interdisciplinary model of literary studies—like the one attempted by this book—risks dissolving the robust understanding of our field's particular object and methods of explication without which there can be no discipline to bridge with others.[10] At the same time, it is becoming increasingly clear that to survive under the conditions of early twenty-first-century austerity, literary studies needs to move more definitively beyond the restrictive dichotomy between literary signs and the other objects in the world that is part of our field's inheritance from formalism.

Victorian literary practices of reading with the senses have something to offer us at this moment of methodological ferment in literary studies. Victorian literature models an attentiveness to sensations as such that looks ahead to formalist reading. But for Victorian writers such attentiveness to sensory signs serves to draw readers closer to (rather than separate them from) the intentional objects to which those signs direct us. Pater, for instance, privileges figurative language, but insists on the kinky satisfactions of reading it literally. He thickly describes *La Gioconda* as a figuration of Hegelian universal history, but his essay still takes pains to stipulate that the portrait's model was a real person and asks his readers to meditate on "the relationship of a living Florentine to this creature of . . . thought" (98). Pater, in other words, asks us to reflect on the connecting links between the description, the portrait, and the portrait's subject. The sustained interest in the connecting links of reference and intentionality throughout Pater's work can, I think, be taken as consonant with James's radical empiricism. James, too, wanted a philosophy of experience adequate to the way that the intentionality of knowledge by description—its intrinsic direction to an object—is not just something that connects our experiences but is instead part of our experience. For James and Pater, in other words, even the most palpable of signs do not end in themselves like a globed fruit but rather, just by being palpable, lead us on and involve us further in the world.

In this regard, Victorian literature can show us a path not taken by our discipline. These literary models of what it means to read with the senses are best characterized as intentional rather than representational. Representationalism understands perception in terms of detachment and mediation, viewing the act of perception, as in James Gibson's words again, "a representation in the theater of consciousness" (*Ecological Approach*, 256). In contrast, the literary practices of reading with the senses I have examined in this book frame perception and reading in terms of direction toward objects. Each of these reading practices sought to bring the intentional objects of perception into a more intimate presence, refusing perceptual detachment by, paradoxically, eroticizing or otherwise intensifying it in the way of kink (Pater and Lee), vagueness (Eliot), and blindness (Hardy). The remainder of this epilogue sketches what I think literary studies might take from Victorian literature's radical empiricism by turning briefly to Wilde's *The Portrait of Mr. W. H.* (1889), a Victorian novella about reading, portraits, and the theater.

The plot of *The Portrait of Mr. W. H.* revolves around the ways that reading about something can become a mode of experiencing it. The novella follows three main characters—Cyril, Erskine, and the unnamed narrator—as they struggle to convert each other to an apparently naïve belief in a literary text: the belief that Shakespeare's sonnets recount the history of his involvement with a young actor named Willie Hughes who inspired the female protagonists in his plays, even though the name Willie Hughes is absent from the historical record and only appears very obliquely in the sonnets themselves. The sheer oddity of this scenario itself gestures at the late-Victorian fascination with the questions around intentionality and descriptive knowledge this book has charted. In the novella, the absence of external evidence for this reading of the sonnets generates the story's conflict, as well as its eponymous portrait—a forged Elizabethan painting of Willie Hughes that Cyril, the originator of the Willie Hughes reading, commissions in order to win over his initially skeptical friend, Erskine. Given the relative ease of of forging a document, Cyril's choice of a forged painting is strange. For one thing, the forged portrait must be painted on the basis of poetic descriptions of a person whose actual existence is dubious. The representational complexity of such an effort torques the principles of mimetic fidelity that Wilde would later that same year playfully invert in his more famous essay "The Decay of Lying." There, he argued that life imitates art rather than the other way around. But the portrait also signals that the problems of belief and evidence in the novella hinge on the relationship between descriptive and empirical knowledge. Noting that the initial warrant for the Willie Hughes reading of the sonnets lies in Cyril's "artistic sense," Rachel Ablow suggests that the aim for the novella's characters as they work to convert each other to belief in the theory is just that they want to bypass "inference or logical conclusions based on evidence," claiming for a reading of a literary text the unreserved belief we routinely accord only to sense experience.[11] By commissioning the forged portrait, then, Cyril attempts to transform text into portrait, knowledge by description into knowledge by acquaintance.

Wilde's novella thus rehearses a dilemma immanent to our critical understanding of the historical relationship between empiricism and literature, a relationship most directly evident in the novel, the form that grew up with empiricism in the eighteenth century. As Ian Watt influentially recounted that history in *The Rise of the Novel* (1957), the empiricist "belief in the individual apprehension of reality through the senses" gave the novel its distinctive formal aim—to convey the impression of being "an authentic account of the actual experiences of individuals."[12] The novel here piggybacks on our implicit belief in the senses to solicit a subordinate and provisional kind of belief. Where sense experience is believed, the novel is, at most, a believable account of such beliefs. If Watt's historical narrative helps account for the emergence of "fiction" as an epistemological and literary category during this period, in doing so it also renders any claims for objective accuracy in an interpretation of a novel (or, by extension, any other literary text) highly dubious, as Wilde's characters discover to their intense frustration. On this understanding, as Ablow glosses the problem in Wilde's novella, "beliefs founded on sensations can simply not be transmitted to others," least of all through literary texts.[13]

Worse still, as scientists continued to investigate perception within the representationalist framework of mainline empiricism, sense perception likewise became vulnerable to a corrosive skepticism. As this book has demonstrated, nineteenth-century science came to view much of the individual apprehension of reality through the senses as itself just another kind of propositional account, a descriptive knowledge that we reflexively apply to our sensations. Wilde leveraged just this perceptual skepticism to support the antimimetic argument of "Decay of Lying," arguing that art is what supplies us with the language of perception through which we apprehend the world, and so art must be considered originary rather than imitative. If we follow its logic, the established critical narrative around empiricism and literature thus commits us to some surprisingly solipsistic conclusions: both when we read and when we perceive, we are in the Cartesian theater of consciousness where each mind keeps as a solitary prisoner its dream of a world.

The Portrait of Mr. W. H. shows us how the robust empiricism of reading with the senses that this book has traced in Victorian literature and science can break this impasse. David Kurnick's work has taught us how theater shaped novelists' efforts to open the interiority of its individual subjects outward.[14] Wilde's novella does something similar with the Cartesian theater. As Jonathan Loesberg points out, the Willie Hughes theory requires the reader of the sonnets to take what seems to be figurative language literally.[15] To identify the sonnets' fair youth with the actor Willie Hughes, for example, Wilde's unnamed narrator points to the first four lines of

Sonnet 53: "What is your substance, whereof are you made, / That millions of strange shadows on you tend? / Since everyone hath, every one, one shade, / And you, but one, can every shadow lend."[16] The wordplay here depends on the metaphorical meaning of shadows as images. The fair youth exceeds the mortal allotment of one shadow because the speaker sees all other beautiful things as insubstantial images, or pale imitations, of him. Wilde's narrator, though, insists on reading shadow literally, as a technical term for an actor.[17] These moments of reading figurative language literally in particular sonnets perform in the small what the Willie Hughes theory does for the sonnets collectively—insist on supplying them with a referent, an intentional object, namely, Willie Hughes.

While this kind of biographical reading was a fixture of Victorian literary criticism, Loesberg demonstrates that it typically used historical evidence (correspondence and so on) to decode literary texts as putatively secret messages to historical addressees. In supplying such a secret addressee, these readings of the sonnets sought to explain away the queer desire they articulate chiefly by refusing to read them literally, choosing instead to read homoerotic elements as coded allegories. Wilde's unnamed narrator comments on this refusal of the literal in common readings of sonnets by Michelangelo, noting that one consequence is failure to grasp the way the sonnets' figurative language plays with their referent: "Michel Angelo addresses the young Tommaso Cavalieri in such fervent and passionate terms that some have thought that the sonnets in question must have been intended for . . . the widow of the Marchese di Pescara. . . . But that it was to Cavalieri that they were written, and that the literal interpretation is the right one, is evident . . . from the fact that Michel Angelo plays with his name, as Shakespeare plays with the name of Willie Hughes" (66). Along these lines, Wilde's readers supply Shakespeare's sonnets with a referent so as to explain, rather than explain away, their very evident queer eroticism. Loesberg suggests that *The Portrait of Mr. W. H.* thus models a "method of perverse formalist reading" that "shows how private fixations can become public meanings and how queer desire can become a work's constitutive literary element."[18] That is, Wilde's novella forges an erotic formalism out of its refusal to divest figurative language of intentionality.

The queer formalist reading in *Portrait of Mr. W. H.* bears out Deidre Lynch's recent observation that the affective labor of loving has long lodged ambivalently at the core of literary studies. Surveying the emergence of the modern understanding of literature during the long eighteenth century, Lynch's *Loving Literature* provides a genealogy of close reading, with its tendency to approach the text as if it were a kind of person. Lynch traces the origin of this understanding of the text back to eighteenth-century readers who came to see "their intensely felt transactions with their reading matter . . . as the locus of ethical transactions whose essence was human contact."[19] Lynch shows us, that is, how reading began to seem like touching another person, so that studying literature demanded that one also somehow love literature. The role of touch here—the way the essence of loving literature seems to be human contact—has clear affinities with the way the theories of perception tracked in this book led writers to envision reading as a practice of becoming intimate with the world. When compared with perceiving, there are, of course, limits to the intimacy reading affords. The back of a tomato is "present as absent, but available to perception through appropriate movement" (Noë, 58) in a way that, to even the closest reading, Willie Hughes is not. Reading and perceiving involve different degrees of presence, different distances and pathways we must travel through a connecting world to become acquainted with (or get closer to acquaintance with) their objects.

The obstacle for the characters in *The Portrait of Mr. W. H.* is that those paths through a connecting world do not exist. There are no records, no descriptive accounts of him outside the sonnets themselves. Loesberg suggests that the absence of that extratextual evidence marks the difference between a historical claim that requires objective accuracy and a formalist claim that simply has to convincingly account for the text. The Willie Hughes theory works as a formalist reading as long as it satisfactorily explains the sonnets, regardless of whether the historical Willie Hughes actually existed. But there are other ways that the Willie Hughes reading could be objectively accurate even if his existence is not a verifiable historical fact.

Willie Hughes belongs to what chapter 2 described as the extended realm of entities common to fictional characters, perceptual illusions, and forgeries; he is semiveridical. Neither a star nor Willie Hughes is available for perceptual exploration in the way of the tomato right in front of you. Even so, Willie Hughes makes aspects of the world present to readers of the sonnets by virtue of the way he involves them in different routes through the connecting world. Belief in Willie Hughes involves Wilde's unnamed narrator in an unexpectedly dense (Ablow calls it "impossibly dull") course of reading on Renaissance-era Neoplatonism and its relationship with the history of pederastic friendships in Greece and early modern Europe, as well as on the history of Elizabethan theatrical practices, especially of the boy actors who played female roles.[20] The narrator recounts this intellectual and cultural history using the same descriptive style that Wilde would shortly employ to describe Dorian Gray's collections of aesthetic objects in *The Picture of Dorian Gray.* All this reading climaxes in a moment of intense anamnesis, in which the narrator seems himself to have lived the experiences recounted in his reading of the sonnets. There is much to be said about this moment of anamnesis and its relationship to Wilde's aesthetic philosophy as well as to late Victorian understandings of queer desire. What I want to note here, though, is that it is also the moment in the novella where description begins to yield something like knowledge by acquaintance: "As I read and re-read [the sonnets] in garden or chamber, it seemed to me that . . . Art, as so often happens, had come to take the place of personal experience" (91).

Seen one way, the description of Willie Hughes in *The Portrait of Mr. W. H.* has all the excessive thickness of Pater's description of *La Gioconda,* a thickness all the more noticeable for the fact that La Gioconda was a real person and Willie Hughes merely a fictional one. In this light, the nagging resemblance between the narrator's historicism and our own lends credibility to Heather Love's charge that the literary critical preoccupation with absence led new historicists, like the aesthetes before them, to lose touch with the hard, material surfaces of life, focusing their own thick descriptions on "what is not there, rather than what is" ("Close Reading and Thin Description," 427).

New postcritical variations on literary studies such as Love's thin description aim to redirect our attention to what is there, to observable reality and to the surfaces of texts as opposed to the hidden depths supposedly sought by suspicious or symptomatic readings in the grip of a paranoid impulse to expose the powerful forces arrayed just out of view. That impulse to expose the ruses of power gave critique a clear political mandate, however, where postcritical work has at times seemed, even to its practitioners, to acquiesce too much to the way things are. When the choice is framed this way, literary studies faces the kind of predicament dramatized by Hardy's *Return of the Native,* where Eustacia's rebelliousness against a patriarchal authority leads her to see deeply into things but also to misrecognize them while Thomasin sees things clearly but at the cost of a docility that prevents her from aspiring to the transformative power of critique.

In the recent debates about method, literary studies thus finds itself presented with two alternatives that, in different ways, are both circumscribed by the dichotomy between signs and objects ratified by early twentieth-century formalism. Under the influence of post-structuralism, politically ambitious projects of critique have often tended to deepen that dichotomy. That widened gulf has afforded those projects the means of revealing the apparently natural objects of our experience as the contingent effects of an illicit mistaking of language for the world. For post-structuralists like Paul de Man, such confusion is nothing less than ideology itself.[21] In contrast, postcritical and descriptive methods must bridge the gap between signs and other objects before their claims about literary texts can have empirical or scientific purchase. Even so, that dichotomy reappears in the form of a fundamental ambiguity in the way surface reading and thin description construe what is there and what is not there when we read.

What is there when we read is both less (when conceived of as the stimulus, the letters on the page) and more (when conceived of as the background skills and knowledge required to see letters as letters in the first place) than advocates of surface reading and thin description have allowed. The way reading weaves together what is actually present with what is virtually present made it a master metaphor for nineteenth-century perception science. When they encountered that science, Victorian literary writers experimented with ways that its core insight about the complex perceptual presence of letters and words might scale up to the larger figures populating literary texts—characters, authors, tropes, and so on. Willie Hughes is one such complex figural presence. As an erotic object, Willie Hughes incites the sonnets' readers to follow the descriptive pathways that bring them closer to the early modern lifeworld of which Shakespeare's sonnets were part. Just as the Holy Mother embodied by Romola was a perceptual illusion that nonetheless secured her observers' greater involvement in the world, the importance of Willie Hughes lies in the way he facilitates the reader's being there, even while he is not, in any straightforward sense, there himself.

Wilde's novella, then, asks us to think about reading literature in terms of what Noë calls different perceptual styles of access to the world. Thinking about literature as a style of access to the world can, I suggest, move us beyond the dichotomy between signs and objects. On this understanding, literature is not defined by its separateness from objects but rather by the connective pathways it affords to other things in the world. To give due attention to those connective pathways would unavoidably commit literary studies to a certain thickness in its accounts of literary texts. As Jonathan Kramnick notes, adding complicating variables to its objects by tracing out their unexpected connections is a core feature of literary studies.[22] Hence the ready home that thick description found in our discipline in the first place. I am convinced by Love's argument that thick descriptions in literary studies have tended to try to go without the fundamental layer of observable reality indispensable to that method in the social sciences ("Close Reading and Thin Description," 410). The root of the problem, though, seems to me to be found not in thick description itself as a literary critical method (which would thus necessitate a corrective change of course to thin description), so much as in the severing of language from its intentional objects that founded modern literary studies. Restore those cut ties, and literature's canniness in apprehending webs of significance can more meaningfully contribute to genuinely interdisciplinary efforts to understand and explain the world.

Now, as in the nineteenth century, literature models for us the complex forms of presence the world can take in our experience. One of the important lessons the Victorian literary encounter with perception science might hold for us is that there are good epistemological reasons to oppose austerity as a methodology as well as a policy in our political economy. We should not need to starve ourselves, much less to die, in order to know. Like James when he radicalized empiricism, Victorian literary writers came to understand reading and perception as experiences of irreducible complexity. The objects of our direct acquaintance—the sensation, the statue, the painting, the building, the landscape—as well as those we know by description—the character, the author, the word, the sentence, the trope—all bristle with a fringe of relations that lead outward to other objects of experience. Reading intentionally is not a mistake or an ideology but rather a corollary of the most basic processes involved in reading as a perceptual act. When we read as when we perceive, we are always in the midst of things, always directed toward the world. In enticing us to recognize this fundamental fact, Victorian literature affords us a perceptual understanding of perception itself and points us toward a justification of literary studies that is, perhaps, clarifying in its simplicity: literary studies matters because it offers us styles of understanding the world in which both literature and its readers are entangled.

GLOSSARY OF SELECTED SCIENTIFIC AND TECHNICAL TERMS

acquaintance, knowledge by An epistemological category first proposed in the 1860s for the kind of knowledge obtained by the presentation of a thing to the senses. The category is an approximate English translation of the verbs in many other European languages denoting something like "to be acquainted with" (*connaître, kennen,* and so on).

association The mental process whereby one idea or sensation brings to mind others on the basis of resemblance, contiguity in experience, or contrast. Association was supposed to explain how the mind perceives a stable world of objects even as the sense data it uses to do so is unstable and fragmentary (the phenomenon that is today referred to as perceptual constancy).

description, knowledge by The compliment to knowledge by acquaintance, this epistemological category signified the kind of knowledge obtained through a propositional account. To know something by description is an English-language version of verbs signifying more formal ways of knowing (*savoir, wissen,* and so on).

intentionality The direction or reference toward an object that defines mental states as opposed to physical ones.

local signs The specific quality of a sensation produced by the particular location of the stimulated nerve within a sensory organ and/or the nervous system more broadly. The theory of local signs was the cornerstone of empiricist theories of the visual perception of space in the nineteenth century. According to these theories, we learn to see spatially by coordinating the local signs deriving from where on the eye a stimulus falls and which muscular movements will change the location of that visual stimulus.

unconscious inference The logical process performed reflexively by the mind in which a given sensation forms the minor premise of a syllogism whose major premise comprises prior sensory experience. Unconscious inference was supposed to allow the mind to infer spatial location (by reading local signs) and the presence of recognizable objects from sense data.

NOTES

Introduction

1. Of course, you might not be reading this with your eyes. I address questions of disability (particularly blindness) and its effects on reading in chapter 3.
2. See Sherrington, *The Integrative Action of the Nervous System*, 129–32.
3. I borrow the term "grip" as a description of how we visually perceive words from Alva Noë's *The Varieties of Presence*, 10. Further citations will be incorporated parenthetically. Vision has often been understood as having a particularly intimate relation with touch since George Berkeley's *Essay Towards a New Theory of Vision* appeared in 1709. Later accounts of vision in the nineteenth and twentieth centuries, however, revised Berkeley's argument by stressing that visual perception synthesizes visual sensations not with those of touch but rather with the feelings of muscular exertion and bodily position. Hence grip better reflects what we are doing when we see.
4. The currently dominant theory in psychology is that there are two "routes" for reading: a direct lexical route that involves only visual perception and a phonological route that detours through a phonetic recoding of the written sign. For an overview, see Dehaene, *Reading in the Brain*, 25–31. For a more detailed discussion, see Kennedy et al., *Reading as a Perceptual Process*, 377–490.
5. Scarry, *Dreaming by the Book*, 5.
6. An important exception here is Paul Armstrong's recent work on neuroscience and literature. See Armstrong, *How Literature Plays with the Brain*, 26–53.
7. I think the sense in which literary criticism understands reading as a technology of perception can be broadly characterized in the terms set forth by Martin Heidegger in *The Question Concerning Technology*. Heidegger there emphasizes the etymological connection between technology (from the Greek root *technē*) and poetry; both, he contends, originally name ways of making something present. See *The Question Concerning Technology*, 10–12.
8. Reading thus seems subject to the dilemma that Heidegger famously saw as bedeviling all tool work: we can either use tools or be aware of them but never both at the same time. When we have our tools in hand to work with them, they cease to be present to thought. They can only become really present to thought when they break so that the

flow of work is broken or when we stand back to contemplate them independently of our immediate needs.

9. Best and Marcus's account of deep or symptomatic reading owes much to Eve Sedgwick's "Paranoid Reading and Reparative Reading." In retrospect, Sedgwick's essay marks the moment that literary criticism began a so-far unfinished major reassessment of its methods.
10. Best and Marcus, "Surface Reading," 9. Best and Marcus's polemic in favor of surface reading generated considerable controversy, and this method has been rigorously criticized for its apparent political quietism.
11. The scientific aspirations driving the turn to description are evident from the subsequent 2016 special issue of *Representations* on description that Marcus and Best coedited together with Heather Love: in contrast to the exclusively literary critical focus of their earlier issue on surface reading, this one put together essays in literary studies with essays in anthropology, psychology, and the history of science. Of course, this would not be the first time description has brought together literary criticism and social science. The New Historicism famously drew its own reading methods from the thick description advocated by the anthropologist Clifford Geertz. Geertz's thick description, though, is a method for supplementing direct observations with attention to the larger semiotic structures of meaning that make up a culture; in effect, thick description makes direct observation more like reading. The new description, Heather Love has remarked, instead aims to make reading more like direct observation. See Love, "Close Reading and Thin Description," 404. Further citations will be incorporated parenthetically in the text.
12. Latour, *Reassembling the Social,* 117; italics in original.
13. Shklovsky, *Theory of Prose,* 3, 6. Further citations will be incorporated parenthetically. Shklovsky contrasts this enlivened, defamiliarized mode of perception with how we perceive under normal circumstances, when habit and routine in the service of mental economy slowly drain away our attention to the felt qualities of things until all that is left are absentminded recognitions standing in for a once vividly experienced world.
14. Marcus, Love, and Best, "Building a Better Description," 14; italics in original.
15. This philosophical tradition of defining aesthetic experience as disinterested begins with Immanuel Kant's account of the judgment of the beautiful in the third critique. See Kant, *The Critique of the Power of Judgment,* 89–96.
16. Daston and Galison, *Objectivity,* 203, 241.
17. Levine, *Dying to Know,* 2.
18. Indeed, Jameson sometimes casts the antinomies of affect in terms of the scientific distinction between sensation and perception, as when he notes that "perception is . . . a rationalization of the sensory and its expression a codified form of rhetoric under the rubric of description." See Jameson, *Antinomies of Realism,* 47.
19. Kramnick, "An Aesthetics and Ecology of Presence," 315.
20. For a detailed account, see Jackson, *Science and Sensation in Romantic Poetry.*
21. See Jones, "Theories of Language in the Eighteenth Century."
22. See Ahmed, *Archaeology of Babel,* 1–49. Ahmed argues that such textualization was substantially driven by the administrative needs of colonial governance, and that therefore philology should be understood as a technology of empire.

23. Wordsworth, "Lines Written a Few Miles above Tintern Abbey," in *William Wordsworth,* 134. Further citations will be incorporated parenthetically.
24. Beer, *Darwin's Plots,* 6.
25. Favret, "The Pathos of Reading," 1318–19.
26. Rancière, *The Politics of Literature,* 4.
27. Rancière, *The Politics of Literature,* 7.
28. Examples here are numerous but for one that tracks closely with the epistemological tension between description and direct acquaintance at the center of this book, see Pond, "Harriet Martineau's Epistemology of Gossip," on the relationship between empiricism and gossip as a feminized form of discursive access to the world in Harriet Martineau's work.
29. Rachel Ablow has collected essays representing many of these approaches in *The Feeling of Reading.*

1. Knowing Things by Description in Victorian Science

1. Morgan, "Critical Empathy," 31.
2. Dames, *The Physiology of the Novel,* 39.
3. Gibson, *The Senses Considered as Perceptual Systems,* 306.
4. See Locke, *An Essay Concerning Human Understanding,* 119.
5. See Hartley, *Observations on Man,* 65–84.
6. Reid, *An Inquiry into the Human Mind on the Principles of Common Sense,* 289. Further citations will be incorporated parenthetically.
7. Brentano, *Psychology from an Empirical Standpoint,* 88. It is worth noting that despite their aims (like Reid, Brentano wanted to sharpen the distinction between physiological responses and mental states) Brentano seems unaware of just how important Reid was in making his own work possible. He only cites Reid's later books and so perhaps he never read his *Inquiry into the Human Mind.*
8. See Reed, *From Soul to Mind,* 26. Further citations will be incorporated parenthetically.
9. Bacon, *The New Organon,* 36. For a detailed discussion of Whewell's attempt to renovate Baconian induction, see Snyder, *Reforming Philosophy,* 33–155.
10. Snyder notes that Whewell's reading of Reid and his followers (particularly Dugald Stewart) preceded his reading of Kant and was likely to have been his first encounter with critiques of empiricism and the "sensationalist school." See Snyder, *Reforming Philosophy,* 46.
11. Whewell, *The Philosophy of the Inductive Sciences,* 36. Further citations will be incorporated parenthetically.
12. For "ideas" here, we should read perceptions. In the service of his own critique of Locke, Whewell frequently refers to perceptions with the Lockean terminology of "ideas," but he defines sensations in opposition to ideas. In that regard, Whewell's argument remains within the framework Reid established.
13. Duncan, "George Eliot's Science Fiction," 16.
14. Whewell was not the straightforward follower of Kant that Mill took him to be. For a detailed account of the Mill's attack on Whewell, see Snyder, *Reforming Philosophy,* 95–155.

15. Mill, *A System of Logic*, 420.
16. Helmholtz, "The Facts in Perception," in *Science and Culture*, 355. Further citations will be incorporated parenthetically.
17. For an overview of Helmholtz's understanding of unconscious inference in light of his conflict with Kantian idealism, see Hatfield, *The Natural and the Normative*, 195–208. I discuss Helmholtz's theory of spatial perception in more detail in chapter 2.
18. Helmholtz, "The Recent Progress of the Theory of Vision," in *Science and Culture*, 201. See also 176–77.
19. Helmholtz, *Treatise on Physiological Optics*, 3:8. Further citations will be incorporated parenthetically.
20. See Reid, *Essay on the Intellectual Powers of Man*, 32.
21. In this regard, he steadfastly defended his mentor Johannes Müller's so-called law of specific nerve energies—the principle that sensory qualities derive from the anatomy of the nerves and not from any inherent property in the forces stimulating them.
22. Crary, *Suspensions of Perception*, 321. The disjunction between epistemology and ontology in Helmholtz's work is one instance of a broader problem that Quentin Meillassoux diagnoses in philosophy after Kant, when, in his telling, philosophers began to append a tacit "for us" to any scientific statement about the world. In *After Finitude*, Meillassoux proposes to bypass the problem of the empirical observer altogether by modeling a descriptive formal language on mathematics. In contrast to ordinary language in which meaning is determined by a community of speakers, numbers derive their significance purely from the logical consistency of the system of which they are part. Mathematical language is therefore maximally independent of its users. As Devin Griffiths notes in his critique of Meillassoux, the supposed purity of ontological statements in a formalized language "comes at the cost of greater semantic *distance* from the world." Griffiths, *The Age of Analogy*, 43; italics in original. In other words, Meillassoux's turn to mathematics does not offer resources for thinking beyond the jarring divide (between epistemology and ontology) in work like that of Helmholtz, but rather accepts that divide as given and irreparable.
23. As Edward Reed puts it, Victorian empiricists "had to offer an account of these truths of inference that differed from their account of truths of intuition (sensation)" (133).
24. I take the term "theater of consciousness" here from James Gibson's *Ecological Approach to Visual Perception*. Daniel Dennett has also memorably described this model of the perceiving mind as "the Cartesian theater." See Gibson, *Ecological Approach to Visual Perception*, 256; and Dennett, *Consciousness Explained*, 101–38.
25. For instance, David Marr's landmark 1979 study, *Vision*, approaches its subject using the same kind of dualistic framework developed by scientists following Reid: "The study of vision . . . must include not only the study of how to extract from images the various aspects of the world that are useful to us, but also an inquiry into the nature of the internal representations by which we capture this information and thus make it available as a basis for decisions about our thoughts and actions," Marr, *Vision*, 3. For a reading that traces the assumptions of Marr (and, implicitly, the Victorians) back to the representationalism of the eighteenth-century empiricists, see Kramnick, "An Aesthetics and Ecology of Presence," 66–68.
26. James, *The Principles of Psychology*, 2:2. Further citations will be incorporated parenthetically.

27. In stating this "law of figured consciousness," James's argument resembles twentieth-century gestalt psychology, which likewise claimed that perceptual figures are primary in our experience (2:82–83).
28. James, "Does 'Consciousness' Exist?," in *William James*, 1154.
29. For a discussion of James's understanding of experience as a complex unity and the more robust empiricism it pointed to for later philosophers, see Meyer, "Of 'Experiential Togetherness,'" 332–359. James's radicalization of empiricism reflects wider scientific currents following the probabilistic revolution of the mid-nineteenth century, when developments in physics and statistical modeling led scientists to reconceptualize matter in terms of "ensemble[s] of possible interconnections between individual things, actions, and locations at a given moment." See Tondre, *The Physics of Possibility*, 23.
30. James, "A World of Pure Experience," in *William James*, 1173; italics in original.
31. Levine's interest centers on forms as portable patterns of arrangement that retain their basic features across different social contexts, and perhaps for that reason she takes the concept of affordances from work in design theory (which adapted it from Gibson). See Levine, *Forms*, 6.
32. Gibson, *The Ecological Approach to Visual Perception*, 139. Further citations will be incorporated parenthetically.
33. In support of her call for thin description in literary studies, Heather Love thus cites Bruno Latour's exhortation of social scientists to emulate literary authors: "Those in anthropology, sociology, cultural studies—who pride themselves on 'writing fictional narratives'—should be inspired in being at least as disciplined, as enslaved by reality, as obsessed by textual quality, as good writers can be." Latour, *Reassembling the Social*, 126; see also Love, "Close Reading and Thin Description," 428.
34. James, "The Tigers in India," in *William James*, 854.
35. Gallagher and Greenblatt, *Practicing New Historicism*, 9.
36. James, "The Tigers in India," 854.
37. See Barthes, *The Rustle of Language*, 148; italics in original.
38. Freedgood and Schmitt, "Denotatively, Technically, Literally," 11. Further citations will be incorporated parenthetically.
39. Freedgood, *The Ideas in Things*, 14.
40. See Griffiths, *Age of Analogy*, 27–50. It is worth noting that Griffiths characterizes this mode of analogy with an analogy of his own, comparing it to the perceptual experience of harmony. I discuss Victorian perceptual theories of harmony in detail in chapter 5.

2. Getting Acquainted with Description in *Romola*

1. Lukács, "Narrate or Describe?," 130.
2. Goodlad and Sartori, "The Ends of History," 605.
3. See Love, "Close Reading and Thin Description" 403, 407, 415. The interplay between image and historical or narrative context is one of the main preoccupations in Sontag, *Regarding the Pain of Others*.
4. Pearl Brilmyer highlights the importance of these changing circumstances for Eliot's understanding of characters, arguing that her descriptive techniques treat literary

characters as plastic "material-semiotic figures" that are shaped and reshaped by what they encounter. Brilmyer, "Plasticity, Form, and the Matter of Character in *Middlemarch*," 78.

5. Grote, *Exploratio Philosophica*, 60.
6. For Lukács, the classical historical novel is the prototype for nineteenth-century realism more broadly. The historical novel's eventual development into a specific genre of realism marks all by itself the problem with what he termed the bourgeois realism of post-1848 Europe—that realism had ceased to aim at generating historical self-understanding.
7. Lukács, *The Historical Novel*, 189. Further citations will be incorporated parenthetically.
8. For a critique of Lukács's neglect of women writers' work with the historical novel, see Wallace, *The Woman's Historical Novel*, 8–15.
9. Graham Law reports that the number of *Cornhill* subscribers fell steadily from seventy thousand when the magazine first appeared in 1860 to fifty thousand in 1863 by the time *Romola* had finished its run. Even if it didn't give subscriptions the boost Smith was looking for, *Romola* was clearly not responsible for this decline—*Cornhill* continued to hemorrhage subscribers throughout the 1860s. See Law, *Serializing Fiction in the Victorian Press*, 24–25.
10. *The George Eliot Letters*, 4:49. Italics in original.
11. See Carroll, *George Eliot*, 195–96.
12. James, "The Life of George Eliot," 675.
13. James, "Review: *Middlemarch*," 424.
14. "Current Literature: *Romola*," 29.
15. "Recent Works of Fiction—*Romola*," 457.
16. Kurnick, "Abstraction and the Subject of Novel Reading," 492.
17. Eliot, *Romola*, 400. Further citations will be incorporated parenthetically.
18. Eliot's reading in the early 1860s suggests that names were much on her mind. The *Quarry for Romola* includes a long note Eliot made from Ludovico Muratori's history of the introduction of surnames in Italy during the tenth and eleventh centuries. In January 1862, just as she was beginning *Romola*, Eliot began enthusiastically reading Max Müller's then newly published *Lectures on the Science of Language* with G. H. Lewes, who then went on to address Müller's account of the formation of names at length in his review for *Blackwood's*. See Eliot, "George Eliot's *Quarry for Romola*," 15–16; and Lewes, "A Box of Books," 436–44.
19. Mill, *A System of Logic*, 19.
20. See Kripke, *Naming and Necessity*, 26, 127–28.
21. In contrast to Mill, Kripke argues that both proper and common names are rigid designators. Putnam's account of reference likewise declines to place much trust in the thoughtfulness of individual speakers. Concerned exclusively with common nouns (as opposed to proper names), Putnam strips Mill's connoted attributes down to a bare minimum he calls a stereotype—a lazy impression of what kinds of objects a name refers to that is just good enough to allow a speaker to communicate with others. Stereotypes underpin such baseline linguistic competence, but they are not comprehensive enough to fix a reference. For that, we need experts, a special subclass of speakers whose business it is to keep our linguistic classifications sharp by investigating the

various objects names refer to. So, Putnam observes, most of us know only that gold is a yellow metal, but we refer to it correctly (most of the time) because we defer to the chemists, jewelers, and others who have developed better methods of recognizing it. Putnam thus proposes a "division of linguistic labor" that, for laymen at least, radically empties out names of their descriptive connotations. See Putnam, *Mind, Language, and Reality,* 227–28.

22. I have not counted myself and am relying on the estimate given by Andrew Brown, editor of the Oxford's World Classics *Romola* (549).
23. See Woloch, *The One vs. the Many,* 14–21.
24. Frazer, *Pausanias and Other Greek Sketches,* 21.
25. Searle, "Proper Names."
26. Dames, *Amnesiac Selves,* 216. In Dames's account, Baldassare's peculiar form of amnesia indexes Eliot's paradoxical project of transforming historical memory into a nostalgia in considerable tension with the kind of textual and historical research fundamental to the historical novel and particularly to the overresearched *Romola* itself.
27. See *The Journals of George Eliot,* 107.
28. Müller, "On the Fantastic Apparitions of Vision," 237.
29. Müller, *Elements of Physiology,* 2:1079. Further citations will be incorporated parenthetically.
30. For Lotze's account of local signs, see his *Microcosmus,* 309–10. Lotze did not reject nativism absolutely, although he was less nativist than Müller. For a discussion of Lotze's theory, see Hatfield, *The Natural and the Normative,* 158–63. Helmholtz gives his fullest account of local signs in his *Treatise on Physiological Optics,* vol. 3.
31. For an overview of how Helmholtz drew from Müller as well as the ways their theories of vision and space differed, see Lenoir, "The Eye as Mathematician."
32. On the muscle sense, see Smith, "'The Sixth Sense.'" The role of the muscle sense is where Helmholtz's account of spatial perception departs fundamentally from George Berkeley's classic *Essay Towards a New Theory of Vision,* which suggests that sight and touch are the two senses through which we learn to perceive space.
33. Helmholtz, "Recent Progress in the Theory of Vision," in *Science and Culture,* 198. Further citations will be incorporated parenthetically.
34. Lewes, *Problems of Life and Mind,* 163. Further citations will be incorporated parenthetically.
35. Müller adduces the etymology of logos in order to argue that the primary function of names is to gather "single impressions under one general conception." See Müller, *Lectures on the Science of Language,* 2:71–72.
36. Eliot, "The Natural History of German Life," in *Essays of George Eliot,* 271.
37. Frege, "On Sense and Reference," 37. Further citations will be incorporated parenthetically.
38. Russell, "On Denoting," 483. Further citations will be incorporated parenthetically.
39. See Frege, "On Sense and Reference," 48; and Russell, "On Denoting," 484.
40. Russell, *The Problems of Philosophy,* 58; italics in original. Further citations will be incorporated parenthetically.
41. Compare Lewes, who makes an argument similar to Russell here only to point out the impossibility of distinguishing in experience between what we know by description

and what we know by acquaintance: "We cannot resist belief in a sensation, though we may doubt any of the inferences it awakens . . . but in point of fact pure Observation—i.e. sensation wholly unmingled with Inference—is impossible" (157).

42. See Eames, *Bertrand Russell's Dialogue with His Contemporaries*, 113.
43. For an example, see Chalmers, *The Character of Consciousness*, 284–95.
44. Latour, *Reassembling the Social*, 144.
45. Kripke, *Reference and Existence*, 79. Further citations will be incorporated parenthetically.
46. See Noë, *Varieties of Presence*, 47–73. Noë never explicitly says so, but he does sometimes strongly suggest that he thinks of this kind of sensorimotor understanding as something like knowledge by acquaintance: "To perceive something, you must understand it, and to understand it you must, in a way, already know it, you must have already made its acquaintance" (20). Noë's version of knowledge by acquaintance differs crucially from the way Helmholtz understood it, however, because Helmholtz modeled his account of sensorimotor understanding on propositional logic, whereas Noë contends that we should instead think about propositional knowledge in terms of sensorimotor understanding (see, for instance, 25–29, 65–66). Noë's empiricism is radical, in other words.
47. See Auyoung, "Phantoms and Fictional Characters," 403–4.
48. In his polemical attack on Russell's sense-datum theory of perception, J. L. Austin cautions against conflating illusions and hallucinations. In cases of illusion, we are seeing something erroneously, whereas in hallucinations we see something conjured up, something that has no material presence. See Austin, *Sense and Sensibilia*, 24–25. As we saw when discussing Müller's work on visions, however, hallucinations are typically conjured up *out of* something that is present, and in this regard they differ from illusions in degree rather than kind. Noë for this reason doubts the existence of so-called perfect hallucinations (see *Varieties of Presence*, 43–44).
49. It was through this process that nineteenth-century astronomers discovered the "personal equation"—split-second differences in individual observers' visual perception of when an astronomical event occurs. Such tiny differences could dramatically change astronomical calculations and so became a widespread preoccupation in astronomy and ultimately contributed to early experimental psychology's fascination with clocking the speed of perception. See Canales, *A Tenth of a Second*, 21–58.
50. Henchman, *The Starry Sky Within*, 15.
51. Eliot, *Adam Bede*, 5.
52. Gallagher, "The Rise of Fictionality," 340.
53. Gallagher, "George Eliot," 66; italics in original. Further citations will be incorporated parenthetically.
54. For this reason, Kripke suggests that his analogy between fictional characters and nonveridical perceptions actually works best with historical fiction: "Napoleon [as presented in a story] has out-and-out predicates that really apply to him historically, but some things are true of him only in the sense that they are ascribed to him in a story. Here the star has its out-and-out properties as an astronomical object, but also its properties (analogous to those of Napoleon in a story) as it appears to us visually" (98–99).

55. Griffiths, *The Age of Analogy*, 111. Making a similar argument about the fictional characters in historical novels, Griffiths compares them to well-wrought forgeries in that both tend to "collapse the distance between the imitation and the original." See Griffiths, *The Age of Analogy*, 103–10, 121.
56. Gallagher makes a similar observation about the peculiar truth claims of the historical novel when she observes that historical characters are at once historical and fictional: "When reading historical novels, we make a distinction between the fictional bits, the moments of novelistic characterization that convey judgments and opinions, which seem to come to us in the *subjunctive* voice, and the historical parts, representing the established facts that are under interpretation. Tolstoy's Napoleon may be said, therefore, to have a fictional character, even though the totality of his persona in *War and Peace* is not fictional because it must obey a rule of noncontradiction with the Emperor's personal history." See Gallagher, "What Would Napoleon Do?," 321.
57. Burckhardt, *Civilization of the Renaissance in Italy*, 541–50. Further citations will be incorporated parenthetically.
58. *The George Eliot Letters*, 6:25.
59. If satisfying the expectations raised by the name "George Eliot" weren't enough, Eliot would have picked up a similar lesson in another novel that she was reading while working on *Romola*. She and Lewes began reading Wilkie Collins's *No Name* together when it started running in *All the Year Round* in March 1862 (Lewes describes *No Name* as "rather dreary" in a letter to his son in May—see *The George Eliot Letters*, 4:32). The protagonist of *No Name* is one Magdalen Vanstone, whom Collins introduces as cheerful and prosperous in a way that defies her given name's connotations: "Magdalen! . . . Surely, the grand old Bible name—suggestive of a sad and sombre dignity; recalling, in its first association, mournful ideas of penitence and seclusion—had been here . . . inappropriately bestowed?" As the novel turns out, the answer to this question is both yes and no. Magdalen is secretly illegitimate and thus loses her legal right to her name after her parents die unexpectedly. However, in the course of her desperate and (in the novel's terms) morally dubious efforts to reclaim her birthright and her subsequent penitence, she not only gets her name back in the end but also more fully embodies it by finally conforming to the connotations with which she was initially at odds. See Collins, *No Name*, 9.
60. In a dazzling recent reading of *Middlemarch* and *Daniel Deronda*, Ian Duncan shows how Eliot's scientific and technical terms oscillate between literal and figurative registers, but in *Romola* neither of those registers seem to be working well. See Duncan, "George Eliot's Science Fiction," 15–39.
61. Dames, *Amnesiac Selves*, 231.
62. Wright, "George Eliot's Vagueness," 645.
63. Feuerbach, *The Essence of Christianity*, 12.
64. Eliot's interest in *Romola* in exploring the way that visions entangle belief and doubt is, I would suggest, why the novel seems to lend itself to recent critical debates around the hermeneutics of suspicion. See, for example, Reilly, "Always Sympathize!," 629–46.
65. See Kurnick, "Abstraction and the Subject of Novel Reading," 490–91.
66. Eliot, *Middlemarch*, 4.

3. Reading in the Dark

1. Hardy, *The Life and Work of Thomas Hardy*, 259. Further citations will be incorporated parenthetically.
2. Dale Kramer, for example, cites the note as evidence for his claim, in agreement with Hardy's biographers, that "it is quite likely that . . . Hardy dedicated himself to *Jude* with the idea that this would be his last novel, and with every intention of having his full say in defiance of the convention-ridden reviewers who refused his fictional characters the kind of sympathy and tolerance that in most cases they would have granted their personal acquaintances." Kramer, "Hardy and Readers," 165.
3. Hardy, *The Return of the Native*, 167. Further citations will be incorporated parenthetically.
4. Hardy's autobiography was originally presented as a biography written by his wife, Florence. Therefore, Hardy refers to himself in the third person throughout, except in the quoted personal notes.
5. Hardy's allegory of reading in *The Return of the Native* chimes with many of the arguments in Paul de Man's "The Rhetoric of Blindness." Like Hardy, de Man argues that reading is made possible by a form of blindness. For de Man, this blindness is a confused or mystified attribution of presence—of literal meaning or authorial intention—to a literary text, the language of which is defined first of all by its rhetoricity, its figurative mode and discontinuity with a grounding authorial consciousness. This blindness is not only inevitable (at least to an extent) but also enabling for the critical reader, who anchors her critical interpretations by composing an authorial intending subject standing behind the text. Thus the blindness of de Man's reader, like the blindness of Hardy's, operates partly through an uncritical act of prosopopoeia that nonetheless opens up the possibility of critical interpretive work. See de Man, *Blindness and Insight*, 102–41.
6. For a detailed account of Hardy's engagement with psychology, see Keen, *Thomas Hardy's Brains*.
7. The link between association and semiotics was made as early as David Hume's *Treatise*, in which Hume suggests that association is the mental operation underlying signification. See Hume, *A Treatise on Human Nature*, 64–65.
8. I take this phrase, of course, from Walter Pater's "Style," published in 1888, ten years after *The Return of the Native*. I use Pater's phrase despite its later publication because it encapsulates the notion of authorship that Hardy elaborates in his fiction and criticism. See Pater, *Appreciations*, 1–36.
9. The importance of vision in Hardy's novels and poems has been so thoroughly established in scholarly work that vision has come to seem almost identical to mind itself for Hardy criticism. J. B. Bullen's assertion that "the more clearly something is seen in [Hardy's] work, the more clearly it is understood" has been nuanced by Ruth Bernard Yeazell's recent exploration of light in Hardy's fiction, in which she observes that visual experience is complex and is illusory as often as it is revealing. Nonetheless, Yeazell still maintains that light, and by extension visual experience, is "the medium of subjectivity" in Hardy's novels. Anna Henchman's work on Hardy and Victorian astronomy, while likewise disputing the overemphasis on sight in earlier work on

Hardy, still privileges vision as the sine qua non of sensory perception generally. See Bullen, *The Expressive Eye,* 8; Yeazell, "The Lighting Design of Hardy's Novels," 75; and Henchman, "Hardy's Stargazers and the Astronomy of Other Minds," 37–64. See also Berger, *Thomas Hardy and Visual Structures.* Embodiment more broadly in Hardy's fiction has been analyzed in relation to work by Elaine Scarry and in relation to Deleuze and Guattari's theory of "faciality" by William Cohen. See Scarry, *Resisting Representation,* 49–90; and Cohen, *Embodied,* 86–107.

10. Hardy, "The Profitable Reading of Fiction," in *Life and Art,* 64.
11. In the preface to *The Dynasts,* for example, Hardy claims that the text assumes "a completion of the action by those to whom the drama is addressed" in "supplementary scenes of the imagination." Hardy, *The Dynasts,* viii.
12. See Miele, "'Their Interest and Habit,'" 156.
13. "On Competition amongst Architects," 66.
14. Hardy, "Memories of Church Restoration," in *Life and Art,* 103.
15. Freeman, *Principles of Church Restoration,* 7, 5.
16. On Morris and the continuing work of the SPAB, see Donovan, *William Morris and the Society for the Protection of Ancient Buildings.*
17. Morris, "The Manifesto of the Society for the Preservation of Ancient Buildings."
18. "St. Juliot Church Restoration," 6.
19. Hardy's notion of the associative sense as the basis for a social cohesiveness rooted in the past is decidedly a version of what Rick Rylance has termed the associationist romance. See Rylance, *Victorian Psychology and British Culture,* 66.
20. Alison, *Essay on the Nature and Principles of Taste,* 20. Further citations will be incorporated parenthetically.
21. Ruskin was by his own admission deeply susceptible to accidental associations himself: "Let the eye but rest on a rough piece of branch of curious form during a conversation with a friend, rest however unconsciously, and though the conversation be forgotten . . . yet the eye will, through the whole life after, take a certain pleasure in such boughs which it had not before, a pleasure so slight, a trace of feeling so delicate, as to leave us utterly unconscious of its peculiar power; but undestroyable by any reasoning, a part, thenceforward, of our constitution, destroyable only by the same arbitrary process of association by which it was created. . . . And there is probably no one opinion which is formed by any of us, in matters of taste, which is not in some degree influenced by unconscious association of this kind." Ruskin, *Modern Painters,* 2:37.
22. John Stuart Mill recognized the associationist elements of Ruskin's aesthetics more or less immediately. For two modern critical assessments, see Landow, *Aesthetic and Critical Theories of John Ruskin,* 89–110; and Helsinger, *Ruskin and the Art of the Beholder,* 184–85.
23. Teukolsky, *The Literate Eye,* 50. Teukolsky is particularly interested in the way Ruskin contradicts the rigorous formalism of *Modern Painters,* vol. 2, through descriptions of color perception in J. M. W. Turner's paintings that are grounded in associative chains of signification. See Teukolsky, 57–61.
24. John Ruskin, *The Seven Lamps of Architecture,* 53. Further citations will be incorporated parenthetically.

25. Hardy, "The Science of Fiction," in *Life and Art,* 89.
26. See Bain, *The Senses and the Intellect,* 512–23. Bain's account of similarity parallels arguments by William Whewell (see chapter 1) and Max Müller (see chapter 5) that likewise identify metaphor as fundamental to scientific reasoning.
27. See Rylance, *Victorian Psychology and British Culture,* 219.
28. See James, *The Principles of Psychology,* 2:345–60.
29. James's argument here is especially indebted to Shadworth Hodgson's *Time and Space,* which claims that "no object of representation remains long before consciousness in the same state, but fades, decays, and becomes indistinct. Those parts of the object, however, which possess an interest resist this tendency to gradual decay of the whole object. . . . This inequality in the object—some parts, the uninteresting, submitting to decay; others, the interesting parts, resisting it—when it has continued for a certain time, ends in becoming a new object." Hodgson, *Time and Space,* 266–67.
30. See Jakobson, "Two Aspects of Language," 113; and Freud, *The Interpretation of Dreams,* 35–73, 295–414.
31. Freedgood, *The Ideas in Things,* 13.
32. Hardy's description of authorship here and elsewhere as a process entailing the mutual transformation of self and world suggests that it should be understood as "work," as Scarry has described it in her reading of Hardy's novels. That is, as an embodied process of mutual expression, inscription, and immersion, fraught with ethical complexity and the potential for both benefit and grievous harm. While Scarry focuses on representations of physical labor in Hardy's novels, she notes that for Hardy these forms of creative labor were analogous to the creative labor of novel writing, and she suggests that the same analogy holds between the "reciprocal act of ventriloquism" constituting these forms of labor and literary interpretation itself. This article seeks to extend Scarry's reading by accounting for the specific dynamics and forms of embodiment and interpretive and ethical relationship that characterize reading and authorship for Hardy. See Scarry, *Resisting Representation,* 71.
33. Hardy's aesthetic progress narrative here is obviously indebted to G. W. F. Hegel's account of the transition in art from a serene classical period to a more self-conscious Romantic era. Classical art is serene, according to Hegel, because its artworks perfectly balance sensuous presence and idea, form and content, and are therefore self-sufficient and self-enclosed. In Romantic art, this harmonious balance has given way to a disjunction between form and content because the Idea has outgrown the possibility of adequate sensuous embodiment. Romantic artworks are therefore necessarily imperfect and gesture beyond and outside of themselves; in effect, they have become signs. Hardy, who would have encountered Hegel's argument through Pater's "Winckelmann" in *The Renaissance* (1873), articulates Hegelian art history with associationist psychology in his own theory of reading and aesthetics. See Hegel, *Aesthetics,* 517–28; and Pater, "Winckelmann," in *The Renaissance,* 141–85.
34. In his reading of this passage, Bullen attributes Hardy's northern ideal of "beauty in ugliness" to three sources: Hardy's personal responses to different landscapes, recorded in notes, letters, and diaries; a widespread Victorian fascination with the Arctic in the 1870s that had been stimulated by the Nares and Markham expedition to Greenland in 1876; and the art and art criticism (especially by Ruskin and Pater)

in which Hardy had taken a special interest at the time. While each of these sources undoubtedly influenced Hardy, this list is incomplete without an account of the associationist psychology through which Hardy theorized aesthetic response. Without this account, Bullen cannot adequately explain the distinction between orthodox beauty and associative beauty on which the other distinctions in this passage—between backward and advanced, South and North, and so forth—are founded. See Bullen, *The Expressive Eye*, 90–117 and 259–64.

35. Thomas Blacklock was not, in fact, born blind. He went blind as an infant after suffering from smallpox.
36. J. Hillis Miller notes the tacit identification of Mrs. Yeobright's comprehensiveness of view and that of Hardy himself, pointing out the similarities between her "comprehensiveness of . . . view" and the famous aerial perspectives from which events are often narrated in *The Dynasts*. Miller also assimilates this comprehensiveness of view to the excess of vision that blinds Clym. In Miller's account of the novel, however, blindness is a "punishment for seeing too well," an inevitable consequence of having the "Promethean temerity" to aspire to "sunlike . . . knowledge and broad vision." This knowledge blinds by revealing the inadequacy of any object of desire as a phallus, a figure covering over the lack—the "always-absent source of value"—that structures desire. While Miller's reading is suggestive, it cannot situate Mrs. Yeobright's figurative blindness in relation to the text's other moments of synesthetic, associative perception, and fails to recognize that blindness is not only a consequence and punishment but also a precondition for the type of comprehensive view attained by Mrs. Yeobright here. See Miller, *Topographies*, 43.
37. Saunderson appeared very frequently in Victorian writing on the blind. To take just one example, his is the concluding biographical sketch in Johns, *Blind People*, 174–80.
38. Locke, *An Essay Concerning Human Understanding*, 425.
39. "Blind Workers and Blind Helpers," 604.
40. Hardy, *Tess of the D'Urbervilles*, 265. Anna Henchman likewise underscores that enriched perception for Hardy's characters always requires a diminishment or bracketing of some sensory input. In Henchman's reading, this bracketing is analogous both to reading and to the procedures of astronomy, whose calculations of distance and motion similarly require that the misleading input of unreflective ways of seeing be ignored. See Henchman, "Hardy's Stargazers and the Astronomy of Other Minds," 45, 52–56.
41. Cohen, for example, elides the emotional listener in his reading of Eustacia's vigil as an instance of Hardy breaking down the distinction between an embodied human subject and the objective field of sensations. While I agree with many of Cohen's broader conclusions, I suggest that a focus on modes of embodied perception can more fully account for the representations of embodiment and the near obsession with faces in *The Return of the Native*. See Cohen, *Embodied*, 96–97.
42. Hardy, "The Profitable Reading of Fiction," in *Life and Art*, 61; Arnold, "The Study of Poetry," in *Essays in Criticism*, 281.
43. Arnold's most influential attempt to define criticism is, of course, *Culture and Anarchy*.
44. Hardy draws this parallel himself in his autobiography. See *Life and Work*, 57. For Ford's discussion of the importance of the substantial time Hardy spent in London to his life and writing, see *Thomas Hardy: Half a Londoner*.

45. Arnold, "The Function of Criticism at the Present Time," in *Essays in Criticism*, 1.
46. Hardy's claims about the way artists transform their perceptual objects are broadly representative of the continuing influence of the Romantic cult of genius on Victorian thinking about the arts. Compare Wilhelm Dilthey's 1887 essay "The Imagination of the Poet." One of Dilthey's main arguments is that in the poet's imagination, "images are transformed under the influence of feelings. They are shaped by [the poet's] emotions, just as the uncertain outlines of rocks and trees are transformed by the influence of a traveler in the woods at night." Dilthey, *Selected Works*, 95.
47. See Wimsatt and Beardsley, "The Affective Fallacy." Unlike Hardy, of course, the New Critics Wimsatt and Beardsley are not explicitly invested in an authorial consciousness whose intentions stand behind and ground the text.
48. Barthes, *S/Z*, 4.
49. See Warner, "Uncritical Reading."
50. See Sedgwick, *Touching Feeling*, 136–38.
51. See, for example, Felski, "After Suspicion."
52. Felski, *The Limits of Critique*, 110.
53. On reparative reading, see Sedgwick, *Touching Feeling*, 144–52; on just reading, see Marcus, *Between Women*, 3, 71–100; on surface reading, see Best and Marcus, "Surface Reading"; on postcritical reading, see Felski, *The Limits of Critique*, 171–82.
54. Here again, I follow Sedgwick, who suggested that reparative reading derives in significant part from the recognition that other people are fragile. See Ellis Hanson, "The Future's Eve."
55. In this respect, Eustacia reflects the contradictory meanings assigned to classical art and culture in late-Victorian Britain. Hellenism could be equivalent to an elegant but premodern sensualism, as in Hegel's art history or the passage in *The Return of the Native* that identifies "the Hellenic idea of life" with "the old-fashioned revelling in the general situation" (167). Or it could be equivalent to criticism itself, as in Arnold's definition of Hellenism as the free, spontaneous play of consciousness upon stock notions and habits. This ambivalence in Victorian thinking about Greek and Roman antiquity is, of course, especially crucial for Pater.
56. Ruskin, *Modern Painters*, 3:164.
57. Ibid., 3:167.

4. Tagging the Vatican Museum with Vernon Lee

1. Eliot, *Middlemarch*, 192–93.
2. See Merrills, "The Origins of 'Vandalism.'"
3. Compare Jonah Siegel: "The existence of the whole that is a museum requires a great many things to be broken." See Siegel, *The Emergence of the Modern Museum*, 4. On Victorian disenchantment with the museum, see also Siegel, *Desire and Excess*, 3–10.
4. Lee, *Belcaro*, 6. Further citations will be incorporated parenthetically.
5. Evangelista, "Vernon Lee in the Vatican," 34.
6. Siegel, "The Material of Form," 189–201.
7. Ibid., 195.
8. On the modernist dismissal of Lee, see Maxwell and Pulham, *Vernon Lee*, 2. On Lee and the New Critics, see Morgan, *The Outward Mind*, 242–50.

9. See Dames, *The Physiology of the Novel,* 176–90; and Morgan, *The Outward Mind,* 219–55.
10. See Siegel, *Emergence of the Modern Museum,* 100–101, 284.
11. Lee goes on to refute Hegel's art history by rejecting his argument that art is a vehicle for the Idea, defining it instead as form purely.
12. Ironically, this kind of reconstruction of paleontological animals from fossils itself depended on a biological theory that had just been overturned and so itself become a kind of historical fossil. See Dawson, *Show Me the Bone,* 211–42.
13. For an overview, see Paul, *The First Modern Museums of Art,* x–xix, 1–19.
14. See "Testimony before the Select Committee on the National Gallery (1853)," in Siegel, *Emergence of the Modern Museum,* 144, 153–54.
15. W. Stanley Jevons, "The Use and Abuse of Museums," in Siegel, *The Emergence of the Modern Museum,* 285. Further citations will be incorporated parenthetically.
16. See Yeazell, *Picture Titles,* 31–38.
17. See "Report of the Select Committee on National Monuments and Works of Art (1841)," in Siegel, *Emergence of the Modern Museum,* 93, 95, 105, 122–23.
18. See "Report of the Select Committee on Arts and Their Connexion with Manufactures (1836)," in Siegel, *Emergence of the Modern Museum,* 87.
19. Goode, "The Museums of the Future," 427.
20. Ibid.; italics in original.
21. Pater, *The Renaissance,* xix. Further citations will be incorporated parenthetically.
22. Colby, *Vernon Lee,* 56.
23. Yeazell, *Picture Titles,* 109.
24. Jackson, *Science and Sensation in Romantic Poetry,* 26.
25. So, Reid asks, "How do [sensations] constantly and invariably suggest the conception and belief of external objects, which exist whether they are perceived or not? No philosopher can give any other answer to this, but that such is the constitution of our nature." Reid, *Inquiry into the Human Mind,* 208.
26. For Bain's use of the concept, see *The Senses and the Intellect,* 318.
27. Jackson, *Science and Sensation,* 27.
28. Wilde, "The Critic as Artist," 240–41. Compare Basil's explanation of Dorian's suggestiveness in *The Picture of Dorian Gray:* "I see everything in him. He is never more present in my work than when no image of him is there. He is a suggestion. . . . I find him in the curves of certain lines, in the loveliness and subtleties of certain colours." Wilde, *The Picture of Dorian Gray,* 14.
29. Lee and Anstruther-Thomson, *Beauty and Ugliness,* 15. Further citations will be incorporated parenthetically.
30. Lee, *Juvenilia,* 1:46, 36, 37.
31. Colby, *Vernon Lee,* 58.
32. Henry James, to whom Lee dedicated the novel (much to his embarrassment), summed up the prevailing feeling when he wrote to her in a letter that "you have impregnated all those people too much with the sexual, the basely erotic preoccupation: your hand was too violent, the touch of life is lighter." 10 May 1885, cited in Zorn, *Vernon Lee,* 112.
33. "*Miss Brown*. By Vernon Lee," 20.
34. Lee, *Miss Brown,* 193. Further citations will be incorporated parenthetically.

35. Lee, *Euphorion*, 397.
36. Colby, for instance, suggests that Lee's account of courtly love likewise described her own passionate love for Mary Robinson. See Colby, *Vernon Lee*, 59. For Willis's remarks on Lee's sublimation of sex into aesthetics, see Ehnenn, *Women's Literary Collaboration, Queerness, and Late-Victorian Culture*, 70. Ehnenn likewise treats these claims skeptically, but her primary concern is with the way Lee's aesthetics entail a specifically lesbian subjectification, whereas my focus here is on the way that Lee's notion of chaste passion flattens aesthetic subjects in the service of a kind of masochistic objectivity.
37. See Zorn, *Vernon Lee*, 111–39.
38. Miller, *Versions of Pygmalion*, 3.
39. Jarvis, *Exquisite Masochism*, 14, x.
40. In *Juvenilia*, Lee estimates that free-standing statues on average present between twenty and twenty-five aspects (47–48).
41. Empathy is the English-language rendering (first proposed, coincidentally, by Pater's student, the psychologist E. B. Titchener) of the German word *Einfühlung*. The concept originates with Robert Vischer in the 1870s, but Lee's most important sources were Theodor Lipps and Karl Groos. See Vischer, "On the Optical Sense of Form," 89–123; and Titchener, *Lectures on the Experimental Psychology of the Thought-Processes*, 21. Benjamin Morgan provides a detailed account of empathy in *The Outward Mind*, 222–33.
42. Morgan, *The Outward Mind*, 227.
43. See Groos, *The Play of Man*, 331–32. In this example, Groos is actually quoting Lee and Anstruther-Thomson, who he thinks got a little carried away.
44. Morgan, "Critical Empathy," 34.
45. See the second section of chapter 1.
46. Lee, *The Beautiful*, 32; italics in original. Further citations will be incorporated parenthetically.
47. Compare this passage from *Beauty and Ugliness* that characterizes the perception of things explicitly in terms of reference: "This process is that of . . . naming; and it becomes an ever-shortened and more automatic act of guessing from a minimum of data at the real nature of the seen object and at our proper reactions towards its presence" (28).
48. See Morgan, "Critical Empathy," 33; and Morgan, *The Outward Mind*, 225–33.
49. See Cohn, *Still Life*, 1–29.
50. Lee, *The Handling of Words*, 136. Further citations will be incorporated parenthetically.
51. See Dames, *The Physiology of the Novel*, 176–90.
52. Noting that both Lee and Richards drew from psychology to develop their methods, Morgan points to a substantial difference in the fact that Richards's models were more cognitivist and brain based, while Lee's empathy was a specifically bodily experience. While I take his point here, I want to emphasize that empathy was a brain-based abstraction of bodily experience. In that regard, as in so many others, Lee is a transitional figure between the Victorians and the twentieth century. See Morgan, *The Outward Mind*, 245–46. For a more detailed account of the New Critical debt to psychology, see Gang, "Behaviorism and the Beginnings of Close Reading."

53. Morgan, *The Outward Mind,* 252.
54. Lee, *The Beautiful,* 76–77. For Keats's poem, see *'Bright Star,'* 239.

5. The Sense and Reference of Sound

1. Scarry, *Dreaming by the Book,* 6.
2. Taine, *On Intelligence,* 15–20. Further citations will be incorporated parenthetically. Noting that Pater owned several copies of Taine's books, Billie Inman suggests that Pater derived most of his understanding of psychology from Taine. See Inman, *Walter Pater's Reading,* 230.
3. The aestheticist elevation of music to the highest place among the arts began as early as Arthur Schopenhauer's second volume of *The World as Will and Idea* (1844), where he argues that music alone among the arts bypasses the mediation of abstract ideas and lets us experience the surging life force of the universe directly.
4. For an account of Whistler's titling practices, see Yeazell, *Picture Titles,* 204–24.
5. On Whistler's libel suit against Ruskin, see Dowling, *The Vulgarization of Art,* 41–49.
6. Whistler, *The Gentle Art of Making Enemies,* 126. Further citations will be incorporated parenthetically.
7. Teukolsky, *The Literate Eye,* 118.
8. Compare Ruth Bernard Yeazell on Whistler's call for silence before art: "It would hardly require an Oscar Wilde to register the paradox that Whistler himself never ceased speaking." Yeazell, *Picture Titles,* 220.
9. Gillian Beer compares the prominence of Helmholtz by the end of the 1870s to that of Darwin himself. See Beer, *Open Fields,* 243–49.
10. Out of the 370 articles the British Periodicals database returned when I searched for Helmholtz in the 1870s, a full 287 discussed music.
11. I take the liberty of using "sense" here differently from Gottlob Frege in his famous essay, "On Sense and Reference." Frege defines "sense" as the mode of presentation of a specifically linguistic sign, while he classifies sensory experience as ideas. Neither Helmholtz nor Pater recognized a distinction between these two different categories. See Frege, "On Sense and Reference." For a detailed discussion of the relationship between Frege's philosophy of language and the science of sensory perception, see chapter 2.
12. Donoghue, *Walter Pater,* 139–40.
13. Schmitt, "Tidal Conrad (Literally)," 15.
14. Schmitt, "Technical Maturity in Robert Louis Stevenson," 56.
15. I draw here from Ellis Hanson's recent call for a critical turn to kink. See Hanson, "A Kink in Time."
16. Helmholtz estimated the number of such resonators as around three thousand. See Hatfield, "Helmholtz and Classicism," 526.
17. Helmholtz, *Science and Culture,* 57–58. Further citations will be incorporated parenthetically.
18. For Helmholtz's intervention in the dispute between Ohm and Seebeck, see *On the Sensations of Tone,* 58–61. Further citations will be incorporated parenthetically. For a more detailed discussion, see Turner, "The Ohm-Seebeck Dispute, Hermann von

Helmholtz, and the Origins of Physiological Acoustics"; and Vogel, "Sensations of Tone, Perceptions of Sound, and Empiricism."

19. See *On the Sensations of Tone,* 64. Helmholtz in the 1850s believed that there were five primary colors but subsequently revised the number downward.
20. Pater, *Appreciations,* 67–68.
21. See, for example, Crawford, "Pater's *Renaissance,* Andrew Lang, and Anthropological Romanticism"; Connor, "Myth as Multiplicity in Walter Pater's *Greek Studies* and 'Denys L'Auxerrois'"; and Coates, "Pater and the Myth of Dionysus."
22. Pater, *Greek Studies,* 13. Further citations will be incorporated parenthetically.
23. Williams, *Transfigured World,* 6–7.
24. Volume 2 of Müller's lectures, which Pater borrowed from Brasenose College Library in 1874, in fact contains a discussion of Helmholtz's theory of upper partials and his account of them as the foundations of vowel sounds. See Müller, *Lectures on the Science of Language,* 2:101–14.
25. Müller, *Lectures on the Science of Language,* 1:25.
26. See Connor, "Myth as Multiplicity," 29.
27. Ruskin, *The Queen of the Air,* 8–9.
28. Duncan, "George Eliot's Science Fiction," 19.
29. Connor identifies a similar ambivalence in Pater's attitude toward the way mythic development arrests experience: "On the one hand, he sees growing refinement of a myth as involving a movement towards an ever more fixed and definite form which will concentrate and complete the myth; but on the other, he sees that form itself as by definition limiting, since it reduces the range and variety of significance in the myth." Connor, "Conclusion: Myth and Meta-myth in Max Müller and Walter Pater," 211.
30. For a discussion of Pater's response to Crowe and Cavalcaselle, see Teukolsky, "The Politics of Formalist Art Criticism."
31. Siegel, "Schooling Leonardo."
32. A self-reflectively second-order figuration of a figure representing the historical conditions of the Venetian Renaissance, Pater's "Giorgione" is a signal instance of what Carolyn Williams calls his aesthetic historicism. See Williams, *Transfigured World.*
33. James Eli Adams thus observes that, for Pater, "aesthetic understanding comes to be understood on the model of intimate knowledge of another person." Adams, *Dandies and Desert Saints,* 185.
34. Pater, *Marius the Epicurean,* 192. Further citations will be incorporated parenthetically.
35. Arata, "The Impersonal Intimacy of *Marius the Epicurean,*" 145.
36. On Pater as apostle of aesthetic democracy, see Dowling, *The Vulgarization of Art,* 75–89. On the historicist Pater, see Lecourt, "'To Surrender Himself, in Perfectly Liberal Inquiry.'"
37. Pater, *Plato and Platonism,* 46. Further citations will be incorporated parenthetically.
38. *The Dialogues of Plato,* 614.
39. Plato, *Cratylus,* 71.
40. Arata, "The Impersonal Intimacy of *Marius the Epicurean,*" 132.
41. Love, *Feeling Backward,* 59.
42. We can, I think, also trace Pater's metaphor for reading here back a step further to Ruskin's *Queen of the Air,* where Ruskin characterizes his own strategy for reading

myths in terms of the experiences that generated them using the same figure: "Now you must always be prepared to read Greek legends as you trace threads through figures on a silken damask: the same thread runs through the web, but it makes part of different figures" (27).

43. Walter Pater, *Imaginary Portraits,* 5–6. Further citations will be incorporated parenthetically.

44. The identification of virtue and habit survives etymologically in "ethics," from ethos, which in Ancient Greek denotes both character and habit. Discussing this passage in *De Profundis,* Wilde confirms that "the dull Oxford people thought the phrase a mere willful inversion of the somewhat wearisome text of Aristotelian *Ethics.*" Wilde, *De Profundis,* 53. On the popular Victorian understanding of habits, see Vrettos, "Defining Habits."

45. Morelli published his argument for reattributing the paining to Titian in 1883, just five years after the appearance of Pater's essay, and it steadily gained ground over the ensuing decades. See Morelli, *Italian Masters in German Galleries,* 157. For an overview of the controversy concerning *The Concert*'s attribution, see David Alan Brown's discussion in *Bellini, Giorgione, Titian, and the Renaissance of Venetian Painting,* 264–67.

Epilogue

1. Pater in fact suggests elsewhere in the essay that the rocks might be bituminous—impregnated with hydrocarbons derived from decomposing animal and plant matter, which is to say, impregnated with biological history (*The Renaissance,* 87). He nevertheless chooses not to make much of this highly evocative geological fact in his discussion of the painting.
2. Aestheticism's descriptions were too thick for Clifford Geertz. He warned his fellow anthropologists to avoid the aestheticism of losing touch with the "hard surfaces of life" in their own thick descriptions. Geertz, *Interpretation of Cultures,* 30.
3. See Wilde, "The Critic as Artist," 238–39.
4. Rancière, *The Politics of Literature,* 5. Rancière, I should note, is likewise skeptical of this characterization of modernism.
5. See Jakobson, "Linguistics and Poetics," 70.
6. See Massumi, "The Autonomy of Affect."
7. It's worth noting that Jameson follows Shklovsky in the strong antinomy he deploys between the "naming and representational construction" of affects. See Jameson, *Antinomies of Realism,* 35.
8. In historicizing Shklovsky in this way, I run the risk Cannon Schmitt has described of "prevent[ing] Russian Formalism from being useful to us. Historicizing the isolation of literature repeats that isolation in a different register, cutting off from (continued) life not the literary but Viktor Shklovsky." Here, I hope to outrun that risk by disentangling the strand of Shklovsky's that fits under the modernist paradigm from the parts of his essay that outline a more intentional, object-centered understanding of perception and reading. If this book historicizes the former, I hope it is clear how much it has been thinking with the latter. See Schmitt, "Refamiliarizing Viktor Shklovsky," 189.

9. While the melancholic sense of decline has long been an occupational hazard in the humanities, it has become particularly acute in the aftermath of the financial crisis of 2008. Surveying the precipitous decline in enrollments that followed, Eric Hayot has convincingly demonstrated that the pervasive sense of crisis is, in this environment, actually justified. See Hayot, "The Sky Is Falling."
10. For a detailed account of the risks of interdisciplinarity for literary studies, see Kramnick, *Paper Minds*, 17–36.
11. Ablow, "Oscar Wilde's Fictions of Belief," 175, 178.
12. Watt, *The Rise of the Novel*, 14, 27.
13. Ablow, "Oscar Wilde's Fictions of Belief," 177.
14. For an overview, see Kurnick, *Empty Houses*, 1–28.
15. Loesberg, "Wildean Interpretation and Formalist Reading," 28.
16. *Shakespeare's Sonnets*, 111.
17. See Wilde, *The Portrait of Mr. W. H.*, 50. Further citations will be incorporated parenthetically.
18. Loesberg, "Wildean Interpretation and Formalist Reading," 12, 17.
19. Lynch, *Loving Literature*, 12. Of course, loving literature does not necessarily make us any more ethical, nor does it serve as a reliable alternative to violence (as the roots of the discipline in colonial administration and working-class education make clear). Lynch's readings also reveal the ways that the love of literature "can be a matter of misrecognition, overvaluation, self-congratulation, aggressivity, transference, fetishism, and/or jealousy, that it . . . brings with it (sometimes unreasonable) intimacy expectations, and that, in these relations . . . we rather enjoy taking the presence of the other for granted" (14). She makes clear, in short, that just loving literature won't magically prevent us from being bad lovers.
20. Ablow, "Oscar Wilde's Fictions of Belief," 178.
21. De Man thus argues, "It is very difficult not to conceive the pattern of one's past and future existence as in accordance with temporal and spatial schemes that belong to fictional narratives and not to the world. This does not mean that fictional narratives are not part of the world and of reality; their impact upon the world may be all too strong for comfort. What we call ideology is precisely the confusion of linguistic with natural reality, of reference with phenomenalism." See de Man, *The Resistance to Theory*, 11. This study of course risks just such a confusion.
22. Kramnick, *Paper Minds*, 34.

BIBLIOGRAPHY

Ablow, Rachel, ed. *The Feeling of Reading: Affective Experience and Victorian Literature.* Ann Arbor: Univ. of Michigan Press, 2010.

———. "Oscar Wilde's Fictions of Belief." *Novel: A Forum on Fiction* 42, no. 2 (2009): 175–82.

Adams, James Eli. *Dandies and Desert Saints: Styles of Victorian Manhood.* Ithaca, NY: Cornell Univ. Press, 1995.

Ahmed, Siraj. *Archaeology of Babel: The Colonial Foundations of the Humanities.* Stanford, CA: Stanford Univ. Press, 2018.

Alison, Archibald. *Essay on the Nature and Principles of Taste.* New York: Harper and Brothers, 1853.

Arata, Stephen. "The Impersonal Intimacy of Marius the Epicurean." In Ablow, *The Feeling of Reading,* 131–56.

Armstrong, Paul. *How Literature Plays with the Brain: The Neuroscience of Reading and Art.* Baltimore: Johns Hopkins Univ. Press, 2013.

Arnold, Matthew. *Essays in Criticism.* New York: A. L. Burt, n.d.

Austin, J. L. *Sense and Sensibilia.* Oxford: Clarendon, 1962.

Auyoung, Elaine. "Phantoms and Fictional Characters: Hardy's Phenomenology of Loss." Victorian Studies 59, no. 3 (2017): 399–408.

———. *When Fiction Feels Real: Representation and the Reading Mind.* Oxford: Oxford Univ. Press, 2018.

Bacon, Francis. *The New Organon.* Cambridge: Cambridge Univ. Press, 2000.

Bain, Alexander. *The Senses and the Intellect.* London: John Parker, 1855.

Barthes, Roland. *The Rustle of Language.* Translated by Richard Howard. Berkeley: Univ. of California Press, 1989.

———. *S/Z: An Essay.* Translated by Richard Miller. New York: Hill and Wang, 1974.

Beer, Gillian. *Darwin's Plots: Evolutionary Narrative in Darwin, George Eliot, and Nineteenth-Century Fiction.* Cambridge: Cambridge Univ. Press, 2009.

———. *Open Fields: Science in Cultural Encounter.* Oxford: Oxford Univ. Press, 1996.

Berger, Sheila. *Thomas Hardy and Visual Structures: Framing, Disruption, Process.* New York: New York Univ. Press, 1990.

Best, Stephen, and Sharon Marcus. "Surface Reading: An Introduction." *Representations* 108, no. 1 (2009): 1–21.

"Blind Workers and Blind Helpers." *Cornhill* 9, no. 53 (May 1864): 603–17.

Brake, Laurel, et al., eds. *Walter Pater: Transparencies of Desire*. Greensboro, NC: ELT, 2002.

Brentano, Franz. *Psychology from an Empirical Standpoint*. Translated by Antos Rancurello et al. New York: Routledge, 1995.

Brilmyer, Pearl. "Plasticity, Form, and the Matter of Character in *Middlemarch*." *Representations* 130, no. 1 (2015): 60–83.

Brown, David Alan. *Bellini, Giorgione, Titian, and the Renaissance of Venetian Painting*. New Haven, CT: Yale Univ. Press, 2006.

Bullen, J. B. *The Expressive Eye: Fiction and Perception in the Work of Thomas Hardy*. Oxford: Clarendon Press, 1986.

Burckhardt, Jacob. *Civilization of the Renaissance in Italy*. Translated by S. G. C. Middlemore. New York: Macmillan, 1890.

Cahan, David, ed. *Hermann von Helmholtz and the Foundations of Nineteenth-Century Science*. Berkeley: Univ. of California Press, 1993.

Canales, Jimena. *A Tenth of a Second: A History*. Chicago: Univ. of Chicago Press, 2009.

Carroll, David, ed. *George Eliot: The Critical Heritage*. New York: Routledge, 1971.

Chalmers, David. *The Character of Consciousness*. Oxford: Oxford Univ. Press, 2010.

Coates, John. "Pater and the Myth of Dionysus." *English* 56, no. 216 (2007): 265–82.

Colby, Vineta. *Vernon Lee: A Literary Life*. Charlottesville: Univ. of Virginia Press, 2003.

Cohen, William A. *Embodied: Victorian Literature and the Senses*. Minneapolis: Univ. of Minnesota Press, 2009.

Cohn, Elisha. *Still Life: Suspended Development in the Victorian Novel*. Oxford: Oxford Univ. Press, 2016.

Collins, Wilkie. *No Name*. New York: Penguin, 1994.

Connor, Steven. "Conclusion: Myth and Meta-myth in Max Müller and Walter Pater." In *The Sun Is God: Painting, Literature, and Mythology in the Nineteenth Century*, edited by J. B. Bullen. Oxford: Clarendon Press, 1989, 199–224.

———. "Myth as Multiplicity in Walter Pater's Greek Studies and 'Denys L'Auxerrois.'" *Review of English Studies* 34, no. 133 (1983): 28–42.

Crary, Jonathan. *Suspensions of Perception: Attention, Spectacle and Modern Culture*. Cambridge MA: MIT Press, 2001.

Crawford, Robert. "Pater's Renaissance, Andrew Lang, and Anthropological Romanticism." *ELH* 53, no. 4 (1986): 849–79.

"Current Literature: *Romola*." *Reader*, 11 July 1863, 28–29.

Dames, Nicholas. *Amnesiac Selves: Nostalgia, Forgetting, and British Fiction, 1810–1870*. Oxford: Oxford Univ. Press, 2001.

———. *The Physiology of the Novel: Reading, Neural Science, and the Form of Victorian Fiction*. Oxford: Oxford Univ. Press, 2007.

Daston, Lorraine, and Peter Galison. *Objectivity*. New York: Zone Books, 2007.

Dawson, Gowan. *Show Me the Bone: Reconstructing Prehistoric Monsters in Nineteenth-Century Britain and America*. Chicago: Univ. of Chicago Press, 2016.

Dehaene, Stanislas. *Reading in the Brain: The New Science of How We Read*. New York: Viking, 2009.

de Man, Paul. *Blindness and Insight: Essays in the Rhetoric of Contemporary Criticism*. Minneapolis: Univ. of Minnesota Press, 1983.

———. *The Resistance to Theory.* Minneapolis: Univ. of Minnesota Press, 1986.

Dennett, Daniel. *Consciousness Explained.* New York: Back Bay, 1991.

Dilthey, Wilhelm. *Selected Works.* Vol. 5, *Poetry and Experience,* edited by Rudolf A. Makkreel and Frithjof Rodi. Princeton, NJ: Princeton Univ. Press, 1985.

Donoghue, Denis. *Walter Pater: Lover of Strange Souls.* New York: Knopf, 1995.

Donovan, Andrea. *William Morris and the Society for the Protection of Ancient Buildings.* New York: Routledge, 2008.

Dowling, Linda. *The Vulgarization of Art: The Victorians and Aesthetic Democracy.* Charlottesville, VA: Univ. Press of Virginia, 1996.

Duncan, Ian. "George Eliot's Science Fiction." *Representations* 125, no.1 (2014): 15–39.

Eames, Elizabeth Ramden. *Bertrand Russell's Dialogue with His Contemporaries.* New York: Routledge, 1989.

Ehnenn, Jill. *Women's Literary Collaboration, Queerness, and Late-Victorian Culture.* Burlington, VT: Ashgate, 2008.

Eliot, George. *Adam Bede.* Oxford: Oxford Univ. Press, 1996.

———. *Daniel Deronda.* Oxford: Oxford Univ. Press, 1988.

———. *Essays of George Eliot.* Edited by Thomas Pinney. New York: Columbia Univ. Press, 1963.

———. *The George Eliot Letters.* 9 vols. , edited by Gordon Haight. New Haven, CT: Yale Univ. Press, 1954–78.

———. "George Eliot's *Quarry for Romola:* An Edition of the Notebook Held in the Morris L. Parrish Collection at Princeton University Library." Edited by Andrew Thompson. *George Eliot—George Henry Lewes Studies* 66, no. 1–2 (2014): 5–99.

———. *The Journals of George Eliot.* Edited by Margaret Harris and Judith Johnston. Cambridge: Cambridge Univ. Press, 1998.

———. *Middlemarch.* New York: Penguin, 1994.

———. *Romola.* Oxford: Oxford Univ. Press, 1994.

Evangelista, Stefano. "Vernon Lee in the Vatican: The Uneasy Alliance of Aestheticism and Archaeology." *Victorian Studies* 52, no.1 (2009): 31–41.

Favret, Mary. "The Pathos of Reading." *PMLA* 130, no. 5 (2015): 1318–31.

Felski, Rita. "After Suspicion." *Profession* (2009): 28–35.

———. *The Limits of Critique.* Chicago: Univ. of Chicago Press, 2015.

Feuerbach, Ludwig. *The Essence of Christianity.* Translated by George Eliot. Amherst, NY: Prometheus, 1989.

Frazer, J. G. *Pausanias and Other Greek Sketches.* London: Macmillan, 1900.

Freedgood, Elaine. *The Ideas in Things: Fugitive Meaning in the Victorian Novel.* Chicago: Univ. of Chicago Press, 2005.

Freedgood, Elaine, and Canon Schmitt. "Denotatively, Technically, Literally." *Representations* 125, no. 1 (2014): 1–14.

Freeman, E. A. *Principles of Church Restoration.* London: Joseph Masters, 1846.

Frege, Gottlob. "On Sense and Reference." In *Translations from the Philosophical Writings of Gottlob Frege,* edited by P. Geach and M. Black. Oxford: Blackwell, 1960, 36–56.

Freud, Sigmund. *The Interpretation of Dreams.* Translated by James Strachey. New York: Basic Books, 2010.

Ford, Mark. *Thomas Hardy: Half a Londoner.* Cambridge, MA: Harvard Univ. Press, 2016.

Gallagher, Catherine. "George Eliot: Immanent Victorian." *Representations* 90, no. 1 (2005): 61–74.

———. "The Rise of Fictionality." In *The Novel,* vol.1, *History, Geography, and Culture,* edited by Franco Moretti Princeton, NJ: Princeton Univ. Press, 2007, 336–63.

———. "What Would Napoleon Do? Historical, Fictional, and Counterfactual Characters." *New Literary History* 42, no. 2 (2011): 315–36.

Gallagher, Catherine, and Stephen Greenblatt. *Practicing New Historicism.* Chicago: Univ. of Chicago Press, 2000.

Gang, Joshua. "Behaviorism and the Beginnings of Close Reading." *ELH* 78, no. 1 (2011): 1–25.

Geertz, Clifford. *The Interpretation of Cultures.* New York: Basic Books, 1973.

Gibson, James J. *The Ecological Approach to Visual Perception.* New York: Taylor and Francis, 1986.

———. *The Senses Considered as Perceptual Systems.* Boston: Houghton Mifflin, 1966.

Goode, George Brown. *The Museums of the Future.* Washington: Government Printing Office, 1891.

Goodlad, Lauren, and Andrew Sartori. "The Ends of History: Introduction." *Victorian Studies* 55, no. 4 (2013): 591–614.

Griffiths, Devin. *The Age of Analogy: Science and Literature between the Darwins.* Baltimore: Johns Hopkins Univ. Press, 2016.

Groos, Karl. *The Play of Man.* Translated by Elizabeth Baldwin. New York: Appleton, 1913.

Grote, John. *Exploratio Philosophica.* Cambridge: Deighton, Bell, 1865.

Hanson, Ellis. "The Future's Eve: Reparative Reading after Sedgwick." *South Atlantic Quarterly* 110, no. 1 (2011): 101–119.

———. "A Kink in Time." *b20 review,* 6 October 2016, https://www.boundary2.org/2016/10/ellis-hanson-kink-in-time/.

Hardy, Thomas. *The Dynasts.* Vol. 1. London: Macmillan, 1920.

———. *Life and Art.* Edited by Ernest Brenneke. New York: Haskell House, 1966.

———. *The Life and Work of Thomas Hardy.* Edited by Michael Millgate. Athens: Univ. of Georgia Press, 1985.

———. *The Return of the Native.* New York: Penguin, 1999.

———. *Tess of the D'Urbervilles.* New York: Penguin, 1998.

Hartley, David. *Observations on Man.* Vol. 1. London: S. Richardson, 1749.

Hatfield, Gary. "Helmholtz and Classicism." In Cahan, *Hermann von Helmholtz and the Foundations of Nineteenth-Century Science,* 522–58.

———. *The Natural and the Normative: Theories of Spatial Perception from Kant to Helmholtz.* Cambridge, MA: MIT Press, 1990.

Hayot, Eric. "The Sky Is Falling." MLA Profession, 2018, https://profession.mla.org/the-sky-is-falling/.

Hegel, G. W. F. *Aesthetics: Lectures on Fine Art.* Vol. 1. Translated by T. M. Knox. Oxford: Clarendon, 1975.

Heidegger, Martin. *The Question Concerning Technology.* Translated by William Lovitt. New York: Garland, 1977.

Helmholtz, Hermann von. *On the Sensations of Tone.* Translated by Alexander Ellis. New York: Dover, 1954.

———. *Science and Culture: Popular and Philosophical Essays.* Edited by David Cahan. Chicago: Univ. of Chicago Press, 1995.

———. *Treatise on Physiological Optics.* Vol. 3, translated by James Southall. New York: Dover, 1962.

Helsinger, Elizabeth. *Ruskin and the Art of the Beholder.* Cambridge, MA: Harvard Univ. Press, 1982.

Henchman, Anna. "Hardy's Stargazers and the Astronomy of Other Minds." *Victorian Studies* 51, no. 1 (2008): 37–64.

———. *The Starry Sky Within: Astronomy and the Reach of the Mind in Victorian Literature.* Oxford: Oxford Univ. Press, 2014.

Hodgson, Shadworth. *Time and Space: A Metaphysical Essay.* London: Longman, 1865.

Hume, David. *A Treatise on Human Nature.* Oxford: Oxford Univ. Press, 2000.

Inman, Billie. *Walter Pater's Reading: A Bibliography.* New York: Garland, 1981.

Jackson, Noel. *Science and Sensation in Romantic Poetry.* Cambridge: Cambridge Univ. Press, 2008.

Jakobson, Roman. "Linguistics and Poetics." In *Language in Literature,* edited by Krystyna Pomorska. Cambridge, MA: Harvard University Press, 1987, 62–94.

———. "Two Aspects of Language and Two Types of Aphasic Disturbances." In *Language and Literature,* edited by Krystyna Pomorska. Cambridge, MA: Harvard University Press, 1987, 95–119.

James, Henry. "The Life of George Eliot." *Atlantic Monthly* 55 (1885): 668–78.

———. "Review: *Middlemarch.*" *Galaxy Magazine* 15, no. 3 (1873): 424–28.

James, William. *The Principles of Psychology.* 2 vols. New York: Dover, 1918.

———. *William James: Writings 1902–1910.* New York: Library of America, 1987.

Jameson, Fredric. *The Antinomies of Realism.* New York: Verso, 2013.

Jarvis, Claire. *Exquisite Masochism: Marriage, Sex, and the Novel Form.* Baltimore: Johns Hopkins Univ. Press, 2016.

Johns, B. G. *Blind People: Their Works and Ways.* London: John Murray, 1867.

Jones, Tom. "Theories of Language in the Eighteenth Century." *Oxford Handbooks Online,* October 2015. http://www.oxfordhandbooks.com/view/10.1093/oxfordhb/9780199935338.001.0001/oxfordhb-9780199935338-e-100.

Kant, Immanuel. *The Critique of the Power of Judgment.* Translated by Paul Guyer and Eric Matthews. Cambridge: Cambridge Univ. Press, 2000.

Keats, John. *"Bright Star": Complete Poems and Selected Letters.* London: Vintage, 2010.

Keen, Suzanne. *Thomas Hardy's Brains: Psychology, Neurology, and Hardy's Imagination.* Columbus: Ohio State Univ. Press, 2014.

Kennedy, Alan, et al., eds. *Reading as a Perceptual Process.* New York: Elsevier, 2000.

Kramer, Dale. "Hardy and Readers: *Jude the Obscure.*" In *The Cambridge Companion to Thomas Hardy,* edited by Dale Kramer. Cambridge: Cambridge Univ. Press, 1999, 164–82.

Kramnick, Jonathan. "An Aesthetics and Ecology of Presence." *European Romantic Review* 26, no. 3 (2015): 315–27.

———. *Paper Minds: Literature and the Ecology of Consciousness.* Chicago: Univ. of Chicago Press, 2018.

Kripke, Saul. *Naming and Necessity.* Malden, MA: Blackwell, 1972.

———. *Reference and Existence: The John Locke Lectures.* Oxford: Oxford Univ. Press, 2013.

Kurnick, David. "Abstraction and the Subject of Novel Reading: Drifting through *Romola.*" *Novel: A Forum on Fiction* 42, no. 3 (2009): 490–96.

———. *Empty Houses: Theatrical Failure and the Novel.* Princeton, NJ: Princeton Univ. Press, 2012.

Landow, George. *The Aesthetic and Critical Theories of John Ruskin.* Princeton, NJ: Princeton Univ. Press, 1971.

Latour, Bruno. *Reassembling the Social: An Introduction to Actor-Network-Theory.* Oxford: Oxford Univ. Press, 2005.

Law, Graham. *Serializing Fiction in the Victorian Press.* New York: Palgrave, 2000.

Lecourt, Sebastian. "'To Surrender Himself, in Perfectly Liberal Inquiry.'" *Victorian Studies* 53, no. 2 (2011): 231–53.

Lee, Vernon. *The Beautiful: An Introduction to Psychological Aesthetics.* Cambridge: Cambridge Univ. Press, 1913.

———. *Belcaro: Being Essays on Sundry Aesthetical Questions.* London: T. Fisher Unwin, 1887.

———. *Euphorion: Being Studies of the Antique and Medieval in the Renaissance.* London: T. Fisher Unwin, 1885.

———. *The Handling of Words and Other Studies in Literary Psychology.* Lincoln: Univ. of Nebraska Press, 1968.

———. *Juvenilia: Being a Second Series of Essays on Sundry Aesthetical Questions.* Vol. 1. London: T. Fisher Unwin, 1887.

———. *Miss Brown.* Doylestown, PA: Wildside, n.d.

Lee, Vernon, and Clementina Anstruther-Thomson. *Beauty and Ugliness and Other Studies in Psychological Aesthetics.* London: John Lane, 1912.

Lenoir, Timothy. "The Eye as Mathematician." In Cahan, *Hermann von Helmholtz and the Foundations of Nineteenth-Century Science,* 109–53.

Levine, Caroline. *Forms: Whole, Rhythm, Hierarchy, Network.* Princeton, NJ: Princeton Univ. Press, 2015.

Levine, George. *Dying to Know: Scientific Epistemology and Narrative in Victorian England.* Chicago: Univ. of Chicago Press, 2002.

Lewes, G. H. "A Box of Books." *Blackwood's Edinburgh Magazine,* April 1862, 436–51.

———. *Problems of Life and Mind: The Foundations of a Creed.* Vol. 1. Boston: James Osgood, 1874.

Locke, John. *An Essay Concerning Human Understanding.* Oxford: Clarendon, 1975.

Loesberg, Jonathan. "Wildean Interpretation and Formalist Reading." *Victorian Studies* 58, no. 1 (2015): 9–33.

Lotze, Hermann. *Microcosmus.* Vol. 1. Translated by Elizabeth Hamilton and Constance Jones. Edinburgh: T and T Clark, 1885.

Love, Heather. "Close but Not Deep: Literary Ethics and the Descriptive Turn." *New Literary History* 41, no. 2 (2010): 371–91.

———. "Close Reading and Thin Description." *Public Culture* 25, no. 3 (2013): 401–34.

———. *Feeling Backward: Loss and the Politics of Queer History.* Boston: Harvard Univ. Press, 2007.

Lukács, Georg. *The Historical Novel.* Translated by Hannah Mitchell and Stanley Mitchell. Boston: Beacon, 1962.

———. "Narrate or Describe?" In *Writer and Critic,* translated by Arthur Kahn. New York: Merlin, 1970, 110–48.

Lynch, Deidre. *Loving Literature: A Cultural History.* Chicago: Univ. of Chicago Press, 2015.

Marcus, Sharon. *Between Women: Friendship, Desire, and Marriage in Victorian England.* Princeton, NJ: Princeton Univ. Press, 2007.

Marcus, Sharon, Heather Love, and Stephen Best. "Building a Better Description." *Representations* 135, no. 1 (2016): 1–21.

Marr, David. *Vision: A Computational Investigation into the Human Representation and Processing of Visual Information.* Cambridge, MA: MIT Press, 2010.

Massumi, Brian. "The Autonomy of Affect." *Cultural Critique* 31 (Autumn 1995): 83–109.

Maxwell, Catherine, and Patricia Pulham, eds. *Vernon Lee: Decadence, Ethics, Aesthetics.* New York: Palgrave Macmillan, 2006.

Meillassoux, Quentin. *After Finitude: An Essay on the Necessity of Contingency.* London: Continuum, 2010.

Merrills, A. H. "The Origins of 'Vandalism.'" *International Journal of the Classical Tradition* 16, no. 2 (2009): 155–75.

Meyer, Steven. "Of 'Experiential Togetherness': Toward a More Robust Empiricism." In *The Lure of Whitehead,* edited by Nicholas Gaskell and A. J. Nocek. Minneapolis: Univ. of Minnesota Press, 2014, 332–59.

Miele, Chris. "'Their Interest and Habit': Professionalism and the Restoration of Medieval Churches, 1837–77." In *The Victorian Church: Architecture and Society,* edited by Chris Brooks and Andrew Saint. Manchester: Manchester Univ. Press, 1995, 151–71.

Mill, John Stuart. *A System of Logic, Ratiocinative and Inductive.* London: Longmans, 1906.

Miller, J. Hillis. *Topographies.* Stanford, CA: Stanford Univ. Press, 1995.

———. *Versions of Pygmalion.* Cambridge, MA: Harvard Univ. Press, 1990.

"*Miss Brown.* By Vernon Lee." *Spectator,* 13 December 1884, 20.

Morelli, Giovanni. *Italian Masters in German Galleries.* Translated by Louise Richter. London, 1883.

Morgan, Benjamin. "Critical Empathy: Vernon Lee's Aesthetics and the Origins of Close Reading," *Victorian Studies* 55, no.1 (2012): 31–56.

———. *The Outward Mind: Materialist Aesthetics in Victorian Science and Literature.* Chicago: Univ. of Chicago Press, 2017.

Morris, William. "The Manifesto of the Society for the Preservation of Ancient Buildings." *SPAB,* https://www.spab.org.uk/about-us/spab-manifesto.

Müller, Johannes. *Elements of Physiology.* Vol. 2. Translated by William Baly. London: Taylor and Walton, 1842.

———. "On the Fantastic Apparitions of Vision." Translated by G. E. Berrios. *History of Psychiatry* 16, no. 2 (2005): 229–46.

Müller, Max. *Lectures on the Science of Language.* 2 vols. New York: Scribner's, 1890–91.

Noë, Alva. *The Varieties of Presence.* Cambridge, MA: Harvard Univ. Press, 2012.

"On Competition amongst Architects." *Ecclesiologist* 5 (March 1842): 65–67.

Pater, Walter. *Appreciations, With an Essay on Style.* London: Macmillan, 1895.

———. *Greek Studies.* London: Macmillan, 1901.

———. *Imaginary Portraits.* New York: Allworth, 1997.

———. *Marius the Epicurean*. Kansas City, MO: Vancourt, 2008.

———. *Plato and Platonism*. London: Macmillan, 1901.

———. *The Renaissance: Studies in Art and Poetry*. Berkeley: Univ. of California Press, 1980.

Paul, Carole, ed. *The First Modern Museums of Art: The Birth of an Institution in 18th- and Early 19th-Century Europe*. Los Angeles: J. Paul Getty Museum, 2012.

Pond, Kristen. "Harriet Martineau's Epistemology of Gossip." *Nineteenth-Century Literature* 69, no. 2 (September 2014): 175–207.

Plato. *Cratylus*. Translated by C. D. C. Reeve. Indianapolis: Hackett, 1998.

———. *The Dialogues of Plato*. Vol. 1. Translated by Benjamin Jowett. New York: Scribner, Armstrong, 1873.

Putnam, Hilary. *Mind, Language, and Reality*. Cambridge: Cambridge Univ. Press, 1979.

Rancière, Jacques. *The Politics of Literature*. Translated by Julie Rose. Malden, MA: Polity, 2011.

"Recent Works of Fiction—*Romola*." *British Quarterly Review* 76 (October 1863): 448–65.

Reed, Edward. *From Soul to Mind: The Emergence of Psychology from Erasmus Darwin to William James*. New Haven, CT: Yale Univ. Press, 1997.

Reid, Thomas. *Essay on the Intellectual Powers of Man*. Edinburgh: John Bell, 1785.

———. *An Inquiry into the Human Mind on the Principles of Common Sense*. Edinburgh: A. Millar, A. Kincaid, and J. Bell, 1765.

Reilly, Arianna. "Always Sympathize! Surface Reading, Affect, and George Eliot's *Romola*." *Victorian Studies* 55, no. 4 (2013): 629–46.

Ruskin, John. *Modern Painters*. Vols. 2 and 3. London: George Allen, 1906.

———. *The Queen of the Air*. London: George Allen, 1874.

———. *The Seven Lamps of Architecture*. New York: Dover, 1989.

Russell, Bertrand. "On Denoting." *Mind* 14, no. 56 (1905): 479–93.

———. *The Problems of Philosophy*. London: Oxford Univ. Press, 1959.

Rylance, Rick. *Victorian Psychology and British Culture, 1850–1880*. Oxford: Oxford Univ. Press, 2000.

Scarry, Elaine. *Dreaming by the Book*. Princeton, NJ: Princeton Univ. Press, 2001.

———. *Resisting Representation*. Oxford: Oxford Univ. Press, 1994.

Schmitt, Cannon. "Refamiliarizing Viktor Shklovsky." *Victorian Literature and Culture* 47, no. 1 (Spring 2019): 187–201.

———. "Technical Maturity in Robert Louis Stevenson." *Representations* 125, no. 1 (2014): 54–79.

———. "Tidal Conrad (Literally)." *Victorian Studies* 55, no. 1 (2012): 7–29.

Searle, John. "Proper Names." *Mind* 67, no. 266 (April 1958): 166–73.

Sedgwick, Eve Kosofsky. *Touching Feeling: Affect, Pedagogy, Performativity*. Durham, NC: Duke Univ. Press, 2003.

Siegel, Jonah. *Desire and Excess: The Nineteenth-Century Culture of Art*. Princeton, NJ: Princeton Univ. Press, 2000.

———, ed. *The Emergence of the Modern Museum: An Anthology of Nineteenth-Century Sources*. Oxford: Oxford Univ. Press, 2008.

———. "The Material of Form: Vernon Lee at the Vatican and Out of It." *Victorian Studies* 55, no. 2 (2013): 189–201.

———. "Schooling Leonardo." In Brake et al., *Walter Pater: Transparencies of Desire*, 133–150.

Shakespeare, William. *Shakespeare's Sonnets.* New York: Simon and Schuster, 2004.

Sherrington, C. S. *The Integrative Action of the Nervous System.* New Haven, CT: Yale Univ. Press, 1906.

Shklovsky, Viktor. *Theory of Prose.* Translated by Benjamin Sher. Champaign, IL: Dalkey Archive, 1990.

Smith, Roger. "'The Sixth Sense': Towards a History of Muscular Sensation." *Gesnerus* 68, no.1 (2011): 218–71.

Sontag, Susan. *Regarding the Pain of Others.* New York: Picador, 2003.

Snyder, Laura. *Reforming Philosophy: A Victorian Debate on Science and Society.* Chicago: Univ. of Chicago Press, 2010.

"St. Juliot Church Restoration." *Royal Cornwall Gazette,* 27 April 1872, 6.

Taine, Hippolyte. *On Intelligence.* Vol. 2, translated by T. D. Haye. London: Reeve, 1871.

Teukolsky, Rachel. *The Literate Eye: Victorian Art Writing and Modernist Aesthetics.* Oxford: Oxford Univ. Press, 2013.

———. "The Politics of Formalist Art Criticism." In Brake et al., *Walter Pater: Transparencies of Desire,* 151–69.

Titchener, E. B. *Lectures on the Experimental Psychology of the Thought-Processes.* New York: Macmillan, 1909.

Tondre, Michael. *The Physics of Possibility: Victorian Fiction, Science, and Gender.* Charlottesville: Univ. of Virginia Press, 2018.

Turner, R. Steven. "The Ohm-Seebeck Dispute, Hermann von Helmholtz, and the Origins of Physiological Acoustics." *British Journal for the History of Science* 10, no. 1 (1977): 1–24.

Vischer, Robert. "On the Optical Sense of Form." In *Empathy, Form, and Space: Problems in German Aesthetics, 1873–1893,* translated and edited by Harry Mallgrave and Eleftherios Ikonomou. Santa Monica, CA: Getty Center for the History of Art and Humanities, 1994, 89–123.

Vogel, Stephen. "Sensations of Tone, Perceptions of Sound, and Empiricism." In Cahan, *Helmholtz and the Foundations of Nineteenth-Century Science,* 259–89.

Vrettos, Athena. "Defining Habits." *Victorian Studies* 42, no. 3 (2000): 399–426.

Wallace, Diana. *The Woman's Historical Novel.* New York: Palgrave, 2005.

Warner, Michael. "Uncritical Reading." In *Polemic: Critical or Uncritical,* edited by Jane Gallop. New York: Routledge, 2004, 13–38.

Watt, Ian. *The Rise of the Novel: Studies in Defoe, Richardson, and Fielding.* Berkeley: Univ. of California Press, 2001.

Whewell, William. *The Philosophy of the Inductive Sciences.* Vol. 1. London: John Parker, 1847.

Wilde, Oscar. "The Critic as Artist." In *The Soul of Man under Socialism and Selected Critical Prose.* Oxford: Oxford Univ. Press, 2001, 213–79.

———. "The Decay of Lying." In Wilde, *The Soul of Man under Socialism.* Oxford: Oxford Univ. Press, 2001, 163–192.

———. *De Profundis.* New York: Penguin, 2013.

———. *The Picture of Dorian Gray.* New York: Norton, 2007.

———. *The Portrait of Mr. W. H.* In Wilde, *The Soul of Man under Socialism and Selected Critical Prose.* Oxford: Oxford Univ. Press, 2001, 31–103.

Williams, Carolyn. *Transfigured World: Walter Pater's Aesthetic Historicism.* Ithaca, NY: Cornell Univ. Press, 1989.

Wimsatt, W. K., and Monroe C. Beardsley. "The Affective Fallacy." In *The Verbal Icon: Studies in the Meaning of Poetry.* Lexington: Univ. Press of Kentucky, 1954, 21–39.

Whistler, James Abbott McNeill. *The Gentle Art of Making Enemies.* London: William Heinemann, 1904.

Woloch, Alex. *The One vs. the Many: Minor Characters and the Space of the Protagonist in the Novel.* Princeton, NJ: Princeton Univ. Press, 2003.

Wordsworth, William. *William Wordsworth: The Major Works.* Edited by Stephen Gill. Oxford: Oxford Univ. Press, 2000.

Wright, Daniel. "George Eliot's Vagueness." *Victorian Studies* 56, no. 4 (2014): 625–48.

Yeazell, Ruth Bernard. "The Lighting Design of Hardy's Novels." *Nineteenth-Century Literature* 64, no. 1 (2009): 48–75.

———. *Picture Titles: How and Why Western Paintings Acquired Their Names.* Princeton, NJ: Princeton Univ. Press, 2015.

Zorn, Christa. *Vernon Lee: Aesthetics, History, and the Victorian Female Intellectual.* Athens: Ohio Univ. Press, 2003.

INDEX

Page numbers in italics refer to illustrations.

Recent Books in the
Victorian Literature and Culture Series

Reading with the Senses in Victorian Literature and Science
DAVID SWEENEY COOMBS

Parting Words: Victorian Poetry and Public Address
JUSTIN A. SIDER

The Physics of Possibility: Victorian Fiction, Science, and Gender
MICHAEL TONDRE

Willful Submission: Sado-Erotics and Heavenly Marriage in Victorian Poetry
AMANDA PAXTON

Pirating Fictions: Ownership and Creativity in Nineteenth-Century Popular Culture
MONICA F. COHEN

Mathilde Blind: Late-Victorian Culture and the Woman of Letters
JAMES DIEDRICK

Poetry and the Thought of Song in Nineteenth-Century Britain
ELIZABETH K. HELSINGER

The Antagonist Principle: John Henry Newman and the Paradox of Personality
LAWRENCE POSTON

Personal Business: Character and Commerce in Victorian Literature and Culture
AERON HUNT

Second Person Singular: Late Victorian Women Poets and the Bonds of Verse
EMILY HARRINGTON

The Ghost behind the Masks: The Victorian Poets and Shakespeare
W. DAVID SHAW